T0355517

Medieval
Clothing and Textiles

Volume 19

Medieval
Clothing and Textiles

ISSN 1744-5787

Medieval Clothing and Textiles

Volume 19

edited by

MELANIE SCHUESSLER BOND

and

CORDELIA WARR

THE BOYDELL PRESS

First published 2025
The Boydell Press, Woodbridge

ISBN 978-1-83765-278-5

The Boydell Press is an imprint of Boydell & Brewer Ltd
PO Box 9, Woodbridge, Suffolk IP12 3DF, UK
and of Boydell & Brewer Inc.
668 Mt Hope Avenue, Rochester, NY 14620-2731, USA
website: www.boydellandbrewer.com

Our Authorised Representative for product safety in the EU is Easy Access System Europe -
Mustamäe tee 50, 10621 Tallinn, Estonia, *gpsr.requests@easproject.com*

A CIP catalogue record for this book is available
from the British Library

The publisher has no responsibility for the continued existence or accuracy of URLs for
external or third-party internet websites referred to in this book, and does not guarantee that
any content on such websites is, or will remain, accurate or appropriate

Contents

Illustrations

Full credit details are provided in the captions to the images in the text. The editors, contributors, and publishers are grateful to all the institutions and persons listed for permission to reproduce the materials in which they hold copyright. Every effort has been made to trace the copyright holders; apologies are offered for any omissions, and the publishers will be pleased to add any necessary acknowledgement in subsequent editions.

Tables

Contributors

MELANIE SCHUESSLER BOND (Editor) is Professor of Costume Design at Eastern Michigan University. She focuses on clothing in sixteenth-century Western Europe with particular attention to material culture and the sociological implications of clothing. In addition to her book, *Dressing the Scottish Court, 1543–1553: Clothing in the Accounts of the Lord High Treasurer of Scotland* (2019), she has published articles and chapters on various topics, including French hoods, children's clothing, and treason and clothing. She has also presented numerous papers on sixteenth-century clothing, including wedding attire, ladies-in-waiting, movie costumes, and Scottish clothing. Her current project is a book on the wardrobe of Mary, Queen of Scots.

CORDELIA WARR (Editor) is Professor of Medieval and Renaissance Art at the University of Manchester. Her research focuses on clothing, its representation, and its problematic relationship with the spiritual realm. She has published widely on the representation of religious dress. Her book *Dressing for Heaven: Physical and Spiritual Dress in Italian Art 1215–1545* (2010) investigates clothes as liminal objects, drawing on areas such as material culture, Renaissance models of consumption and devotion, and gender studies. Her recent publications include "*In persona Christi*: Liturgical Gloves and the Construction of Public Religious Identity" (*Bulletin of the John Rylands Library*, 2019), and a chapter on "Dress and Belief" for volume 3 of the *Bloomsbury Cultural History of Dress and Fashion* (2016).

ROBIN NETHERTON (Reviews Editor) is a costume historian specializing in Western European clothing of the Middle Ages and its interpretation by artists and historians. Since 1982, she has given lectures and workshops on practical aspects of medieval dress and on costume as an approach to social history, art history, and literature. Her published articles have addressed such topics as fourteenth-century sleeve embellishments, the cut of Norman tunics, and medieval Greenlanders' interpretations of European female fashion. A journalist by training, she also works as a professional editor. With Gale R. Owen-Crocker, she co-founded and for fifteen years co-edited *Medieval Clothing and Textiles*.

SARAH-GRACE HELLER is an Associate Professor in the Department of French and Italian at Ohio State University, specializing in medieval French and Occitan literature, language, and material culture. She is the author of *Fashion in Medieval France* (2007), editor of *A Cultural History of Fashion in the Medieval Age* (2016), and co-editor of *Troubadour Texts and Contexts* (2024). She has published articles on topics such as attitudes towards consumption and fashion, consumer practices of beauty, the *Roman de la Rose* and other medieval romances, and the semiotics of culture. She is president of the Société Guilhem IX, which promotes Occitan scholarship, and serves on the editorial board of the journals *Medieval Clothing and Textiles* and *Tenso*. She has also served as director and associate director of Ohio State University's Center for Medieval and Renaissance Studies.

CLAIRE W. KILGORE received her master's degree in Art History from the University of Nebraska–Lincoln in 2017 and is currently a Ph.D. candidate at the University of Wisconsin–Madison. Her dissertation examines depictions of pregnancy, childbirth, and reproductive anatomy, including depictions of dress and household linens in scenes of sacred birth, in German-speaking lands between the fourteenth and mid-sixteenth centuries. Other research interests include material religion, pilgrimage, and devotional jewelry. She was a co-curator of the 2024 exhibition "Material Muses: Medieval Devotional Culture and Its Afterlives" at the Haggerty Museum of Art in Milwaukee, Wisconsin.

TANIA KOLARIK is an Art History Ph.D. candidate at the University of Wisconsin–Madison, where she studies Islamic, Byzantine, Mongol, and Italian textiles circulating in the global medieval Mediterranean and their influence on the art and architecture of fourteenth-century Italy. Her dissertation, "Clothing the Commune: The Culture of Textiles in the Long Fourteenth Century," examines the central role of textiles within Italian trecento culture. It reframes the field of trecento art and architecture by placing textiles at the center of Italian society as well as including a consideration of the role of gender and social class in the production and reception of these textiles within medieval Italian cityscapes.

ALEXANDRA LESTER-MAKIN is a professional embroiderer and textile archaeologist specialising in the early medieval period (450–1100). She holds a Ph.D. from the University of Manchester and was a research associate on Unwrapping the Galloway Hoard, an Arts and Humanities Research Council–funded project run by National Museums Scotland and the University of Glasgow. Currently, she is a Third Century Fellow at Manchester Metropolitan University. She is the author of *The Lost Art of the Anglo-Saxon World: The Sacred and Secular Power of Embroidery* (2019) and co-editor of *Textiles of the Viking North Atlantic: Analysis, Interpretation, Re-creation* (2024). She also presents workshops and lectures and runs a YouTube channel under the name Early Medieval Embroidery.

LESLEY O'CONNELL EDWARDS is an independent scholar who researches the history of hand knitting, using both archives and artefacts. She is particularly interested in knitting in early modern England, especially the production of, and trade in, wool stockings. Her master's dissertation at Oxford University explored the hand knitting industry of later sixteenth-century Norwich. Her other research interests include working English hand knitters and the construction of knitted items. She was part of the Knitting in Early Modern Europe research project. She is also part of the Holy Hands research project, the first systematic study of knitted liturgical gloves, which were used ceremonially by elite Christian prelates from the twelfth century onwards.

CARLA TILGHMAN has been making and thinking about textiles since she was twelve. She earned a Master of Arts in Art History from the University of Kansas and a Master of Fine Arts in Textiles from Kent State University. She continues to be fascinated by representations of textiles in art and parsing out their entangled meanings.

Preface

Medieval Clothing and Textiles continues to showcase a selection of new research from a range of disciplines. This volume presents material which ranges in date from the fifth to the beginning of the seventeenth century. The geographical span extends from Scotland through to present-day Germany, France, and Italy. Authors use literary and archival material, visual sources including illuminated manuscripts and panel paintings, and—of course—archaeological evidence.

The opening essay, by Alexandra Lester-Makin, explores the sensory relationships people of early medieval Britain and Ireland had with textiles. It investigates how early medieval perceptions and culture(s) affected the ways in which people understood different fabrics and used them. To do so, the paper uses sensory archaeology as a vehicle for unlocking sensory interactions between human and fabric and in order to learn more about early medieval society's understanding of its world(s). Firstly, it introduces the available textiles from the period and outlines how they have been studied to date. It then explores the early medieval sensorium. Finally, a discussion of several case studies demonstrates how this fresh scholarly approach can give nuanced insights into our understanding of textile perception and use in Britain and Ireland between 450 and 1100.

Tania Kolarik examines the thirteenth-century green-and-white marble intarsia motifs on the facades of the Cathedral of San Martino and the church of San Michele in Foro in Lucca. She focuses on their likely inspiration by the textiles designed, made, traded, and worn within the city. Kolarik argues that the unified building campaign of the two facades functioned to assert the power of the bishop and cathedral canons within the old city center, organized around the cathedral, and the new city center at San Michele and the adjoining municipal palace. These facades created the appearance of a shared, specifically Lucchese, identity through the "textile mentality" of Lucca that was rooted in its status as a major hub of textile production and trade in the global Mediterranean.

The third essay, by Claire W. Kilgore, focuses on the cult of Saint Ursula and the Eleven Thousand Virgins in late medieval Cologne. Through a consideration of some of the reliquary busts associated with the cult, she argues that the fashionable clothing depicted on the busts would have resonated with the women of Cologne, both those involved with the textile industries in which women were dominant—silk weaving and gold spinning—and elite women who may have worn similar clothing to that depicted on the reliquaries. Using theories of material culture and lived religion,

Kilgore contextualises the reliquary busts within the city of Cologne, arguing for the multivalency of their meanings.

Sarah-Grace Heller investigates sumptuary legislation in the southern French city of Montauban in the late thirteenth century, comparing the laws of 1275 and 1291 and providing a transcription of the edict of 1291 together with an English translation. Her essay considers clothing regulations in a thriving mercantile town and analyses the vernacular Occitan in which they were written in order to establish details of dress and accessories that were current there. She looks at the possible rationale behind the stringent regulations in Montauban, as well as placing some of the prohibitions within a wider southwestern European context.

Carla Tilghman takes a look at representations of men's underwear in the art of Northern Europe. Using panel paintings and manuscript illuminations, she considers the different ways in which *braies* were represented and how they could have been understood by viewers and commissioners. The works which she considers range from secular subjects, such as the labours of the months, to altarpieces showing the martyrdoms of saints. She argues that context changed the ways in which underwear was understood and represented. Viewers were able to admire men stripped for work in the fields, to consider the sacrifice of Christ on the cross, and to meditate on the deaths of the saints who were made vulnerable during their martyrdoms through their lack of outer clothing, as well as demonstrating their purity through their shining white underwear.

In the final paper in this volume, Lesley O'Connell Edwards provides a detailed study of the trade in knitted jersey stockings in Norwich and Yarmouth around the end of the sixteenth century and discusses the ways in which children were actively involved. Drawing on a wide range of sources, O'Connell Edwards is able to consider cargos, destinations, and traders, and link some of the latter to Norwich. Her material points to the existence of child knitters both in Norwich and elsewhere, and she discusses how widespread child labour may have been within the stocking trade. Finally, evidence from a contemporary document is used to consider the possibility of estimating the volume and value of the trade in stockings in the area around Norwich and Yarmouth at the end of the sixteenth and beginning of the seventeenth centuries.

As announced in volume 18, Melanie Schuessler Bond has now joined Cordelia Warr in the editorship of this journal. Robin Netherton continues to act as reviews editor. We are profoundly grateful as well for our editorial board in helping us ensure that *Medieval Clothing and Textiles* maintains its position as one of the foremost journals in its field.

We continue to consider for publication in this journal both independent submissions and papers read at sessions sponsored by DISTAFF (Discussion, Interpretation, and Study of Textile Arts, Fabrics, and Fashion) at the international congresses held annually in Kalamazoo, Michigan, and Leeds, England. Proposals for potential conference speakers should be sent to distaff.org@gmail.com (for Kalamazoo) or gale. owencrocker@ntl.world.com (for Leeds). Potential authors for *Medieval Clothing and*

Textiles should read the author guidelines at http://www.distaff.org/MCTguidelines. pdf, and send a 300-word synopsis to mbond5@emich.edu and cordelia.warr@ manchester.ac.uk.

Authors of larger studies interested in submitting a monograph or collaborative book manuscript for our subsidia series, Medieval and Renaissance Clothing and Textiles, should apply using the publication proposal form on the website of our publisher, Boydell and Brewer, at https://boydellandbrewer.com/boydell-brewer-prospective-authors. We encourage potential authors to discuss their ideas with the General Editors, Robin Netherton (robin@netherton.net) and Gale R. Owen-Crocker (gale.owencrocker@ntlworld.com), before making a formal proposal.

Archaeological Textiles, Senses, Perception, and Use: How Sensory Perceptions Affected Textile Use in Early Medieval Britain (450–1100)

Alexandra Lester-Makin[1]

Early medieval objects told stories that were embedded in the cultures that made and used them, whether these were always the same or changed throughout the object's life. These societies used their understanding of the senses to help them navigate their worlds and, by extension, objects were a part of this. Textiles were components of everyday and ceremonial life and their uses were influenced by the sensory and physical worlds they inhabited.

Textiles can be used in performative ways and no matter how they are deployed, for example as clothing or display, they interact with the human body through the senses. These interactions are cultural, learned through social norms, but they can also change over time.[2] As a result, textiles and humans create bonds—relationships that speak to each other through their sensory interactions—whether from a distance or up close and personal. Within these parameters choices are made about what each textile means, how it can and should be used, whether it is considered culturally correct or subversive, and what messages and stories are projected. As a result, the approach known as sensory archaeology is a good vehicle for probing these choices. This theoretical approach uses the human sensory experience to help researchers understand how people in past societies understood, conceptualised, and engaged with their

1   This article was developed from a presentation the author gave at the EuroWeb conference *Making, Wearing, Displaying: Textiles and the Body in Pre-modern Societies*, which was held in Lisbon in May 2023. The original presentation, "How the Senses Informed Textile Use in Early Medieval England (450–1100 CE): The Galloway Hoard as a Case Study," was the result of research I undertook as part of my wider scholarly interests while employed as a research associate at the University of Glasgow on the Arts and Humanities Research Council–funded Unwrapping the Galloway Hoard project (AH/Y012218/1; Principal Investigator Martin Goldberg, National Museums Scotland; Co-investigator Susanna Harris, University of Glasgow). I would like to thank Gale R. Owen-Crocker, Peter Lester, and Martin Goldberg for reading earlier versions of this paper.
2   See for example, Elyse Stanes, "Clothes-in-Process: Touch, Texture, Time," *Textile* 17, no. 3 (2019): 224–45.

worlds.[3] Despite the criticism that people today can never really know or share how past individuals experienced their world(s),[4] sensory archaeology has become a popular way of probing how artefacts, sensory-scapes, and people interrelated. A second criticism, that senses should be treated as a group, not individually—because this is how they work in reality to create multisensory encounters[5]—is now being addressed.[6]

Using sensory archaeology to analyse textiles can help researchers move away from simple data gathering and discussions of fabric's technical attributes to a more interpretative approach,[7] embedded in the sensory environment(s) of the society in which the textile was made and used. Its use in the study of textiles has, in my opinion, only scratched the surface. It has been used as a tool that places textile objects within a purely physical world, but it can also be used to unlock more nuanced ways of understanding a society's whole cosmos, including belief systems, their understanding of things beyond the known world or reality, and generational collective memory.

Due to its multicultural dynamics early medieval Britain provides a rare window through which to study textiles via the senses. The idea of identity across early medieval Britain is complex. The early medieval populations were formed of the Britons, Irish, Scots, Picts, and people descended from populations across what had been the Roman Empire who had settled in Britain during the Roman period. These communities were joined by Germanic tribes, missionaries from Christian Europe and Ireland and, later, the Vikings.[8] In his *Ecclesiastical History* Bede also tells of at least two men from further afield living in England: a monk named Hadrian, who originally came from north Africa, and Theodore of Tarsus, who was Archbishop of Canterbury between 668 and 690.[9] The result was a melting pot where peoples, ideas, and beliefs merged,

3 See Jo Day, "Introduction: Making Senses of the Past," in *Making Senses of the Past: Toward a Sensory Archaeology*, ed. Jo Day (Carbondale, IL: Southern Illinois University Press, 2013), 1–31; Yannis Hamilakis, *Archaeology and the Senses: Human Experience, Memory, and Affect* (Cambridge: Cambridge University Press, 2013).

4 For a discussion about this difficulty see Robin Skeates, *An Archaeology of the Senses: Prehistoric Malta* (Oxford: Oxford University Press, 2010), 3.

5 Day, "Introduction," 7–9; Hamilakis, *Archaeology and the Senses*, 73–101, 113–14.

6 For examples of work incorporating all the senses see Alexandra Lester-Makin, "Embroidery and Its Early Medieval Audience: A Case Study of Sensory Engagement," *World Archaeology* 51, no. 2 (2021): 298–312; Alexandra Lester-Makin, "The Sensory Archaeology of Early Medieval Fabrics from the North Atlantic," in *Textiles in the Viking North Atlantic: Analysis, Interpretation, Re-creation*, ed. Alexandra Lester-Makin and Gale R. Owen-Crocker (Woodbridge, UK: Boydell, 2024), 91–108; Gale R. Owen-Crocker, "Smelly Sheep, Shimmering Silk: The Sensual and Emotional Experience of Textiles," in *Sense and Feeling in Daily Living in the Early Medieval English World*, ed. Maren Clegg Hyer and Gale R. Owen-Crocker (Liverpool: Liverpool University Press, 2020), 97–218.

7 Susanna Harris, "The Sensory Archaeology of Textiles," in *The Routledge Handbook of Sensory Archaeology*, ed. Robin Skeates and Jo Day (London: Routledge, 2020), 210–32.

8 Nancy Edwards, *Life in Early Medieval Wales* (Oxford: Oxford University Press, 2023), 105–33; Nicholas J. Higham and Martin J. Ryan, *The Anglo-Saxon World* (New Haven, CT: Yale University Press, 2013), 6–11, 126–65, 232–70.

9 Bede, *Ecclesiastical History of the English People*, ed. Bertram Colgrave and R. A. B. Mynors (Oxford: Clarendon Press, 1969), book 4, chaps. 1 and 2, 328–37.

coalesced, and morphed, creating ever-evolving perceptions and meanings that were expressed through material culture and understood through the senses. As a result, an analysis of the surviving textiles from a sensory archaeology stance can bring to light a more nuanced and detailed understanding of how they functioned in this unique multicultural sensory environment.

To explore these ideas further the following article investigates how sensory perceptions affected textile use in early medieval Britain by fibre—wool, flax (used to make linen), and silk—drawing out the sensory stories of extant fabrics through a series of small case studies. However, in order to understand the contribution this discussion makes to the fields of both early medieval archaeological textiles and sensory studies, the paper will first outline how textiles have been analysed and interpreted to date and the development of our understanding of sensory perceptions in the early Middle Ages.

STUDYING EARLY MEDIEVAL TEXTILES

Surviving archaeological evidence for textiles from the early medieval period demonstrates that they can be divided into three main categories based on fibre: wool, linen (made predominantly from flax but some nettle and hemp), and silk. Much of the textile corpus from early medieval Britain is fragmentary: it exists as small extant pieces, mineralised fabric, or impressions on other objects. The state of preservation of the textiles is dependent on the conditions in which they were buried. Animal (wool, silk) and plant (flax, hemp) fibres need different conditions in order to survive, but preservation can also be affected by the type of object(s) they were in contact with, which can lead to different fibres, protein and cellulose, surviving together.[10] Many of these—especially those from early in the period—have been found within burial contexts, but material also remains in some later urban sites. Places such as York, London, and Winchester in England have provided good environments for the preservation of wool and silk fabrics in particular but also for some linen.[11] This

---

10 Alexandra Lester-Makin, *The Lost Art of the Anglo-Saxon World: The Sacred and Secular Power of Embroidery* (Oxford: Oxbow, 2019), 32–38.

11 Elisabeth Crowfoot, "Personal Possessions: Textiles," in *Object and Economy in Medieval Winchester*, ed. Martin Biddle (Oxford: Clarendon Press, 1990), 467–93; Arthur MacGregor, *Anglo-Scandinavian Finds from Lloyds Bank* (London: Council for British Archaeology, 1982); Frances Pritchard, "Textiles from Recent Excavations in the City of London," in *Archäologische Textilfunde: Textilsymposium Neumünster 6.5–8.5.1981*, ed. Lise Bender Jørgensen and Klaus Tidow, NESAT 1 (Neumunster, Germany: Textilmuseum Neumunster, 1982), 193–208; Frances Pritchard, "Late Saxon Textiles from the City of London," *Medieval Archaeology* 28 (1984): 46–71; Frances Pritchard, "Self-Patterned Twills from Late Saxon London," *Weavers' Journal* 130 (1984): 11–14; Penelope Walton, *Textiles, Cordage and Raw Fibre from 16-22 Coppergate* (London: Council for British Archaeology, 1989); Penelope Walton Rogers, "Textiles, Cords, Animal Fibres and Human Hair," in *28–9 High Ousegate, York, UK*, ed. Neil Macnab and Jane McComish, report no. AYW3 (York: York Archaeological Trust, 2004), 14–41.

means that the corpus of extant textiles is skewed, something that has to be kept in mind when exploring how they were perceived and used.

The majority of textile analysis and research examines technical components and attributes of the fabric, makes comparisons with other extant pieces, and draws conclusions. This information is used to interpret what the textile may have been used for.[12] Work has generally focused on dress but more recently research centring on textiles as soft furnishings has garnered some interest.[13] Textiles from religious settings such as the shrine of St. Cuthbert have also come under the microscope with their technical attributes and woven designs being used as markers for possible places and dates of production, and discussions about the networks that could have brought them first to Britain and then to their final resting place.[14]

From the 1980s a small number of surveys, such as C. R. Dodwell's *Anglo-Saxon Art: A New Perspective* and Gale Owen-Crocker's *Dress in Anglo-Saxon England*, drew together and critiqued comparative textile evidence from archaeology, art, and text

---

12 There is much published on this subject and it is not possible to list all here. Therefore, only what may be deemed significant publications have been included. All relevant publications to 2007 are cited in Elizabeth Coatsworth and Gale R. Owen-Crocker, *Medieval Textiles of the British Isles AD 450–1100: An Annotated Bibliography* (Oxford: Archaeopress, 2007). Post-2007 publications include Elisabeth Crowfoot, "The Textiles," in *Excavations at Mucking*, vol. 3, *The Anglo-Saxon Cemeteries*, part 1, *Introduction, Catalogues and Specialist Reports*, ed. Sue Hirst and Dido Clark (London: Museum of London, 2009), 428–35; Elisabeth Crowfoot, "Textiles," in *Early Medieval (Later 5th–Early 8th Centuries AD) Cemeteries at Boss Hall and Buttermarket, Ipswich, Suffolk*, ed. Christopher Scull (Leeds, UK: Society of Medieval Archaeology, 2009), 70–71, 228–31; Sue Harrington, "Textiles from the Chamber" and "Textile Analysis," both in *The Prittlewell Princely Burial: Excavations at Priory Crescent, Southend-on-Sea, Essex, 2003*, ed. Lyn Blackmore et al. (London: MOLA, 2019), 264–73, 442–43; Alan Lane and Mark Redknap, "The Early Medieval Textiles," in *Llangorse Crannog: The Excavation of an Early Medieval Royal Site in the Kingdom of Brycheiniog* (Oxford: Oxbow, 2019), 276–316; Caroline Paterson et al., *Shadows in the Sand: Excavation of a Viking-Age Cemetery at Cumwhitton, Cumbria* (Lancaster, UK: Oxford Archaeology North, 2014). A bibliography of Alexandra Makin's textile analysis reports can be found at https://alexandramakin.com/publications (accessed Jan. 10, 2024); Penelope Walton Rogers's work dating to between 1980 and 2021 is available at https://www.aslab.co.uk/bibliography (accessed Jan. 10, 2024).

13 Elizabeth Coatsworth, "Cushioning Medieval Life: Domestic Textiles in Anglo-Saxon England," *Medieval Clothing and Textiles* 3 (2007): 1–12; Sue Harrington, "Soft Furnished Burial: An Assessment of the Role of Textiles in Early Anglo-Saxon Inhumations, with Particular Reference to East Kent," *Anglo-Saxon Studies in Archaeology and History* 14 (2007): 110–16.

14 The textiles from the tomb of St. Cuthbert are a rarity for both number and surviving condition. As a result, they have been examined multiple times since their rediscovery in 1827. See Gerard Brett, "The 'Rider' Silk," in *The Relics of Saint Cuthbert*, ed. C. F. Battiscombe (Oxford: Oxford University Press, 1956), 470–83; J. F. Flanagan, "The Figured-Silks," in the same volume, 484–525; and the following chapters in Gerald Bonner, David Rollason, and Clare Stancliffe, eds., *St. Cuthbert, His Cult and His Community to A.D. 1200* (Woodbridge, UK: Boydell, 1989); Hero Granger-Taylor, "The Weft-Patterned Silks and Their Braid: The Remains of an Anglo-Saxon Dalmatic of c. 800?," 303–27; Hero Granger-Taylor, "The Inscriptions on the Nature Goddess Silk," 339–41; Clare Higgins,

sources.[15] During the 1990s, funded programmes such as the Manchester Medieval Textiles Project created overviews of excavated Anglo-Saxon textiles that wider audiences could access.[16]

In the 2000s scholars began to ask bigger questions, drawing on the evidence to propel discussions around textiles and their use across society, for example, Penelope Walton Rogers's archaeological survey of clothing and textiles,[17] and the Arts and Humanities Research Council–funded project The Lexis of Cloth and Clothing in Britain c. 700–1450.[18] Meanwhile, two articles explored silk's many uses, reuses, and recyclings within Anglo-Saxon society.[19] These ideas had been accepted within scholarly circles but not explored in detail. Adding to the questions about the utilisation of textiles within society, Sue Harrington's thought-provoking article about the representation of gender through textile objects led to the conclusion that Anglo-Saxon society was not necessarily a binary one but had a more nuanced and fluid understanding of gender, particularly before the conversion to Christianity.[20] The recent Unwrapping the Galloway Hoard project, jointly run by National Museums Scotland and the University of Glasgow, has explored the use of textiles within hoards.[21]

The new millennium also brought about the specific incorporation of theory as object biography and entanglement theory were successfully incorporated into studies.[22] Since the first decade of the twenty-first century, sensory archaeology has

---

"Some New Thoughts on the Nature Goddess Silk," 329–37; Anna Muthesius, "Silks and Saints: The Rider and Peacock Silks from the Relics of St. Cuthbert," 343–66.

15 C. R. Dodwell, *Anglo-Saxon Art: A New Perspective* (Manchester, Manchester University Press, 1982); Gale R. Owen-Crocker, *Dress in Anglo-Saxon England* (Manchester: Manchester University Press, 1986). A revised and enlarged edition was published in 2004 (Woodbridge, UK: Boydell).

16 The Manchester Medieval Textiles Project was a collaboration between Gale Owen-Crocker, then at the University of Manchester, and Elizabeth Coatsworth, then at Manchester Metropolitan University. The project started in 1994 and eventually culminated in a published volume, Coatsworth and Owen-Crocker, *Medieval Textiles of the British Isles AD 450–1100* (Oxford: Archaeopress, 2007), and a database that has not been published; Gale Owen-Crocker, pers. comm, 2024.

17 Penelope Walton Rogers, *Cloth and Clothing in Early Anglo-Saxon England, AD 450–700* (York: Council for British Archaeology, 2007).

18 The Lexis of Cloth and Clothing Project is accessible at http://lexisproject.arts.manchester. ac.uk (accessed Jan. 9, 2024).

19 Robin Fleming, "Acquiring, Flaunting, and Destroying Silk in Late Anglo-Saxon England," *Early Medieval Europe* 15, no. 2 (2007): 127–58; Maren Clegg Hyer, "Reduce, Reuse, Recycle: Imagined and Reimagined Textiles in Anglo-Saxon England," *Medieval Clothing and Textiles* 8 (2012): 49–62.

20 Sue Harrington, "From Warp and Weft to Spear and Spindle: Gender Identity and Textile Manufacture in Early Medieval England," in *Gendered Labor in Specialized Economics: Archaeological Perspectives on Female and Male Work*, ed. Sophie E. Kelly and Traci Arden (Denver: University of Colorado Press, 2016), 339–68.

21 Martin Goldberg and Mary Davis, *The Galloway Hoard: Viking-Age Treasure* (Edinburgh: National Museums Scotland, 2021).

22 Elizabeth Coatsworth and Gale R. Owen-Crocker, *Clothing the Past: Surviving Garments from Early Medieval to Early Modern Western Europe* (Leiden, Netherlands: Brill, 2018);

been used to great effect.[23] It has been utilised by early medievalists working in art history, in cultural studies, and with objects and texts,[24] and it has brought together scholars, practitioners, and re-enactors in collaborative research ventures.[25] It is within this evolving research milieu that this paper sits, hoping to develop ideas and ways of thinking about how people and textiles interacted with each other within early medieval Britain.

THE EARLY MEDIEVAL SENSORIUM

The prevailing consensus among scholars is that societies in early medieval Britain followed the Aristotelian view of the five senses, placing them in a set hierarchy—sight, hearing, taste, smell, touch.[26] Many surviving sources and objects—typically works associated with the educated milieu of a Christian population—provide evidence for

---

Lester-Makin, *Lost Art*; Alexandra Lester-Makin, "The Embroidered Fragments from the Tomb of Bishop William of St. Calais, Durham: An Analysis and Biography," in *Art and Worship in the Insular World: Papers in Honour of Elizabeth Coatsworth*, ed. Gale R. Owen-Crocker and Maren Clegg Hyer (Leiden, Netherlands: Brill, 2021), 170–205. An all-day conference session, "The Entangled Making, Uses, and Visualisations of Textiles in the Early Medieval Period, 450–1100," took place at the Leeds International Medieval Congress in July 2023.

23 Owen-Crocker, "Smelly Sheep, Shimmering Silk"; Lena Hammarlund, Heini Kirjavain-en, Kathrine Vestergård Pedersen, and Marianne Vedeler, "Visual Textiles: A Study of Appearance and Visual Impression in Archaeological Textiles," *Medieval Clothing and Textiles* 4 (2008): 69–98; Lester-Makin, "Embroidery and Its Early Medieval Audience"; Lester-Makin, "Sensory Archaeology of Early Medieval Fabrics."

24 See chapters in Hyer and Owen-Crocker, *Sense and Feeling*; Annette Kern-Stähler, Beatrix Busse, and Wiestse de Boer, ed., *The Five Senses in Medieval and Early Modern England* (Leiden, Netherlands: Brill, 2016); Richard G. Newhauser, ed., *A Cultural History of the Senses in the Middle Ages* (2014; repr., London: Bloomsbury Academic, 2019); Simon Thomson and Michael Bintley, eds., *Sensory Perception in the Medieval West* (Turnhout, Belgium: Brepols, 2016). Also, Catherine E. Karkov, *The Art of Anglo-Saxon England* (Woodbridge, UK: Boydell, 2011).

25 See for instance Eva Andersson Strand, Stefan Lindgren, and Carolina Larsson, "Captur-ing Our Cultural Intangible Textile Heritage, MoCap and Craft Technology," in *Digital Heritage: Progress in Cultural Heritage: Documentation, Preservation, and Protection*, ed. Marinos Ioannides et al. (New York: Springer, 2016), 10–15; Eva Andersson Strand, Stefan Lindgren, and Carolina Larsson, "Motion Capture and Textile Experimental Archaeolo-gy, a Possible Combination," *Origini* 40 (2017): 129–40, at 131; Lise Bender-Jørgensen, "Introduction to Part II: Technology as Practice" and "Spinning Faith," both in *Embod-ied Knowledge: Historical Perspectives on Belief and Technology*, ed. Marie Louise Stig Sørensen and Katerina Rebay-Salisbury (Oxford: Oxbow Books, 2013), 91–94, 128–36; Lester-Makin and Owen-Crocker, *Textiles of the Viking North Atlantic*; Ulla Mannering and Charlotte Rimstad, *From Analysis to Reconstruction* (Copenhagen: National Museum of Denmark and Centre for Textile Research, 2023).

26 See discussions in Lester-Makin, "Embroidery and Its Early Medieval Audience," 299–301; Lester-Makin, "Sensory Archaeology of Early Medieval Fabrics."

this.[27] Although this evidence demonstrates that this section of early medieval society followed Aristotle's view of the senses, how, if indeed at all, this played out in everyday life across early medieval society is a different question, and one that is difficult to answer because of the nature of the extant evidence.

While taking into account that the senses work together in order to give a holistic understanding of what is encountered, particularly on a daily basis, this does not happen in isolation. The primary role of the senses is to help a person understand and function within the world they inhabit. Therefore, cultural setting(s) and societal conditioning play an important role in determining how sensory messages are understood and acted upon.[28] Interestingly, research by Elyse Stanes investigating innate knowledge of cloth for her work on contemporary fashion has also shown that these understandings can evolve and change over time, as the individual does.[29] Therefore, decoding sensory input is not a constant, but instead it changes with the individual and the society in which they are living. As a result, the social value of objects would have played an important role in how the community and the individual sensorially interpreted objects and environments they encountered.

Everyday sensory engagement with the world would have taken into account all facets of life and the role the person played in society. Therefore, the idealised Aristotelian sensory hierarchy may not have functioned so neatly in everyday life, if it was taken into account at all. For instance, Catherine Karkov has highlighted that while sight was used by the educated to gain enlightenment on a mystical level, it was used by everyone to *see*, to witness events that could be interpreted in the mind, or to *look* at something but leave the interpretation to others. It also enabled the witnessing of an individual's own power through the objects they had made,[30] used, and donated to others.

Meanwhile, the clamour of the living world may not only have augmented a visual presence but enhanced it, especially when the initiator of the sound could not be seen. For the populace of Britain in the early Middle Ages, sounds appear to have defined land- and built-scapes. For example, Kristopher Poole and Eric

---

27 One example is the late-ninth-century Fuller Brooch (London, British Museum, no. 1952,0404.1) which can be viewed at https://www.britishmuseum.org/collection/object/H_1952-0404-1 (accessed Jan. 9, 2024). See Elizabeth Coatsworth and Michael Pinder, "Sight, Insight and Hand: Some Reflections on the Design and Manufacture of the Fuller Brooch," in *The Material Culture of Daily Living in the Anglo-Saxon World*, ed. Maren Clegg Hyer and Gale R. Owen-Crocker (Liverpool: Liverpool University Press, 2013), 258–74; Katherine O'Brien O'Keeffe, "Hands and Eyes, Sight and Touch: Appraising the Senses in Anglo-Saxon England," *Anglo-Saxon England* 45 (2016): 105–40, at 106, 111–17.

28 David Howes, *The Sensory Studies Manifesto: Tracking the Sensorial Revolution in the Arts and Human Sciences* (Toronto: University of Toronto Press, 2022), 136–38.

29 Stanes, "Clothes-in-Process," 224–45.

30 Catherine Karkov, "Sight and Vision in Early Medieval English Art," in Hyer and Owen-Crocker, *Sense and Feeling*, 12–32, at 31–32.

Lacey have shown that everyday understandings of landscapes were created by the noises of the animals and birds that people encountered.[31] Jill Frederick highlights that due to the amount of cloth each early medieval community needed, the sound of whirring shuttles, as described in Aldhelm's Latin riddle 35 in the *Exeter Book*, which is thought to have been written in the latter half of the tenth century,[32] would have been a constant background noise, despite their noise being soft.[33] The sounds connected with the making of cloth thus formed part of a known and safe place in the unconscious mind.

Taste and smell were complex senses incorporating the ingestion of either the object or its aroma; thus being imparted into the person encountering them, creating a physical bond between object, sensation, and person. For both senses the idea of pleasant or nice equated to goodness and health while an unpleasant taste or smell was deemed negative, bad, or relating to ill health. For doctors, therefore, these senses were considered the most important, with taste taking precedence.[34] More generally, early medieval society appears to have considered smell in ways that are still familiar today. Maren Clegg Hyer has shown that in towns dating to the latter part of the period smell affected where industries were located. For example, smelly textile trades such as flax retting (whereby the fibres are removed from the rest of the plant) and dyeing were located away from people and at locations where the waste could be disposed of easily.[35]

The evidence for how medieval people experienced touch is slight. Javier E. Díaz-Vera has shown that stylised physical motion and interaction was linked to emotion—stroking and love, seizing and anger, trembling and fear. However, he also points out that whether these highly visual representations of touch and emotion were played out in this way in everyday life is, as yet, unknown.[36] But, as Constance

31 Kristopher Poole and Eric Lacey, "Avian Aurality in Anglo-Saxon England," *World Archaeology* 46, no. 3 (2014): 400–15.

32 Maren Clegg Hyer and Gale R. Owen-Crocker, "Woven Works: Making and Using Textiles," in Hyer and Owen-Crocker, *The Material Culture of Daily Living*, 157–84, at 157–58; G. P. Knapp and E. V. K. Dobbie, eds., *Anglo-Saxon Book of Poetic Records* (New York: Columbia University Press, 1936). The *Exeter Book* is a collection of works ranging in theme from saints' lives, wisdom and heroic poems, gnomic and elegy verses to over 100 riddles. It is thought to have been written by a monk between 960 and 990 and was given to the monastery at Exeter by Leofric, Bishop of Exeter, upon his death in 1072.

33 Jill Frederick, "'Þær wæs hearpan sweg, swotol sang scopes': Sounds of Pre-Conquest Community," in Hyer and Owen-Crocker, *Sense and Feeling*, 13–53, at 47.

34 Charles Burnett, "The Superiority of Taste," *Journal of the Warburg and Courtauld Institutes* 54 (1991): 230–38.

35 Maren Clegg Hyer, "The Blossoms' Sweet Stench: Smell in Early Medieval England," in Hyer and Owen-Crocker, *Sense and Feeling*, 70–86, at 83.

36 Javier E. Díaz-Vera, "The Sense of Touch: The Haptic Communication of Emotions in Anglo-Saxon England from a Linguistic Perspective," in Hyer and Owen-Crocker, *Sense and Feeling*, 87–106, at 105.

Classen has argued, medieval life was largely a communal and shared experience.[37] Therefore, people would have been in near-constant contact with each other, whether intentionally or not.

With regards to textile production, Valerie L. Garver has shown, through an examination of textile-making tools and buildings from Büraburg bei Fritzler and Wijnaldum-Tjitsma, two sites in the Carolingian Empire with evidence dating in the range of the eighth and ninth centuries, that the production of flax linen textiles was often a tortuous affair that included cuts and scratches from turning the rough flax plants into usable fibre.[38] This continued work would probably have led to the development of callouses on the hands which would have changed the way both the workers and people who touched them would have sensed each other. In a similar example, the development of arthritis from doing textile work in a seated position has been found in the skeleton of an elderly woman buried in the late ninth to tenth century at Scar, on the island of Sanday, Orkney.[39] In this instance, someone touching the woman would have encountered differently shaped bones under her skin while the lady herself may have had her ability to touch hampered. The active engagement of touch was therefore one that could easily be obstructed or disabled, creating different sensations to those that would be expected.

So, while the educated milieu desired a hierarchy of sensory engagement, the general populace does not appear to have been so dogmatic. Instead, the senses were used together to explain and define the world around them and how they should engage with it. Scholars have shown that early medieval society experienced and understood material culture through multifaceted sensory and perspectival lenses.[40] Objects and

37 Constance Classen, *The Deepest Sense: A Cultural History of Touch* (Chicago: University of Illinois Press, 2012), 180.

38 Valerie L. Garver, "Sensory Experiences of Low-Status Female Textile Workers in the Carolingian World," in *Sensory Reflections: Traces of Experience in Medieval Artifacts*, ed. Fiona Griffiths and Kathryn Starkey (Berlin: De Gruyter, 2020), 50–76.

39 D. H. Lorimer, "The Bodies: The Female Skeleton," in *Scar: A Viking Boat Burial on Sanday, Orkney*, ed. Olwyn Owen and Magnar Dalland (East Linton, UK: Tuckwell Press, 1991), 56–58.

40 Dieter Bitterli, "Strange Perceptions: Sensory Experience in the Old English 'Marvels of the East,'" in Kern-Stähler, Busse, and de Boer, *Five Senses*, 137–62; Meg Boulton, "'The End of the World as We Know It': Viewing Eschatology and Symbolic Space/s in Late Antique and Insular Art," in *Making Histories: Proceedings of the Sixth International Conference on Insular Art*, ed. Jane Hawkes (Donington, UK: Shaun Tyas, 2013), 279–90; Meg Boulton, "Art History in the Dark Ages: (Re)considering Space, Stasis, and Modern Viewing Practices in Relation to Anglo-Saxon Imagery," in *Stasis in the Medieval West? Questioning Change and Continuity*, ed. Michael D. J. Bintley et al. (New York: Palgrave Macmillan, 2017), 69–86; Meg Boulton, "Looking Down from the Rothbury Cross: (Re) viewing the Place of Anglo-Saxon Art," in *Insular Iconographies: Essays in Honour of Jane Hawkes*, ed. Meg Boulton and Michael D. J. Bintley (Woodbridge, UK: Boydell, 2019), 217–34; Javier E. Díaz-Vera, "Coming to Past Senses: Vision, Touch and Their Metaphors in Anglo-Saxon Language and Culture," in Kern-Stähler, Busse, and de Boer, *Five Senses*, 36–66; Katherine Hindley, "Sight and Understanding: Visual Imagery as Metaphor in the

viewers interacted with each other, changing when encountered in distinct ways, for example, when textiles were experienced at different angles or heights, in varying light or settings,[41] and at specific times of the year. By incorporating these ideas into studies of material culture, it is possible to gain an understanding of these personal and publicly shared experiences.

The senses also had positive and negative values attributed to them, which theologians argued could either help the soul gain spiritual understanding and enlightenment and therefore save it, or lead it down the path of damnation.[42] This had implications for people in their everyday lives because the senses formed part of a world where anything and everything could represent good or evil and all had potency. It can be seen particularly well in early medieval myths and sagas. People go unrecognised because of the clothes they are wearing, shamans can move between this and other realms, and the natural world is not always what it seems.[43] Many of these experiences engulf multiple senses creating immersive encounters and memories. This, then, was a world where everything contained multiple meanings, layered with suggestions and significance and hidden in riddles. Research on surviving material culture indicates that there was a deep-seated understanding that all matter expressed these meanings, and that this was a trait that continued throughout the period.

These ideas can be understood well when exploring the early medieval use of colour and bejewelled decoration, especially in ecclesiastical settings. At this time the church was considered a manifestation of the heavenly Jerusalem and a transitional/liminal place. It was therefore only right that it should be decorated as such, embodying its sanctity as well as its association with heaven. This was also true of the objects

---

Old English *Boethius* and *Soliloquies*," in Kern-Stähler, Busse, and de Boer, *Five Senses*, 21–35; Karkov, *The Art of Anglo-Saxon England*, 135–78; O'Brien O'Keeffe, "Hands and Eyes, Sight and Touch"; Simon C. Thomson, "Sensory Perception in the Medieval West: Introduction," in Thomson and Bintley, *Sensory Perception in the Medieval West*, 1–5. Also see chapters in Hyer and Owen-Crocker, *Sense and Feeling*; Cynthia Thickpenny, Katherine Forsyth, Jane Geddes, and Kate Mathis, eds., *Peopling Insular Art: Practice, Performance, Perception* (Oxford: Oxbow, 2020).

41 Meg Boulton, "(Re-) Viewing *Iuxta Morem Romanorum*: Considering Perception, Phenomenology, and Anglo-Saxon Ecclesiastical Art and Architecture," in Thomson and Bintley, *Sensory Perception in the Medieval West*, 207–26; Melissa Herman, "All that Glitters: The Role of Pattern, Reflection, and Visual Perception in Early Anglo-Saxon Art," in the same volume, 159–79.

42 Bitterli, "Strange Perceptions," 137–46; Hindley, "Sight and Understanding"; Herbert L. Kessler, *Seeing Medieval Art* (Toronto: Toronto University Press, 2011), 172; Richard G. Newhauser, "Foreword: The Senses in Medieval and Renaissance Intellectual History," *The Senses and Society* 5, no. 1 (2010): 5–9, at 6–7; O'Brien O'Keeffe, "Hands and Eyes, Sight and Touch"; Eric Palazzo, "Art, Liturgy, and the Five Senses in the Early Middle Ages," *Viator* 41, no. 1 (2010): 25–56, at 29–30.

43 For a discussion on this topic in relation to the senses see Lester-Makin, "Sensory Archaeology of Early Medieval Fabrics," 97–105.

displayed within,[44] which included many textiles used as hangings and vestments, as can be seen depicted on an eleventh-century carved ivory box from Winchester.[45]

Many of the objects would have been illuminated by candles and windows, often small and set high in the walls. Direct light was thought to be the divine *presence* of God, with reflected light spiritually elevating whatever it touched.[46] As this celestial light touched and refracted off the brilliant colours, jewels, and metals, so God was revealing the whole building and drenching it in his divine being. He was essentially illuminating heaven on earth.[47]

To this can be added the idea that the two-dimensional depiction of three-dimensional space did not mean that it should be engaged with as a flat surface. Artworks surrounded and engulfed the viewer, enclosing them in the work, creating "a fluid series of interrelations between us and the object."[48] Meg Boulton argues that this was a "transformative process that involved an exchange between eyes, mind and soul" that was often embedded in cultural associations known to the viewer.[49] This can be seen in the Kempston embroidery, a 24-by-54-millimetre fragment of fine wool cloth with wool embroidery that was found in a small bronze box in a seventh-century female burial at Kempston, Bedfordshire.[50] Dyed purple and embroidered with entwined beasts or knots in yellow/white, green/blue, and red threads, it was probably a band or border on a garment. I have argued elsewhere that it was most likely worn by a holy person.[51] From a distance only indistinct colours would have been visible. As the viewer got closer the details would have become clearer and more recognisable. As the wearer moved or the fabric was caught by a breeze, the entwined beasts would have undulated. At first, the effect would have been simply light against dark, which might have led to feelings of either apprehension or excitement. Then, the multicoloured and finely wrought design would have come into focus, seeming to live, writhing around the person wearing it and building on the previous emotions evoked by it. Within the early medieval mindset, this piece of theatre may well have

---

44 Boulton, "(Re-) Viewing *Iuxta Morem Romanorum*," 219, 222; Kessler, *Seeing Medieval Art*, 19–42, at 34.

45 The box is now at the Victoria and Albert Museum, London (no. 268-1867), and photographs are available at http://collections.vam.ac.uk/item/O92588/box-unknown (accessed Jan. 29, 2024).

46 Heather Hunter-Crawley, "Embodying the Divine: The Sensational Experience of the Sixth-Century Eucharist," in Day, *Making Senses of the Past*, 160–76, at 164; Kessler, *Seeing Medieval Art*, 34, 174–75.

47 Lester-Makin, "Embroidery and Its Early Medieval Audience," 309.

48 Boulton, "(Re-) Viewing *Iuxta Morem Romanorum*," 214.

49 Boulton, "(Re-) Viewing *Iuxta Morem Romanorum*," 217; also Boulton, "The End of the World"; Boulton, "Art History in the Dark Ages."

50 London, British Museum, no. 1891,0624.141. Originally analysed by Elisabeth Crowfoot, "Textile Fragments from 'Relic-Boxes' in Anglo-Saxon Graves," in *Textiles in Northern Archaeology: NESAT III Textile Symposium in York, 6–9 May 1987*, ed. Penelope Walton and John Peter Wild (London: Archetype Publications, 1990), 47–56. It was reanalysed by Lester-Makin, *Lost Art*, 57–76.

51 Lester-Makin, *Lost Art*, 57–76, pl. 14.

been interpreted as the wearer having power over these multidimensional creatures. The design most likely represented the world serpent which, in Germanic mythology, encircled the earth beneath the sea and had many qualities, both good and bad, including those of protection and healing.[52] Therefore, audiences encountering the "living" entwined creatures on the garment might have surmised that they were protecting a wearer who could tame and control them, possibly for healing but also, maybe, for malign purposes. The embedded cultural meanings of the glimpsed motifs would have been clear. It is therefore easy to understand why the Viking raids of 793 were preceded by "immense flashes of lightning, and fiery dragons were seen flying in the air."[53] In that instance, (mythical) creatures had breached the dividing barrier between our world and theirs, just as they did on the holy person's clothing. While this was a magical sign, it was understood culturally as one that heralded the coming of doom to Northumbria.

When the Vikings arrived with motifs that were their own but also somehow familiar, the cultural meanings and sensory experiences may well have been overwhelming and mentally and physically disquieting for the settled populations. The Scandinavian traditions harked back to pre-Christian times and adherence to kin, tribe, and kingdom, providing a link to the fifth-century Germanic settlers of post-Roman Britain. These tribes, who had arrived from multiple territories including modern-day Germany and Scandinavia, would have had similar concepts, which the populations of early medieval England that had been Christianised knew about through stories and poems such as *Beowulf* (although the date of this poem's original composition is unknown, it was first written down between 975 and 1025). Harald Kleinschmidt has explored the use of senses and perception in the pre-Christian world. He has shown that pre-Christian peoples were orientated by affiliation to and preservation of the group through predetermined action and the senses were used to enable these concepts. Thus, visual and auditory perceptions were dominant in stimulating and drawing in both performers and audience, the result of which was a continued engagement with and control of individuals for the good of the group.[54]

The way people dressed and vocalised therefore formed an integral part of onlookers' sensory comprehension of an individual's affiliations, status, and abilities within this world. As Robin Fleming has argued, in early medieval England monarchs from the latter part of the period wore silk clothing that emulated both ecclesiastical garments and garb worn by German emperors; thus rulers of England were visually identifying the priestly nature of kingship and demonstrating the illustriousness of their own royal position.[55] However, objects that pertained to the individual's position

52 George Speake, *Anglo-Saxon Animal Art and Its Germanic Background* (Oxford: Oxford University Press, 1980), 90–92.
53 Michael Swanton, ed. and trans., *The Anglo-Saxon Chronicles: New Edition* (London: Phoenix, 2000), 53, 55.
54 Harald Kleinschmidt, *Perception and Action in Medieval Europe* (Woodbridge, UK: Boydell, 2005).
55 Fleming, "Acquiring and Flaunting Silk," 157–58.

within society, for instance the embroidered stole and maniple found in the tomb of St. Cuthbert, which name both commissioner, Queen Ælfflæd (d. before 916), and receiver, Bishop Frithestan (d. ca. 932–33),[56] could have their own histories and meanings, so when these were viewed or touched, the owner was connecting himself with all who had previously owned and used the object, and I would argue, the maker(s) as well; it was a sensory link to the ancestors and realms beyond.[57] Thus, both the known and unknown worlds were drawn together through a cosmological construct of dress, object, and sensory understanding.

This was a world that prioritised the visual and aural. Kleinschmidt rightly states that the roles of touch, smell, and taste are difficult to ascertain within these societies.[58] However, taking into account the earlier discussion about the sensory everyday, I would argue that touch, particularly for textiles, was as important, if not more so, in order to fulfil the action(s) required for the survival of the group. It is in these complex and evolving sensory milieux that textiles were woven, used, recycled, buried, and/or discarded.

CASE STUDIES

Wool

Wool was used throughout society during this period and in a range of weave structures, from the most basic plain (tabby) weave to more complex twills. The making and use of these textiles is a complex picture with some weaves being particular to certain communities or territories, for example, 2/1 twills from fifth- and sixth-century graves in certain areas of East Anglia.[59] Others, such as 2/2 twills and diamond-patterned twills, were utilized more widely, especially from the seventh and eighth centuries, when larger centralised estates began to control and standardise production.[60] Fabrics including (possibly) honeycomb weaves were also imported.[61]

---

56 Lester-Makin, *Lost Art*, 156–57; for other textiles embroidered with inscriptions including the names of those who made them, see Elizabeth Coatsworth, "Inscriptions on Textiles Associated with Anglo-Saxon England," in *Writing and Texts in Anglo-Saxon England*, ed. A. R. Rumble (Woodbridge, UK: Boydell, 2006), 71–95.

57 Joe Bazelmans, "Moralities of Dress and the Dress of the Dead in Early Medieval Europe," in *Thinking Through the Body: Archaeologies of Corporeality*, ed. Yannis Hamilakis, Mark Pluciennik, and Sarah Tarlow (London: Kluwer Academic/Plenum, 2002), 71–84.

58 Kleinschmidt, *Perception and Action*, 142.

59 Penelope Walton Rogers, "Continuity Within Change: Two Sites in the Borders of the Former Iceni Territory in East Anglia," in *The Very Beginning of Europe? Cultural and Social Dimensions of Early-Medieval Migration and Colonisation (5th–8th century)*, ed. Rica Annaert et al. (Brussels: Flanders Heritage Agency, 2012), 109–22.

60 Owen-Crocker, *Dress in Anglo-Saxon England*, 293–95; Hyer and Owen-Crocker, "Woven Works: Making and Using Textiles," 182–84; Penelope Walton Rogers, *Textile Production at 16-22 Coppergate* (London: Council for British Archaeology, 1997), 1823–25, 1827–29.

61 Walton, *Textiles, Cordage and Raw Fibre*, 356–58; Rogers, *Textile Production*, 1826.

My own analysis of surviving wool fabrics within their find and use contexts reveals that they often formed outer, protective layers. As clothing, some of these woollen textiles covered inner or under garments, creating a barrier between the individual and the world around them. When woollen textiles were used to wrap objects, sometimes over multiple layers of other textile coverings, the same protective barrier was formed. This was also true when wool cloth was utilised as soft furnishings, for example, bedding. In these situations, people were protected from their interior and exterior living environments, making them more comfortable places to inhabit. This is not to say wool textiles were only used in these ways, but the evidence demonstrates that cloth of this fibre was often employed as a barrier between human or object and the world they occupied, as the following case studies will demonstrate. Why would this be? The obvious practical answer is that wool is a good insulator and protector against inclement weather, while aesthetically it could be woven in multiple colours and patterns, dyed brightly and/or augmented with embroidery, but exploring these ideas through a sensory lens brings other cultural and perceptual reasons to light.

The Orkney hood (fig. 1.1) was discovered in a peat bog near Groatsetter Farm, Tankerness, on Mainland, Orkney.[62] It is a child's hood made from recycled wool cloth and two reused woollen tablet-woven bands,[63] the wider of which incorporates a long fringe measuring 28–33 centimetres (11–13 inches). The hood was originally thought to be Viking because the tablet-woven bands and fringe are typical of Scandinavian textiles at this time.[64] However, the fabric was radiocarbon dated to between 250 and 615,[65] linking it to Pictish culture, although this could also mean that the cloth dates to this period while the tablet-woven bands, which have not been radiocarbon dated, and the construction of the hood are later. The loop stitch used to attach the tablet-woven bands to the hood may also be suggestive, as extant examples of this stitch come from early Germanic and later Viking contexts.[66] The hood's shape is also similar to headcoverings from Viking York, Lincoln, and Dublin.[67] The wool fabric was worn and darned in places, telling of its human-textile biography. As a child's hood it would have enveloped the wearer, keeping them warm and dry while hiding their

---

62 Edinburgh, National Museums Scotland, no. X.NA 3. I am grateful to Martin Goldberg for suggesting this case study.

63 Jo Wood, "The Orkney Hood: An Ancient Re-Cycled Textile," in *Sea Change: Orkney and Northern Europe in the Later Iron Age AD 300–800*, ed. Jane Downes and Anna Ritchie (Balgavies, UK: Pinkfoot Press, 2003), 171–75.

64 Audrey S. Henshall, "Early Textiles Found in Scotland," *Proceedings of the Society of Antiquaries of Scotland* 86 (1951–52): 1–29, at 9–15.

65 Thea Gabra-Sanders, "The Orkney Hood, Re-dated and Re-considered," in *The Roman Textile Industry and Its Influence: A Birthday Tribute to John Peter Wild*, ed. Penelope Walton Rogers, Lisa Bender Jørgensen, and Antoinette Rast-Eicher (Oxford: Oxbow, 2001), 98–104.

66 Alexandra Lester-Makin, "Looped Stitch: The Travels and Development of an Embroidery Stitch," in *The Daily Lives of the Anglo-Saxons*, ed. Carole Biggam, Carole Hough, and Daria Izdebska (Tempe: Arizona Center for Medieval and Renaissance Studies, 2017), 119–36.

67 Coatsworth and Owen-Crocker, *Clothing the Past*, 33.

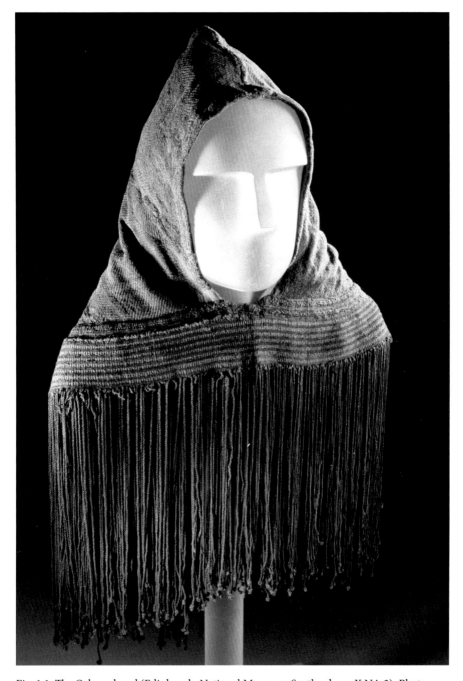

Fig. 1.1: The Orkney hood (Edinburgh, National Museums Scotland, no. X.NA 3). Photo: Copyright © National Museums Scotland, by permission.

face when they did not want to be noticed, possibly in order to feel safe or be alone, maybe when playing with others or when adults called them to do chores. However, they would have been noticeable as the fringe bounced and danced while they ran and played, enabling others to keep an eye on them from a distance. The fringe may have also made a noise, moving the air around it, creating a physical presence beyond the body. At the same time, this extra manifestation may have brought back into "being" those who had previously owned and used the textile and bands. Thus, the ancestors watched over and protected the child while bringing them into communion with the story bound up in the precious fabric: one that the youngster may have been told as they sat with family and/or community elders, connecting them to and placing them within their culture.

The early-seventh-century (possible) pillowcase (fig. 1.2) from the Sutton Hoo ship burial was discovered within a pile of textiles lying between silver vessels and a mail coat.[68] The burial was probably that of Rædwald (d. 624), king of the East Angles.[69] The pillowcase was woven in broken diamond twill with undyed, probably white wool in one system and blue yarn in the other. The thread count is 17–19 by 13–15 per centimetre (about 43–48 by 33–38 per inch),[70] so the woven pattern is small and delicate. The combination of weave structure and dye would have given the fabric an appearance similar to modern taffeta, albeit duller, the colours changing in different light and as the textile moved. From a distance it would have appeared a hazy rippling blue-white. The closer the textile, the clearer the colours and weave structure would become, until—at the moment it was handled or when someone placed their head on it—distinct patterns appeared. The pillow which the case covered would have been stuffed, possibly with feathers, as have been found in other seventh-century ship burials,[71] a luxury compared to lying directly on the ground or on a mattress of straw. It would have rustled when it was plumped up or as the head moved, and the feathers may have poked through the fabrics, pricking the skin. The filling and wool probably smelt: a combined aroma of feathers, wool, and bodily effusions. Throughout all of these sensory encounters the pillow was doing something fundamental: protecting the sleeper's head from a possibly harsh environment and making it more comfortable and restful. This mixture of sensory encounters would have been familiar to the user, forming a welcome and secure (partial) envelopment as they slept. To onlookers it would have demonstrated Rædwald's wealth but just how much would only be ascer-

68 London, British Museum, no. 1939.1010.184.a.
69 Higham and Ryan, *The Anglo-Saxon World*, 124, 133.
70 Elisabeth Crowfoot, "The Textiles," in *The Sutton Hoo Ship-Burial*, vol. 3, ed. Rupert Bruce-Mitford and Angela C. Evans (London: British Museum Publications, 1983), 404–79, at 421; M. C. Whiting, "Appendix 2: Dye Analysis," in the same volume, 465.
71 See Birgitta Berglund and Jørgen Rosvold, "Microscopic Identification of Feathers from 7th Century Boat Burials at Valsgärde in Central Sweden: Specialized Long-Distance Feather Trade or Local Bird Use?," *Journal of Archaeological Science Reports* 36 (2021): 1–14.

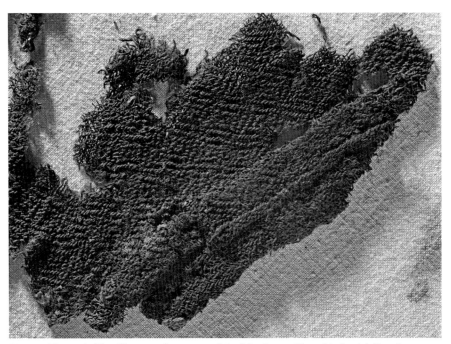

Fig. 1.2: The probable pillowcase from mound 1 of the Sutton Hoo ship burial (London, British Museum, no. 1939,1010.184.a). Photo: Copyright © Trustees of the British Museum, shared under Creative Commons licence CC BY-NC-SA 4.0.

tained if the person got close enough to see the pillow in detail. This was a safe haven for the king and a message restricted to people with access to him.

The Galloway Hoard, which was buried in the ninth century and discovered in Dumfries and Galloway in modern-day Scotland, includes one piece of wool textile, wrapping a silver-gilt lidded vessel (fig. 1.3).[72] This cloth forms the outer barrier between the precious container, which was enveloped in a linen fabric, and the ground in which it was buried. The wool has been radiocarbon dated to between 670 and 780, so it was at least 100 years old when it was taken out of circulation and buried.[73] This was an heirloom piece that may have been through many life cycles before it was chosen to protect the vessel, but despite this heritage, the wool was still placed outermost, forming the first defence between earth and object. As such, it was more likely to have been attacked by bacteria and other microbes in the surrounding soil, resulting in greater deterioration if not complete disintegration. The person burying the wrapped vessel may have understood that the item was likely to degrade, if not the reason for it. While the fabric would have had sensory qualities associated with

72 Edinburgh, National Museums Scotland, no. X.2018.12.71.
73 Goldberg and Davis, *The Galloway Hoard*, 63, 71–72.

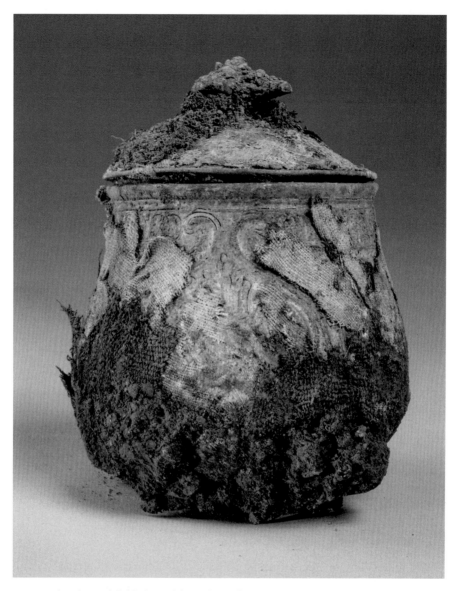

Fig. 1.3: The silver-gilt lidded vessel from the Galloway Hoard, wrapped in two layers of textile (Edinburgh, National Museums Scotland, no. X.2018.12.71). The inner layer is linen, and the outer layer is wool. Photo: Copyright © National Museums Scotland, by permission.

both its biography and physical properties, its primary role within the hoard was to cover and hide the vessel, changing the surface of the container from hard, cold, and smooth with an engraved pattern that could be distinguished by eye and hand, to soft, fibrous, and rough with an unvarying overall texture and, possibly, woolly smell. Thus, the known and sensorially understood stories associated with the lidded vessel were hidden and disguised by those of the heirloom wool textile: a sensory subversion in order to protect the precious vessel and its contents from both the ground in which it was buried and prying humanity.

With these three examples, cultural knowledge led to different sensory encounters and understandings of wool fabrics, but the overriding idea is one of wool as a protective force. Just as the fibre protects sheep, so it also looked after humans and objects, making them feel comfortable and safe (through touch and smell) and making them seem powerful and in control (through sight and sound). These were influential concepts in a cosmos of unknown and unseen dangers.

Linen

In the early medieval period, linen textiles were used by most but not all of society. In England they have been found in archaeological contexts dating throughout the period. Evidence for the appearance of flax in Scotland coincides with the arrival of the Vikings, while in Wales there is confirmation that flax was being grown and processed as an edible crop but not, so far, for weaving.[74] There is also one extant piece, the late-ninth- to tenth-century Llangorse tunic woven from an unidentified bast fibre and embroidered with linen and silk threads, which is thought to have been made in England.[75]

Linen textiles do not appear to have been used in the same way as wool. This smoother-textured fabric was often made into garments worn next to the skin and used for shrouds, which formed a second, tightly wrapped skin. It was also utilized as a wrapper enveloping objects considered precious, a possible example being a piece from the Staffordshire Hoard found in soil inside a gold hilt-collar, which may have come from a sword, although it has not been completely determined if the textile is contemporary with the hilt-collar.[76] Linen was the soft, gentle protector that in-

---

74 This is not to say linen was not being woven in Wales at this time, only that the evidence discovered so far is slight; see Edwards, *Life in Early Medieval Wales*, 195–96, 223–24.
75 Cardiff, National Museum of Wales, no. 91.5H/[412]. Lane and Redknap, *Llangorse Crannog*, 276–316.
76 Staffordshire Hoard, no. 126. The Staffordshire Hoard is jointly held by the Birmingham Museum and Art Gallery, and the Potteries Museum and Art Gallery at Stoke-on-Trent. Caroline Cartwright, "Identification of the Fibres of Textile Fragments Found Embedded in the Soil Inside Silver Gilt Collar K281 from the Staffordshire Hoard," in *Staffordshire Hoard Research Report 13* (York: Archaeological Data Service, 2013). Images of the fabric can be found in this report. See also Tania Dickinson, Chris Fern, and Leslie Webster, "What Does It Mean?" in *The Staffordshire Hoard: An Anglo Saxon Treasure*, ed. Chris Fern, Tania Dickinson, and Leslie Webster (London: Society of Antiquaries, 2019), 352–

corporated connotations of purity due to its connection to the scriptures, especially Revelation 19:8–9 in which an angel sings "His bride is ready, and she has been able to dress herself in dazzling white linen, because her linen is made of the good deeds of saints …."[77] Therefore, linen used as a base layer, closest to the object, brings to mind the idea of purity, concealing and protecting precious, possibly holy objects from human gaze and touch. Once objects were wrapped in linen, humans were not able to interact with them in the same way. The objects were deliberately distanced sensorially, shrouded in purity and hiding their physical truth.

Interestingly Æthelthryth of Ely (d. 679) was noted for refusing to wear linen, as a sign of devotion.[78] As an ascetic she may have felt her body was not pure or holy enough to allow her to wear this fibre. If she had, she would have been metaphorically removed from this world, where her physical form would decay, and preserved as memory until she was unveiled and revealed again. People shrouded in linen were transformed from corrupting corpses into pure and holy individuals. While their souls entered heaven, their personhood was sensorially distanced from the degrading and tainted material world and those who inhabited it. However, their now disassociated physical form could be unwrapped and rewrapped in fabrics that combined heaven and earth, linen then silk, and so be venerated by followers here on earth.

Linen fabric was also used for wall hangings, both woven, like those from the ninth-century Oseberg ship burial,[79] and embroidered, like the eleventh-century Bayeux Tapestry.[80] In these examples, linen is visually taking on the role of the *scop*, the Anglo-Saxon storyteller,[81] who told stories of heroes and great deeds. Whereas when the storyteller spoke and mentally shaped the listening audience, they created a living memory that would dissipate with the last word (until retold and reimagined), the woven and stitched imagery was a constant, unchanging narrative, always visible while the hanging was displayed. Here stories were visually "read" as the viewer progressed along the hanging. If the Bayeux Tapestry was displayed within a castle keep, as has been suggested, the audience would have also seen connections between different scenes.[82] However, the hanging would have moved, caught by the breeze of a person

60, at 359; Peter McElhinney and Chris Fern, "Organics and Pastes," in the same volume, 136–38, at 136.

77 Alexander Jones, ed., *The Jerusalem Bible, Popular Edition* (London: Darton, Longman and Todd, 1974).

78 Bede, *Ecclesiastical History*, 392, 393.

79 Marianne Vedeler, *The Oseberg Tapestries* (Oslo: Spartacus Forlag AS/Scandinavian Academic Press, 2019).

80 Interactive images of the Bayeux Tapestry can be found at the Bayeux Museum website: https://www.bayeuxmuseum.com/en/the-bayeux-tapestry/discover-the-bayeux-tapestry/explore-online (accessed June 10, 2024).

81 Roberta Frank, "The Search for the Anglo-Saxon Oral Poet," *Bulletin of the John Rylands Library* 75 (1993): 11–36.

82 See Gale R. Owen-Crocker, "Brothers, Rivals and the Geometry of the Bayeux Tapestry," in *King Harold II and the Bayeux Tapestry*, ed. Gale R. Owen-Crocker (Woodbridge, UK: Boydell, 2005), 109–23; Chris Henige, "Putting the Bayeux Tapestry in its Place," in the

passing by, making the imagery "live," turning the static story into film, inviting the viewer to enter the action more fully than anticipated by the design alone.[83] The bright colours would illuminate and change as light moved across it, horses would gallop, and sails would billow, enhancing the idea of a living story or history. People would be able to touch the textile, lean against it, gesticulate, and brush it as they discussed what they saw. Noise would have ebbed and flowed within the enclosed space but sound from outside would be muffled, encapsulating the audience in a private world. This was theatre in the round and a show that the audience was invited to participate and believe in: an immersive experience. The Bayeux Tapestry was also a postwar sensory bombardment and propaganda campaign, a soft-touch approach that was the antithesis of the violent subjugation taking place outside.

Linen can therefore be seen as incorporating similar ideas to silk (see below), but it was more widely available than that exotic fibre. It was a powerful but locally made fabric that contained cosmological constructs within its weave and decoration, drawing together people and communities in both this world and the next.

Silk

Silk was the most prestigious fabric. The fibre is made from the cocoon of the *Bombyx mori* (silkworm moth) pupa, and it could not be cultivated in Britain. Evidence for silk textiles in early medieval England is negligible before the seventh-century conversion period, indicating that it probably arrived through Christian contacts on the Continent.[84] These fabrics came from weaving centres in Byzantium and along the Silk Road, and possibly from as far as China once the Vikings had established their river-based trading routes in the ninth century.[85]

During the early part of the period silk was available only to secular and religious elites, through social contact and/or gift exchange networks. The earliest surviving examples come from contexts dating to the seventh century. One, a length of white silk thread, was discovered with a piece of plain-weave flax textile in a small box from

---

same volume, 125–37. It should be noted that the original location of the Bayeux Tapestry is still debated. For discussions about other possibilities for where it could have been displayed, including Bayeux Cathedral, see Elizabeth Carson Paston and Stephen D. White with Kate Gilbert, *The Bayeux Tapestry and Its Contexts: A Reassessment* (Woodbridge, UK: Boydell, 2014), 19–24; Mike Hagger, "The Making and Meaning of the Bayeux Tapestry," *Journal of Medieval History* 50, no. 2 (2024): 214–35; Christopher Norton, "The Helmet and the Crown: The Bayeux Tapestry, Bishop Odo and William the Conqueror," in *Anglo-Norman Studies 43: Proceedings of the Battle Conference 2020*, ed. S. D. Church (Woodbridge, UK: Boydell, 2021), 123–48.

83 For a discussion about the design drawing in viewers see Linda Elaine Neagley, "Portals of the Bayeux Tapestry: Visual Experience, Spatial Representation and Oral Performance," in *The Bayeux Tapestry: New Approaches*, ed. Michael J. Lewis, Gale R. Owen-Crocker, and Dan Terkla (Oxford: Oxbow, 2011), 136–46.

84 Rogers, *Cloth and Clothing*, 240.

85 See Marianne Vedeler, *Silk for the Vikings* (Oxford: Oxbow, 2014).

a child's grave at Updown, Kent. Grave goods within this burial suggest Frankish and therefore Christian connections. A second, a piece of undyed plain-weave silk cut into a circle and wrapped around a spherical object, possibly a button from rich clothing or a knob for soft furnishings, was unearthed in the grave of a smith at Tattershall Thorpe, Lincolnshire. Meanwhile, the silk cloths found in the tomb of St. Cuthbert in Durham Cathedral show the variety available in early medieval Britain.[86]

Later in the period silk also arrived via Viking trade routes and Anglo-Saxon merchants, as described in Aelfric's tenth-century colloquy.[87] There is evidence for (probable) silk thread being used to decorate shoes dating to ca. 1070–80 in London.[88] Excavations in Lincoln have produced fragments of silk headcoverings that date to the Viking period, as do silk hairnets, headcoverings, and tablet weaving discovered in Dublin.[89] These may have come from Byzantium or centres in the Near East.[90] By the end of the period in 1100, silk, while not available to everyone, was being acquired by wider sections of society, particularly people living and working in cosmopolitan urban centres.

Silk had many meanings. In ecclesiastical settings such as the cells at Lindisfarne,[91] silk hangings depicting the life of Christ were used not only to teach people visually about Jesus, enhance buildings, and emulate churches in Rome but also to physically represent heaven on earth.[92] These were conduits through which the invisible heaven was actually here in this visual and material world. As light passed through and around the building, so the reflective silk changed, turning the static woven or embroidered imagery into a moving picture, following the viewer as they moved; Jesus, saints,

---

86 For the textiles discovered in the tomb of St. Cuthbert, see Brett, "The 'Rider' Silk"; Flanagan, "The Figured-Silks," 484–535.

87 G. N. Garmonsway, ed., *Ælfric's Colloquy* (1939; repr., Exeter, UK: University of Exeter Press, 1991), 33.

88 Penny MacConnoran with Alison Nailer, "Complete Catalogue of Leather Items," on CD-ROM accompanying *The London Guildhall: An Archeological History of a Neighbourhood from Early Medieval to Modern Times, Part II*, ed. David Bowsher et al. (London: Museum of London Archaeology, 2007).

89 Anna Muthesius, "The Silk Fragment from 5 Coppergate," in *Anglo-Scandinavian Finds from Lloyds Bank, Pavement, and Other Sites*, ed. Arthur MacGregor (London: Council for British Archaeology, 1982), 132–36; Elizabeth Heckett, "Some Silk and Wool Head-Coverings from Viking Dublin: Uses and Origins—an Enquiry," in Walton and Wild, *NESAT III*, 85–96; Elizabeth Wincott Heckett, *Viking Age Headcoverings from Dublin* (Dublin, Royal Irish Academy, 2003); Frances Pritchard, "Silk Braids and Textiles of the Viking Age from Dublin," in *Archaeological Textiles: Report from the 2nd NESAT Symposium 1.-4.V.1984*, ed. Lise Bender Jørgensen, Bente Magnus, and Elisabeth Munksgaard (Copenhagen: Arkæologisk Institut, 1988), 149–61; Frances Pritchard, "Evidence of Tablet Weaving from Viking-age Dublin," in *Crafting Textiles: Tablet Weaving, Sprang, Lace and Other Techniques from the Bronze Age to the Early 17th Century*, ed. Frances Pritchard (Oxford: Oxbow, 2021), 37–52.

90 Heckett, "Viking Age Headcoverings from Dublin," 111.

91 Joseph Stevenson, ed., "De Abbatibus Abbendoniae," in *Chronicon Monasterii de Abingdon*, 2 vols. (London: Longman, 1858), 2:267–95.

92 Kessler, *Seeing Medieval Art*, 34.

apostles, prophets, and popes joining the congregation and clergy from their textile portraits. As the threads glowed and God's divine light reflected off them, so the souls of those present were able to join with the heavenly hosts, if only for a little while, touching heaven through reflected light. Indeed, these concepts can be seen in the depiction of silk clothing in Irish manuscripts such as the Book of Kells;[93] except here, the representation of these expensive fabrics was within intimate touching distance, a personal, individual experience between viewer and image. As voices intoned and incense burned, as light from candles flickered over the image, so the two-dimensional, brightly coloured fabrics highlighted with gold would undulate, creating an immersive experience, drawing in the person, sensorially engulfing them, enabling the soul to reach out and touch heaven.

In the secular world, elite men and women dressed themselves in silk clothing such as a cloak and tunic mentioned in the *Liber Eliensis*, which is a collated history and inventory of Ely produced by a monk in the twelfth century.[94] These were *purpura*, a word used to describe not the colour but the characteristics of the cloth—shimmering, gleaming, and glowing.[95] These descriptive terms conform to Anglo-Saxon writers' use of Latin to describe things sensorially through their associated characteristics.[96] By wearing such clothing, the elite population of Britain was emulating powerful Christian princes on the Continent. They appeared the same, even if, like the Llangorse tunic, the clothing was not completely made of silk (see above, page 19).[97] Here the visual impact of the garment was more important than the fibres used to create it. As the decoration was worked in silk and linen yarn, the motifs would have both reflected and absorbed light, creating striking effects as wearer and tunic moved. Not all of the garment may have been visible to onlookers if it was partially covered by outer clothing. In this way, the mystique surrounding the small exotic motifs would have

---

93 Dublin, Trinity College Library, MS 58, available at https://digitalcollections.tcd.ie/concern/works/hm50tr726 (accessed Jan. 18, 2024); see image of the Virgin Mary at 7v. Mary's clothing is depicted as transparent, which has been argued as an indication that the fabric is high-quality silk. See Niamh Whitfield, "Dress and Accessories in the Early Irish Tale 'The Wooing of Becfhola,'" *Medieval Clothing and Textiles* 2 (2006): 1–34, at 25.

94 "Enim vero clamidem suam de insigni purpura admodum lorice auro undique contextam illuc contulit …" ("For, to be specific, he [King Edgar] contributed his cloak of striking *purpura* in the style of a hauberk, embroidered with gold all around …") and "… et tunicam ex rubea purpura per girum …" ("For they [Lustwine and Leowaru] gave to God and St Æthelthryth … also a tunic of red *purpura* bordered all round the hem and from the shoulders with orphrey …"). E. O. Blake, ed., *Liber Eliensis* (London: Royal Historical Society, 1962), 117, 158; Janet Fairweather, trans., *Liber Eliensis: A History of the Isle of Ely from the Seventh Century to the Twelfth* (Woodbridge, UK: Boydell, 2005), 140, 188.

95 Dodwell, *Anglo-Saxon Art*, 145–46.

96 For a discussion on this in relation to colour see Carin Ruff, "Aldhelm's Jewel Tones: Latin Colors Through Anglo-Saxon Eyes," in *Anglo-Saxon Styles*, ed. Catherine E. Karkov and George Hardin Brown (New York: SUNY Press, 2003), 223–38.

97 More images of the Llangorse textile can be found at https://museum.wales/collections/online/object/a8517d11-2b52-312a-80a0-d26039fb27e2/Early-Medieval-textile (accessed June 27, 2024).

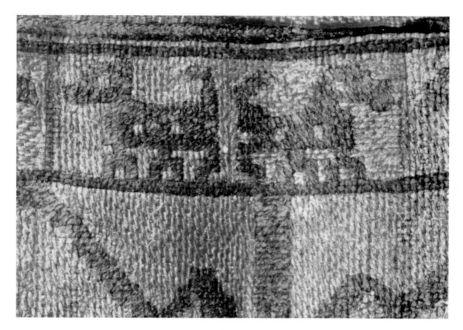

Fig. 1.4: Part of the remains of the Llangorse textile, with digital simulation of colour to delineate the pattern (Cardiff, National Museum of Wales, no. 91.5H/[412]). Photo: Copyright © National Museum of Wales.

been enhanced, as they appeared and disappeared from view. The images are small; for example, the lions in their individual blocks measure approximately 12 millimetres by 14 millimetres (about half an inch square; fig. 1.4).[98] They were designed for intimate viewing. People who saw them at a distance would only have seen the colours and reflections of light, giving the impression of gleaming silk. In this case the senses were misleading, unless one had knowledge and access to examine the textile closely. The Llangorse tunic was therefore an object with multiple layered meanings. It gave the appearance of silk and worldwide connections when viewed from a certain distance, but it was not to be touched by those outside a close circle of knowing individuals. Touching would break the visual spell because such interactions would tell the truth: this garment was not what it appeared to be, actually being made of *linen* and silk.

While linen was used to shroud and sensorially distance the holy and potential saints, silk textiles were used to elevate them beyond the earthly realm. Good examples of this are the numerous silk textiles donated to St. Cuthbert by visiting members of the early medieval elite.[99] Many of these were discovered enveloping the body of the

98 Hero Granger-Taylor, "Comments on the Embroidery Technique and Construction of the Llangorse Textile," in Lane and Redknap, *Llangorse Crannog*, 300.
99 See Ted Johnson South, ed., *Historia de Sancto Cuthberto* (Cambridge: D. S. Brewer, 2002).

saint when his tomb was opened in 1827.[100] Textile donations were normally made by followers after the holy individual had died and their soul was "proven" to have entered heaven through the exhumation and inspection of the physical body, which was often found to be incorrupt, and the performing of miracles. By shrouding the deceased in silk and therefore taking the exotic textiles out of circulation, the patrons were displaying their wealth and power; likewise, by donating such meaningful and precious objects, they were displaying their devotion. The textiles may have been displayed before they were interred with the saint.[101] The removal of a silk textile from the sensorially engaging material world to the hidden and sensorially detached shrine or coffin was a ceremonial burial that metaphorically converted the fabric from a physical object into a heavenly one. In doing so, the human senses, which understood the textile as representing heaven on earth, were now completely decoupled from it. By enveloping the saint, the textile was aligned with the deceased already in heaven. As the textile was sensorially removed from the physical world it became a conduit between realms, a channel between God and humanity through the saint.

Shrouding the human form in silk textiles would not only have been a privilege for those chosen to view and handle both the textile and the potentially saintly corpse; it also enveloped the hard form of the lifeless, fetid body with soft, floating, draping silk, changing it, hiding what it truly was. This was a softening, a gentler encounter between the living and the dead with the smooth colourful silk providing a barrier between the two. While hiding the body from view, such bejewelled and patterned fabrics would have also been a visual feast for onlookers. This appears to have been the case for those who witnessed the burial of King Edward (the Confessor) at the church of St. Peter the Apostle, now Westminster Abbey, in 1066. Scene 26 of the Bayeux Tapestry (fig. 1.5) depicts the king's body wrapped in striking textiles; meanwhile, surviving fragments of silk found in the tomb demonstrate that his body was wrapped in silk fabrics.[102] Here, silk touched the corruptible human body in emulation of precious fabrics wrapping the incorruptible vessels of deceased saints and thus starting a propaganda campaign to canonise the deceased king. Through this public performance the deceased was remembered as glorious, and for Edward's followers, this was a crusade that continued in ever more stylised depictions of him.[103] A sensorially charged performance of sights, noise, and smells formed a living memory carried

---

100 See Battiscombe, *The Relics of Saint Cuthbert*.

101 For a discussion on this topic see Alexandra Lester-Makin, "Textiles and Hoarding in Early Medieval England: The Textiles Given to St. Cuthbert, a Case Study" (in preparation).

102 Information on the silk fragments (London, Victoria and Albert Museum, no. T.2-1944) can be found at https://collections.vam.ac.uk/item/O261251/woven-silk (accessed Oct. 7, 2024).

103 See Gale R. Owen-Crocker, "Refashioning St. Edward: Clothing and Textiles," in *Refashioning Medieval and Early Modern Dress: A Tribute to Robin Netherton*, ed. Gale R. Owen-Crocker and Maren Clegg Hyer (Woodbridge, UK: Boydell, 2019), 95–122.

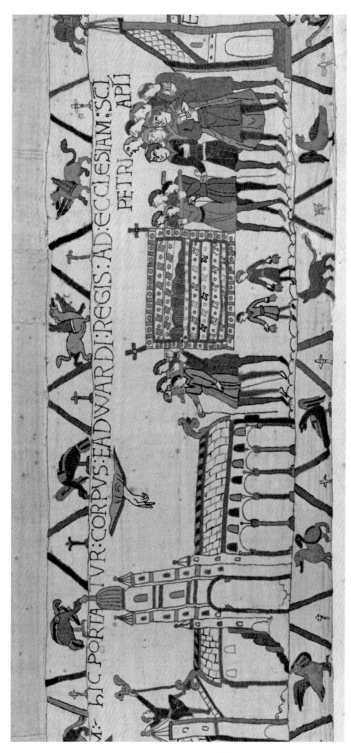

Fig. 1.5: The Bayeux Tapestry, Scene 26: "Here the body of King Edward is taken to the Church of St. Peter the Apostle." Photo: With special permission from the City of Bayeux.

from generation to generation by its retelling and re-depictions, giving power to Edward in the next realm and to his followers on earth in this.

CONCLUSION

This article has shown that by using sensory archaeology we can delve deeper and develop a greater understanding not only of how early medieval textiles were made and used, but also of how cultural perceptions of the sensory world allowed people to engage with them. Textiles were an important and integrated part of early medieval material culture, and while their fragile nature means they do not survive well, extant fragments along with supporting and comparative works can be probed in exciting and innovative ways, of which sensory archaeology is one. This paper has highlighted the entangled sensory connections between object and cosmos, belief and interpretation, memory and storytelling, object and humanity. While textiles do not always incorporate images they can, nevertheless, impart ideas through colour, texture, movement, and sensation, and it is through these that we can unlock the deeper story of early medieval textiles and people in Britain.

Reflecting a Woven Identity: The Global Textile Trade and Two Lucchese Church Facades

Tania Kolarik[1]

From the mid-thirteenth century onward, visitors to the Tuscan city of Lucca would have encountered two monumental church facades facing the primary public piazzas of the city: the Cathedral of San Martino (ca. 1196–1260) and the church of San Michele in Foro (ca. 1220–22).[2] Both feature superimposed arcades, in which the spandrels are filled with confronted white figures of griffins and dragons, solitary lions, stags, and mounted falconers among other animal and human figures standing out against a green ground of *verde di Prato* marble (figs. 2.1, 2.2, 2.3, and 2.4), made with an inlay technique known as intarsia. Interspersed between the various figures are vegetal and abstract motifs, creating a dynamic pattern across the surface. I argue that the similarities in facade construction and decoration between these two churches were an attempt by the bishop and cathedral canons of San Martino, located in the old city center, to visually assert their power within the new and growing epicenter of Lucca at San Michele in Foro, where the communal palace, controlled by the municipal

---

1 I would like to thank my friends and colleagues who read, commented on, and edited several versions of this paper, especially my doctoral advisor Thomas E. A. Dale, Claire Kilgore, Abby Armstrong Check, Mickey Abel, Jennifer Pruitt, Genesie Miller, and the anonymous reviewers for their extremely helpful insights and suggestions. This article began as a graduate seminar paper for Jennifer Pruitt's cross-cultural Islamic art course in 2018, and versions of this paper have been presented at the Leeds International Medieval Congress, including a session organized by DISTAFF in 2021. Additional thanks to the UW–Madison Graduate School, Department of Art History, and Program in Medieval Studies, whose research travel funds allowed me to conduct fieldwork within Lucca in the summer of 2022.

2 Raffaele Savigni, *Lucca* (Spoleto, Italy: Fondazione Centro Italiano di Studi sull'alto Medioevo, 2022), esp. 142–43. For more information about the Cathedral of San Martino, see Clara Baracchini and Antonio Caleca, *Il Duomo di Lucca* (Lucca: Liberia Editrice Baroni, 1973); and Paolo Bertoncini Sabatini, ed., *San Martino a Lucca: Storie della cattedrale [San Martino in Lucca: Stories of the Cathedral]* (Lucca: PubliEd Editore, 2020). For more information about San Michele in Foro, see Chiara Bozzoli, *"La chiara e snella mole": La Basilica di San Michele in Foro a Lucca, arte e architettura* (Lucca: M. Pacini Fazzi, 2007), esp. 83–84; and Silvia Palla, *La chiesa di San Michele in Foro a Lucca* (San Giuliano Terme, Italy: Felici Editore, 2005).

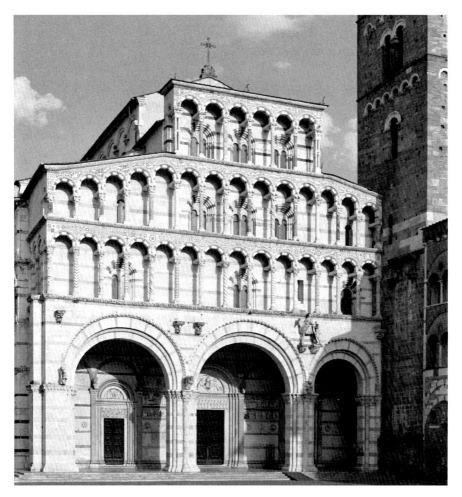

Fig. 2.1: Facade, Cathedral of San Martino, Lucca, Italy, ca. 1196–1260. Photo: Myrabella, Creative Commons license CC BY-SA 3.0, via Wikimedia Commons, cropped from original.

authorities of the *podestà* and *popolo*, was located. Specifically, this unified building campaign further functioned to assert the power of the bishop and cathedral canons to the larger Tuscan region by creating the appearance of a shared, specifically Lucchese, identity through the "textile mentality" of Lucca that was rooted in its status as a major center of textile production and trade in the global Mediterranean.

Expanding upon research that recognizes the connection between contemporaneous textiles and the facades, this analysis will necessarily be limited to comparative examples of luxury textiles due to their increased survival, but also, and more importantly, because the patrons who facilitated the design and construction of these facades had privileged access to this class of textiles through their own wardrobes and business

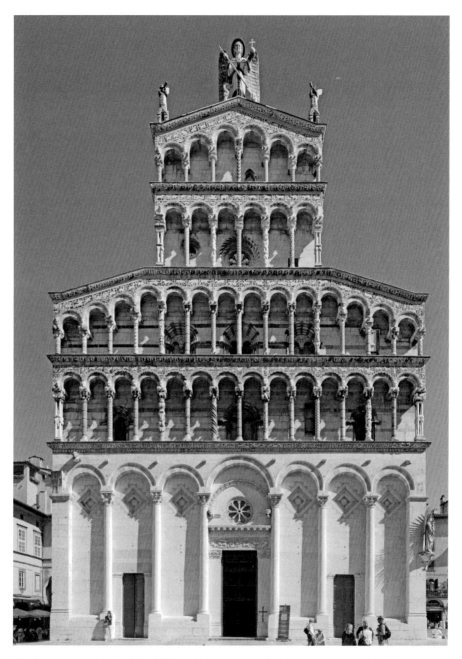

Fig. 2.2: Facade, church of San Michele in Foro, Lucca, Italy, ca. 1220–22, with mid-nineteenth-century restorations. Photo: Spike, Creative Commons license CC BY-SA 4.0, via Wikimedia Commons, cropped from original.

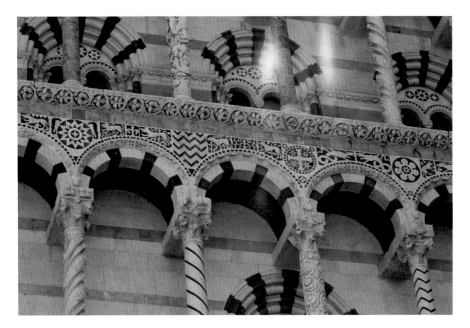

Fig. 2.3: Detail of the first arcade of the facade, Cathedral of San Martino, Lucca, Italy, ca. 1196–1260. Photo: Tania Kolarik.

enterprises.[3] The resonance of projecting textile designs at a monumental scale on the surfaces of the city's most significant public spaces requires understanding the nuances of sociopolitical conflicts in twelfth- and thirteenth-century Lucca. At the time of the construction of the two facades, Lucca simmered with conflict between the bishop, cathedral canons, and their secular allies (*milites*) on the one hand and the *popolo* (municipal authorities made up of merchants, bankers, and artisans) on the other.[4]

To the medieval viewer, the specific figural motifs and patterns depicted on the facades would not have been unfamiliar since they are also representative of various

3 The similarities between the design of these facades and contemporary luxury medieval textiles have been observed by Muriel Wolverton, along with Jamie Sanecki, whose dissertation provides the most in-depth discussion to date about the textile influences on the facade of San Martino. Muriel Beatrice Wolverton, "San Michele in Foro: Representative of Late Romanesque Architecture in Lucca" (M.A. thesis, University of British Columbia, 1972); Jamie Sanecki, "Cathedral and Commune in Medieval Lucca: The Facade of San Martino" (Ph.D. diss., University of Pennsylvania, 2016).

4 The political conflicts between different factions of the Lucchese can be found in Salvatore Bongi, "Prefazione," in Giovanni Sercambi's *Le Croniche di Giovanni Sercambi*, 3 vols. (Rome: Istituto Storico Italiano, 1892), 1:vii–xliii; Alma Poloni, *Lucca nel Duecento: Uno studio sul cambiamento sociale* (Pisa: PLUS-Pisa University Press, 2009); Alma Poloni, "Strutturazione del mondo corporativo e affermazione del Popolo a Lucca nel Duecento," *Archivio Storico Italiano* 165, no. 3 (2007): 449–86; Vito Tirelli, "Lucca nella seconda metà

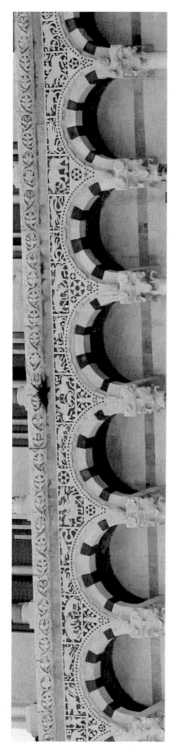

Fig. 2.4: Detail of the second arcade of the facade, Cathedral of San Martino, Lucca, Italy, ca. 1196–1260. Photo: Tania Kolarik.

cloths originating in Lucca's textile workshops. Many members of the local population were employed within the workshops or in a related profession, such as cloth merchants or tailors.[5] These motifs and patterns were also recognizable in textiles from Byzantium, the Islamic world, central Asia, and other Italian textile workshops that would have circulated among the wealthy upper class of Lucca, including the ecclesiastical vestments of the city's bishop. Liturgical processions regularly occurred throughout the city since Lucca practiced a stational liturgy, like Rome, where the bishop and his entourage would move through the streets to churches that were designated for specific liturgies, such as Christmas Eve mass.[6] This allowed for the facades of the churches of origin and destination to act as backdrops for the ritual movement of the clergy. Citizens of all social and economic classes would have been exposed to luxury textiles of the highest quality displayed in the clerical vestments befitting Lucca's position as a bishopric.[7] In addition to liturgical processions, secular public wedding processions of the wealthy noble, mercantile, and banking families would have also provided exposure to luxury clothing outside the grasp of a commoner who could only afford to purchase, spin, and/or weave much plainer fabrics. Therefore, although the physical ownership of luxury textiles was limited to a small group of people, the visual accessibility of these textiles would have been much greater. While all of these motifs are found in textiles produced and traded throughout the medieval Mediterranean,

del secolo XII: Società e istituzioni," in *I ceti dirigenti dell'età comunale nei secoli XII e XIII*, ed. Gabriella Rossetti and Giovanni Vitolo (Pisa: Pacini Editore, 1982), 157–231; and Savigni, *Lucca*, 142–43, 152–53.

5 This interpretation of the medieval viewer is based on Michael Baxandall's concept of the "period eye" from his *Painting and Experience in Fifteenth-Century Italy*, 2nd ed. (Oxford: Oxford University Press, 1988), 29–108; see also Pierre Bourdieu, *The Field of Cultural Production* (New York: Columbia University Press, 1993).

6 For more on the development of the stational liturgy in Christian practice, see John F. Baldovin, *The Urban Character of Christian Worship: The Origins, Development, and Meaning of Stational Liturgy* (Rome: Pont. Institutum Studiorum Orientalium, 1987); Joseph Dyer, "Roman Processions of the Major Litany (*litanie maiores*) from the Sixth to the Twelfth Century," in *Roma Felix: Formation and Reflections of Medieval Rome*, ed. Éamonn Ó Carragáin and Carol Neuman de Vegvar (Farnham, UK: Ashgate, 2007), 113–37. For more on the stational liturgy in Lucca and other cities within Tuscany, see Benjamin Brand, *Holy Treasure and Sacred Song: Relic Cults and Their Liturgies in Medieval Tuscany* (Oxford: Oxford University Press, 2014); Brand, "The Vigils of Medieval Tuscany," *Plainsong and Medieval Music* 17, no. 1 (2008): 23–54; Brand, "Liturgical Ceremony at the Cathedral of Lucca, 1275–1500" (Ph.D. diss., Yale University, 2006).

7 The inventory of the sacristy of the cathedral from 1239 is very sparse in the details as to what luxury items the bishops of Lucca would have worn; see "Inventario del tesoro della sagristia: 18 Febbraio 1239," in *Inventari del Vescovato della Cattedrale e di altre chiese di Lucca*, ed. Pietro Guidi and Ermenegildo Pellegrinetti (Rome: Tipografia Poliglotta Vaticana, 1921), 120–22. However, the will of Bishop Pietro in 1274 is more specific as to the types of luxury garments available to a bishop and worn during religious ceremonies, including a chasuble, dalmatic, and tunic made from Mongol (Tartar) silk, and a garment with gold dragons on the back ("de auro et unum dorzale de auro ad dracones"); see "Disposizioni del Vescovo Pietro circa i suoi beni mobili," in Guidi and Pellegrinetti, *Inventari del Vescovato*, 46–48, esp. 46.

several notable comparisons can be made between the facades and surviving contemporaneous luxury textiles attributed to Lucca and other textile manufacturing centers that existed within the wider global Mediterranean. I will explore how the designs of the two facades appropriate common medieval Mediterranean textile motifs; how their similar programs visually connected the two centers of the city; and how textiles, both real and depicted, functioned to construct both individual and collective identity in thirteenth-century Lucca.

LUCCA: HISTORY AND TEXTILE PRODUCTION

Originally a Roman city that was converted to Christianity sometime in late antiquity, Lucca underwent several intense social and political changes during the twelfth and thirteenth centuries. Following the Peace of Constance in 1183, Emperor Frederick I recognized the legal authority of northern Italian communes and acknowledged Lucca's civil self-rule in 1186.[8] Originally, the civic leaders were part of the long-established nobility, but by the 1190s the *popolo*, mostly comprising the city's merchants and artisans, began to hold communal or municipal offices. This led to clashes between the old nobility, whose members were also the dominant source of the cathedral canons, and the *popolo*, whose main source of wealth derived from Lucca's thriving textile industry.[9] The division between the *popolo* and the cathedral canons further manifested itself in the urban geography of Lucca through two main centers of power, one religious and the other secular, each consisting of a church that faced an open piazza. The members of the *popolo* were headquartered in the communal palace next to San Michele in Foro, and eventually the two structures were connected via a staircase.[10] The bishop and cathedral canons were centered within the episcopal precinct of the Cathedral of San Martino and the adjacent bishop's palace. This duality of urban planning was not unique to Lucca and, as discussed by Maureen Miller and Areli Marina, is still visually evident in the cities of Parma, Florence, Siena, and to a lesser extent, Pisa, among others in the north and central Italian regions.[11]

8   Raffaele Savigni, *Episcopato e Società Cittadina a Lucca da Anselmo II (+1086) a Roberto (+1225)* (Lucca: Edizioni S. Marco Litotipo, 1996), 81.
9   Bongi, "Prefazione," xi, xv–xix, xxv; Poloni, *Lucca nel Duecento*, 69–70; Poloni, "Strutturazione del mondo," 449–86; Tirelli, "Lucca nella seconda metà del secolo XII," 157–231.
10 Giovanni Sercambi, "Come Antonio Guinigi et Nicolao Sbarra volsero suscitare romore in Lucca," *Croniche di parte de' facti di Lucca*, Lucca, Archivio di Stato, Biblioteca Manoscritti, no. 107; in Sercambi, *Le Croniche*, 2:408–10. On page 408 is a line drawing of the manuscript illustration from Sercambi's *Croniche*, which portrays stairs from the church of San Michele in Foro to the communal palace; Graziano Concioni, Claudio Ferri, and Giuseppe Ghilarducci, *Arte e pittura nel Medioevo lucchese* (Lucca: Elia Matteoni, 1994), 222, 230. The permission was obtained in 1277 by the prior and canons of San Michele to build the staircase, which was documented as being used by the *popolo* in 1297.
11 Maureen C. Miller, *The Bishop's Palace: Architecture and Authority in Medieval Italy* (Ithaca, NY: Cornell University Press, 2000), 120; Areli Marina, *The Italian Piazza Transformed: Parma in the Communal Age* (University Park: Pennsylvania State University

In the thirteenth century, Lucca was a major center of banking, textile production, and trade, with connections to artisans and merchants from Sicily and Genoa, who transported Lucchese woven fabrics to Northern Europe and across the Mediterranean and brought Byzantine, Islamic, and Mongol textiles into Italy.[12] While discussions of Lucca have mainly focused on the luxury silk industry, the city was also a known producer of woolen cloth as far back as the Roman period and continued to create non-luxury textiles in addition to luxury cloths woven with silk and metallic threads, such as gold or silver.[13] Genoa provided imported goods and raw materials, mainly from Sicily, while Lucca exported woven textiles and other products to Genoa for further exportation around the Mediterranean.[14] During the thirteenth century, the spinners of Lucca were unable to replicate the quality of silk thread and thereby cloth produced by Byzantine, Islamic, and central Asian workshops. Ignazio Del Punta has shown that during the thirteenth century, the majority of raw silk imported into Lucca by the Genoese came from Greece, Asia Minor, and regions around the Caspian Sea.[15] The ability to source raw materials from international locales further exemplifies the monetary

Press, 2012), 137–39. For further contextualization of this architectural split with the investiture crisis, see also Maureen C. Miller, *Clothing the Clergy: Virtue and Power in Medieval Europe, c. 800–1200* (Ithaca, NY: Cornell University Press, 2014).

12 Rosamond E. Mack, *Bazaar to Piazza: Islamic Trade and Italian Art, 1300–1600* (Berkeley: University of California Press, 2002), 16; David Abulafia, "The Impact of the Orient: Economic Interactions Between East and West in the Medieval Mediterranean," in *Across the Mediterranean Frontiers: Trade, Politics and Religion, 650–1450*, ed. Dionisius A. Agius and Ian Richard Netton (Turnhout, Belgium: Brepols, 1997), 1–40, at 4; Thomas W. Blomquist, "The Castracani Family of Thirteenth-Century Lucca," in his *Merchant Families, Banking and Money in Medieval Lucca* (Aldershot, UK: Ashgate, 2005), 459–76, at 472; Ignazio Del Punta and Maria Ludovica Rosati, *Lucca una città di seta: Produzione, commercio e diffusione dei tessuti lucchesi nel tardo medioevo* (Lucca: Maria Pacini Fazzi Editore, 2017), 5–6. Some of these merchants were also involved in the banking trade.

13 Florence M. Edler, "The Silk Trade of Lucca During the Thirteenth and Fourteenth Centuries" (Ph.D. diss., University of Chicago, 1930), 23–42; Adèle Coulin Weibel, *Two Thousand Years of Textiles: The Figured Textiles of Europe and the Near East* (New York: Pantheon Books, 1952), 59; M. E. Bratchel, *Medieval Lucca and the Evolution of the Renaissance State* (Oxford: Oxford University Press, 2008), 1–3; Thomas W. Blomquist, "The Drapers of Lucca and the Marketing of Cloth in the Mid-Thirteenth Century," in *Economy, Society, and Government in Medieval Italy*, ed. David Herlihy, Robert S. Lopez, and Vsevolod Slessarev (Kent, OH: Kent State University Press, 1969), 65–73, at 65–68. For an overview of the use of gold thread in trecento Italian textiles and artistic depictions, see Tania Kolarik, "Sparkle of Heaven: The Role of *Panni tartarici* or Cloths of Gold to Identify the Divine," in *Bloomsbury Encyclopedia of World Textiles*, vol. 4, *Colour* (London: Bloomsbury, forthcoming).

14 Bratchel, *Medieval Lucca*, 16; Thomas W. Blomquist, "The Dawn of Banking in an Italian Commune: Thirteenth Century Lucca," in Blomquist, *Merchant Families*, 53–75, at 69; Mack, *Bazaar to Piazza*, 16. If there was a medieval industry before the eleventh century it has not been discussed in the literature.

15 Ignazio Del Punta, *Mercanti e banchieri lucchesi nel Duecento* (Pisa: PLUS, 2004), 57–62. Until the fourteenth century, the production of raw silk was limited on the Italian Peninsula to southern Italy and Sicily, mainly in the Calabrian region.

and diplomatic resources that members of the Lucchese mercantile community were able to assemble for the benefit of their city's textile industry, thereby contributing to its economic and civic identity as a center of textiles. Furthermore, this increased the wealth of not only the *popolo* but also the landed nobility and canons who collected rents from buildings in the city and communities in the countryside that supplied the larger textile industry.[16] Even the communal palace of the *popolo* next to the church of San Michele in Foro was owned by the canons of San Martino who then leased the property to the commune until 1370.[17] Due to their increasing wealth, accrued largely from engagement in the textile industry, the upper classes had the ability to invest in lavish clothing as a form of conspicuous consumption.[18]

Woven and embroidered silks functioned as major symbols of medieval status and luxury, with clothing created from expensive fabrics providing nonverbal cues that indicated the wearer's place within the social order.[19] The woven lampas silks of Lucca became renowned for their quality and design, earning the identifying moniker of *lucchese*.[20] Lucchese textiles were the dominant type of cloth exported from Italy to Northern European markets where they were sold by merchant-bankers like Bartolomeo Toringhelli in the 1260s at the Champagne fairs, and during the mid-thirteenth century Lucca-made textiles were regularly sold in eastern Mediterranean markets.[21] These fabrics featured vegetal (such as leaves, vines, rosettes), animal (griffins, lions, dogs, parrots, deer, etc.), and ornamental (stars, castles, Latin and pseudo-Kufic text) motifs in linear registers or roundels. By the fourteenth century, the adaptation of small floriate patterns that were typical of many Mongol *panni tartarici* (cloths woven with metallic thread) began to appear in Lucchese textile design.[22] The end of the century marked the loss of Lucca's dominance as the premier textile production center in Italy. This was due, in part, to political instability at the beginning of the 1300s within the city and region, resulting in some thirty-two textile families relocating to Venice, along with many other families establishing themselves within cities across north and

---

16 Bratchel, *Medieval Lucca*, 49; Blomquist, "The Castracani Family," 460–62. The banking Castracani family had six rental residences around the Cathedral of San Martino in addition to their own personal residence.

17 Archivio di Stato (Lucca), *Il Palazzo pubblico a Lucca dalle origini al periodo ducale* ([Lucca]: M. Pacini Fazzi, 1979), 19; Sanecki, "Cathedral and Commune," 50.

18 Richard A. Goldthwaithe, "The Empire of Things: Consumer Demand in Renaissance Italy," in *Patronage, Art and Society in Renaissance Italy*, ed. F. Kent (Oxford: Clarendon Press, 1987), 153–75; Richard A. Goldthwaithe, *Wealth and the Demand for Art in Italy: 1300–1600* (Baltimore: John Hopkins University Press, 1993). The term "conspicuous consumption" was coined in 1899 by Thorstein Veblen to explain those who buy expensive items to display wealth; Veblen, "Conspicuous Consumption," in *The Theory of the Leisure Class: An Economic Study of Institutions* (New York: B. W. Huebsch, 1919).

19 Mack, *Bazaar to Piazza*, 27.

20 Del Punta and Rosati, *Lucca una città di seta*, 20.

21 Blomquist, "The Dawn of Banking," 70; Del Punta and Rosati, *Lucca una città di seta*, 13.

22 See Del Punta and Rosati, *Lucca una città di seta*, esp. 22–66, for a more detailed discussion on the influence of "Lucca *Chinoiserie*."

central Italy.[23] However, during the early-to-mid-thirteenth century the city's place as a major textile and banking center was at its height, thereby facilitating the influx of wealth needed to complete ecclesiastical projects of a great scale, including the renovated facades of San Martino and San Michele in Foro.

SAN MARTINO AND SAN MICHELE IN FORO: FACADES AND TEXTILE MOTIFS

The Cathedral of San Martino and church of San Michele in Foro predated the early-thirteenth-century construction of the intarsia facades. The Cathedral of San Martino was originally founded in the sixth century, dedicated to Saint Martin of Tours, with the structure reconstructed during 1060–70. The facade of San Martino has three arcades that are covered in green-and-white intarsia, further texturized with ornamental figural and vegetal sculpted columns, capitals, and colonnettes (fig. 2.5). A squat Romanesque portico, begun in the 1190s and completed later in the thirteenth century, sits beneath these arcades (see fig. 2.1).[24] Meanwhile, San Michele was first founded in the eighth century and placed within the centrally located former Roman forum.[25] The church was rebuilt in the eleventh century, but by the latter half of the twelfth century only the plan and lower order of the entire church had been completed.[26] In both cases, the full-scale erection of their facades did not begin until the early thirteenth century and precedence was given to the cathedral, the seat of the bishopric.

An inscription on the first (bottom) arcade of the facade of San Martino gives the date of 1204 and names the artist as Guidetto. His direct oversight came to an end in 1211 after he was hired to oversee the construction of Santo Stefano in Prato. Although this type of authorial inscription onto the building itself is not present in San

23 Del Punta and Rosati (*Lucca una città di seta*, 34) push back against the narrative of the textile industry collapsing after the fourteenth century due to political instability as it remained strong during and long after the upheavals that began in the trecento, and they suggest that the emigration of artisans elsewhere in the region diluted the role of Lucca's textile industry. See also Giovanni Curatola, "Venice's Textile and Carpet Trade: The Role of Jewish Merchants," in *Venice and the Islamic World: 828–1797*, ed. Stefano Carboni (New Haven, CT: Yale University Press, 2007), 205.

24 Baracchini and Caleca, *Il Duomo di Lucca*, 21; Savigni, *Lucca*, 152–53; and Raffaele Savigni, "Lucca Cathedral from the Eleventh to the Sixteenth Century," in Sabatini, *San Martino a Lucca*, 39–60, at 44–45. The construction of the current portico was initiated by the *Opera di S. Martino* (ca. 1180) and the *Opera del Frontespizio* (ca. 1190), who represented the different political factions of the city who competed for control over the civil municipality. The *Opera di S. Martino* was controlled by the canons and the class of *milites*, or traditional nobility, who were politically aligned with the bishop of Lucca. Meanwhile, the *Opera del Frontespizio* was supported by the municipal authorities of the *populus* or *popolo* that consisted of merchants, bankers, artisans, and those nobles who were not politically aligned with the bishop.

25 Bozzoli, *La chiara e snella mole*, 41–42.

26 Bozzoli, *La chiara e snella mole*, 58. This lower order consists of a series of blind arches that wrap around the exterior walls of the church.

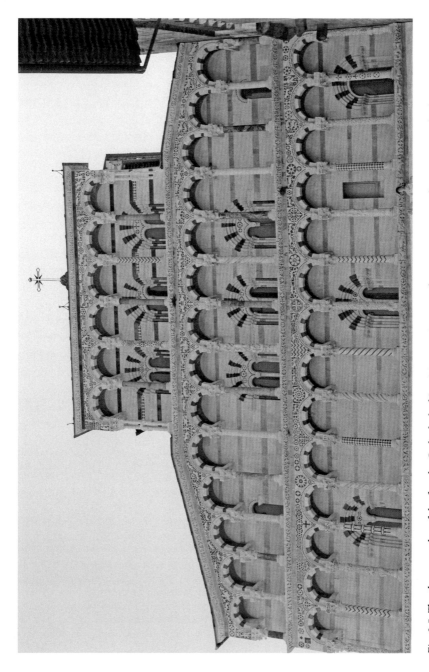

Fig. 2.5: The three arcades of the façade, Cathedral of San Martino, Lucca, Italy, ca. 1196–1260. Photo: Tania Kolarik.

Michele, the facade there may have been raised ca. 1220. Chiara Bozzoli and Carlos Espí Forcén are in agreement that the two facades are by the same workshop, as the stylistic similarities point clearly to that association. Further, the workshop set up by Guidetto in Lucca may have continued under his son Lombardo until ca. 1260.[27] The facades are decorated with the same intarsia inlay technique.[28] The dynamism is enhanced by sculpted and inlaid intarsia columns that create texture across the facade, such as the knotted shafts, carved spirals with rosettes and leaves, along with columns of white and green inlaid with chevron and checkerboard patterning. The columns support arches that have alternating green and white voussoirs, further enhancing their ornamentality.

In general, the scholarship on the churches of San Martino and San Michele, especially on the decoration of the facades, is limited. Further confounding analysis are the nineteenth-century "restorations" of San Michele that fundamentally altered the ornamental program. For example, sculpted and intarsia figures of nineteenth-century political figures such as Victor Emmanuel II and Napoleon, among other notable religious, literary, and political individuals, and motifs of elephants and palm trees were added to the crumbling facade.[29] In his discussion of the radical restoration of San Michele, Espí Forcén suggests that the intarsia on the facade of San Martino reflects more closely the original appearance of San Michele's facade.[30] We can see a glimpse of the pre-restoration facade through the drawings and daguerreotypes made by the famous English art critic John Ruskin in 1846, which allows for the comparison of similar motifs between the two facades and reinforces their creation by the same workshop (fig. 2.6).[31]

27 Bozzoli, *La chiara e snella mole*, 83–84; Savigni, *Lucca*, 143–45; Carlos Espí Forcén, "Una relación simbiótica: La fachada de San Michele de Lucca entre los siglos XIII y XIX," in *Memoria y significado: Uso y reception de los vestigios del pasado*, ed. Luis Arciniega García (Valencia: Universitat de València, 2013), 265–71. As discussed by Bozzoli, the dating for both of these facades is vague, and both are attributed to the sculptor Guidetto (Guido da Argono or Guido da Como), who signed his name to the facade of San Martino in 1204, and his workshop. It is unclear when the building of San Michele in Foro began, but it is considered to have been mostly finished by 1220, with work on the subporch of San Martino coming to an end around 1260.

28 Bozzoli, *La chiara e snella mole*, 79. It is also interesting to note the connection between the source of the green marble from Prato and Guidetto's move to construct Santo Stefano in Prato in 1211.

29 Gigetta Dalli Regoli, "'Sirene animalia sunt mortifera': Animali e mostri in un architrave Lucchese del XII secolo," *Arte Cristiana* 87, no. 795 (1999): 405–12. Regoli makes connections between the carved sculptural motifs on the twelfth-century architrave of San Michele in Foro and medieval bestiaries that were made in the city of Lucca. See also Gabriele Kopp, *Die Skulpturen der Fassade von San Martino in Lucca* (Worms, Germany: Wernersche Verlagsgellschaft, 1981), 80–82; Bozzoli, *La chiara e snella mole*, 74–87; Espí Forcén, "Una relación simbiótica," 270.

30 Espí Forcén, "Una relación simbiótica," 265–71.

31 For images of John Ruskin's daguerreotypes of San Martino and San Michele in Foro, see Ken Jacobson and Jenny Jacobson, *Carrying Off the Palaces: John Ruskin's Lost Daguerreotypes* (London: Quartich, 2015), 41, 284–87. The University of Oxford's Ashmolean

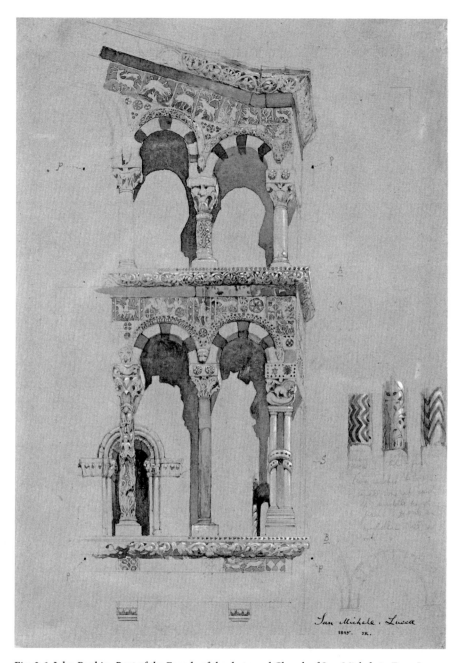

Fig. 2.6: John Ruskin, *Part of the Façade of the destroyed Church of San Michele in Foro, Lucca, as it appeared in 1845* (Oxford, Ashmolean Museum, acc. no. WA.RS.ED.083). Watercolor and bodycolor over graphite on grey wove paper. Photo: Ashmolean Museum, by permission.

In addition to the two facades' similarities to each other, the decorative motifs can be compared to motifs used in the design of contemporaneous textiles within thirteenth-century Lucca and the Mediterranean at large. However, this article will not trace origins of motifs or individual fabrics or make an argument for a particular textile deriving from one specific culture, as the widespread circulation of medieval textiles and the prolific copying of motifs and techniques by the various textile centers around the Mediterranean make this a fairly fruitless endeavor.[32] Even contemporary medieval catalogers within the papal court who created inventories of papal possessions, including garments, were unable to determine the origin of various fabrics: an inventory of Clement V (1264–1314, r. 1305–14) from 1311 listed a white tunic with stripes of red silk and gold as either Mongol or Lucchese in origin.[33] Additionally, the inventory's descriptions of Mongol, Lucchese, and Venetian textiles, among others, list the figural motifs of griffins, birds, leopards, and lions as appearing throughout Clement V's possessions regardless of origin. The Cathedral of San Martino's inventories of the church's material possessions (1305–18) describe fabrics patterned with roundels and stripes filled with animals and outlined with gold thread.[34] This description of striped textiles filled with animals can also be applied to the placement of the sculpted intarsia forms into horizontal registers adorning the arcades of San Martino and San Michele.[35] So, the figural, geometric, and vegetal motifs found on these two facades are commonly used within the design of textiles around the global medieval world.

As noted, specific motifs found on the facade of San Martino include dragons, griffins, boars, stags, dogs, crosses, chevron patterning, and geometric and vegetal

---

Museum has several original drawings and watercolors by Ruskin of San Martino and San Michele in Foro; for further information about Ruskin's representation of the facade of San Michele and links to the rest of the series, see https://ruskin.ashmolean.org/object/WA.RS.ED.083 (accessed Oct. 10, 2024).

32 Luca Molà, "Prefazione," in Del Punta and Rosati, *Lucca una città di seta*, vii–ix, at viii. Molà mentions how Italian textile artisans were able to study the imported fabrics from the Islamic and Mongol worlds and thereby mimic their weaving methods and motifs. David Jacoby, "Silk Economics and Cross-Cultural Artistic Interaction: Byzantium, the Muslim World, and the Christian West," *Dumbarton Oaks Papers* 58 (2004): 197–240. Jacoby's work on the materials used in Mediterranean textile production shows that it is impossible to attribute certain types of gold and silk thread to a precise geographical location.

33 "Inventarium thesauri Ecclesiae Romanae … Clementis Papae V, 1311," *Regestum Clementis Papae … ex vaticanis archetypis sanctissimi domini nostri Leonis XIII pontificis maximi iussu et munificentia …* vol. 1, appendices (Rome: Typographia Vaticana, 1892), 422. The entry for this item states, "Item aliam tuncellam de panno tartarico sive lucano albo laborato per traversum ad virgas rubeas de serico et auro." For other documentary sources of fourteenth-century textiles within Lucchese inventories, see Del Punta and Rosati, *Lucca una città di seta*, 33–46.

34 Guidi and Pellegrinetti, *Inventari del Vescovato*, 191–213; Del Punta and Rosati, *Lucca una città di seta*, 42.

35 An example of this type of textile design consisting of animals depicted within striped registers can be seen in a surviving textile fragment of silk and gold thread at the Cleve-

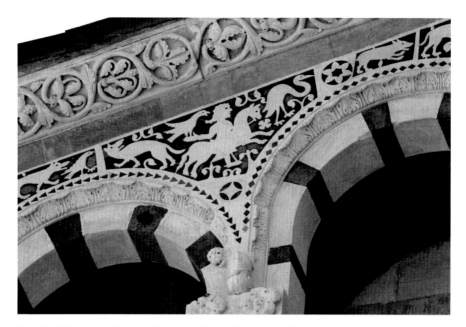

Fig. 2.7: Falconer on horseback, facade detail, Cathedral of San Martino, Lucca, Italy, ca. 1196–1260. Photo: Tania Kolarik.

forms on the first arcade. The second arcade has similar figural motifs, but with the addition of panthers, lions, a bear, a hunter with his dog, and a falconer on a horse (figs. 2.3, 2.4, and 2.7). Likewise, as we see in Ruskin's drawings and watercolors of the facade of San Michele, there are falconers on horseback, dogs, birds, boars, and stags, among other geometric and vegetal patterns (fig. 2.6). These motifs are part of broader medieval court and secular culture and are also visible in metalwork, floor pavements, and fictive textiles in wall paintings.[36] Motifs of a small scale similar to those found

---

land Museum of Art (J. H. Wade Fund, no. 1942.1078). The fragment portrays animals within horizontal registers, consisting of a larger register containing a large feline (lion or panther) and bird (phoenix?), bordered by a register of goats.

36 The relationship between hunting imagery and courtly romance in the medieval Western world has been explored in Mira Friedman, "The Falcon and the Hunt: Symbolic Love Imagery in Medieval and Renaissance Art," in *Poetics of Love in the Middle Ages: Texts and Contexts*, ed. Moshe Lazar and Norris J. Lacy (Fairfax, VA: George Mason University Press, 1989), 157–75; Michael Camille, *The Medieval Art of Love: Objects and Subjects of Desire* (New York: Abrams, 1998); Robin S. Oggins, "Falconry in Medieval Life," in *The Kings and Their Hawks: Falconry in Medieval England* (New Haven, CT: Yale University Press, 2004), 109–38; and Nicholas Perkins, ed., *Medieval Romance and Material Culture* (Cambridge: D. S. Brewer, 2015). For the connection between textiles and floor pavements and their connections to court culture, see Amanda Luyster, *The Chertsey Tiles, The Crusades, and Global Textile Motifs* (Cambridge: Cambridge University Press, 2023).

portrayed in textiles are also on portable ivories whose raw materials would be shipped internationally from African ports to European production centers. These ivories were in the form of caskets and handheld objects like devotional diptychs, mirrors, drinking vessels, and horns for hunting. For example, a carved elephant tusk fragment from the eleventh or twelfth century with an attributed Sicilian origin depicts several birds, boars, dragons, and other mythical beasts that are contained within roundels formed by interlacing vines (fig. 2.8).[37]

Other comparative examples between specific motifs found on both facades and surviving medieval textiles focus on secular hunting imagery. The first of these comparisons features the image of a man on horseback holding a falcon on one hand, which appears multiple times in the intarsia facades of San Martino and San Michele (figs. 2.6 and 2.7). This figural type in textiles was present in Italy during the late twelfth century as evidenced by the gifting of the Fermo Chasuble of St. Thomas Becket to the Italian cathedral of Fermo.[38] The gold-embroidered blue silk fabric contains an Arabic inscription stating that it was created in the Andalusi city of Almería in 1116. While we do not know if the chasuble was seen by textile makers in Lucca, the image of a human figure with a falcon can also be viewed in a Lucchese fragment with a woman training a falcon (fig. 2.9).[39] In addition to the falconry motifs on the facades, the use of dogs and deer further reflects the theme of the hunt present in surviving textile fragments and in the intarsias of both churches, such as the second arcade of San Martino, which contains both a falconer on horseback and a dog attacking a boar (fig. 2.4). For example, a fourteenth-century Lucchese fragment with dogs, deer, birds, and vines brings together several motifs that are apparent on the facades (fig. 2.10).[40]

The presence of falconry and hunting imagery in a dominant position on the facades of two major churches in Lucca is unusual. Scholars of medieval art and literature have shown that this type of secular imagery is most often used as a marker of medieval nobility or as a topos of courtly love and chivalric romance.[41] Yet the examples in Lucca are not without precedent: more explicit representations of chivalric romance than those portrayed in Lucca can be found in Modena in the twelfth-century exterior sculptures on the Ghirlandina tower depicting Roland

37 New York, Metropolitan Museum of Art, acc. no. 17.190.219. For more on the connections between ivories and Italian communes, see Jean C. Campbell, *The Game of Courting and the Art of the Commune of San Gimignano, 1290–1320* (Princeton, NJ: Princeton University Press, 1997).

38 Avinoam Shalem, ed., *The Chasuble of Thomas Becket: A Biography* (Munich: Hirmer, 2017); Annabelle Simon-Cahn, "The Fermo Chasuble of St. Thomas Becket and Hispano-Mauresque Cosmological Silks: Some Speculations on the Adaptive Reuse of Textiles," *Muqarnas* 10 (1993): 1–5.

39 Boston, Museum of Fine Arts, acc. no. 35.80.

40 Cleveland Museum of Art, no. 1977.14.

41 Friedman, "The Falcon and the Hunt"; Camille, *The Medieval Art of Love*, 96–107; Oggins, "Falconry in Medieval Life."

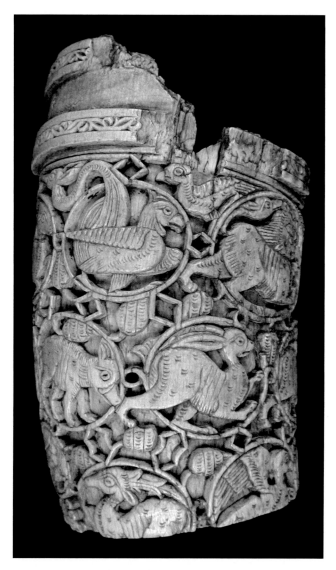

Fig. 2.8: Fragment of a carved elephant tusk, attributed to Sicily, Italy, eleventh to twelfth century (New York, Metropolitan Museum of Art, gift of J. Pierpont Morgan, 1917, acc. no. 17.190.219). Dimensions: 22.2 by 10.5 by 9 centimeters. Photo: Courtesy of the Metropolitan Museum of Art.

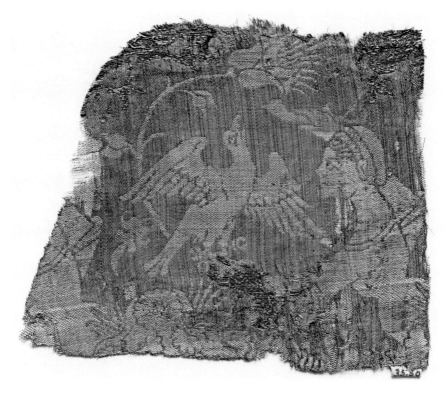

Fig. 2.9: Fragment of silk brocade showing a lady training a falcon, Lucca, Italy, fourteenth century (Boston, Museum of Fine Arts, acc. no. 35.80). Dimensions: 17.5 by 14.5 centimeters. Photo: Museum of Fine Arts, Boston, by permission.

blowing his horn and in the cathedral's Porta della Pescheria portraying King Arthur and his knights attempting to free a damsel in distress.[42]

In addition to the intarsia of San Martino, the sculpted columns on the facade also contain figural motifs used in textile design with addorsed and confronting animal figures framed within vegetal roundels. For example, a colonnette attached to the compound pier between the central and southern arches of the west facade has addorsed birds circled with vegetation (fig. 2.11).[43] Similar textile motifs within a liturgical context can be found among the textiles donated by Pope Boniface VIII (1230–1303, r. 1294–1303) to the cathedral of Anagni. One of the donated red samite copes with silk and gold thread embroidery is covered with roundels that are filled with addorsed birds, two-headed eagles, and griffins.[44] It is possible that the types of

42 Marina, *The Italian Piazza Transformed*, 125–27.
43 Sanecki, "Cathedral and Commune," fig. 210.
44 For more information on the Anagni textiles, see Christiane Elster, *Die Textilen Geschenke Papst Bonifaz' VIII (1294–1303) an Die Kathedral Von Anagni: Päpstliche Paramente des*

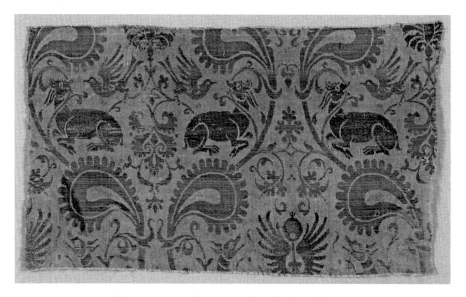

Fig. 2.10: Fragment of lampas-weave silk woven with gold thread, showing dogs and birds amid vines, Italy, 1350–1400 (Cleveland Museum of Art, purchase from the J. H. Wade Fund, no. 1977.14). Dimensions: 21 by 34.9 centimeters. Photo: Cleveland Museum of Art, public domain, Creative Commons license CC0 1.0 Universal.

textiles used for this cope were similar to the luxury textiles the bishop of Lucca would likely have worn during processions and other liturgical celebrations.

Through these comparisons, it has not been my intention to make claims for one-on-one influences, but instead to show that these forms were present and being produced within and around medieval Lucca. Medieval textiles and other compact objects, like ivories, were easily transported along the trade routes of the Mediterranean. As these objects of various media moved across these "pathways of portability," the motifs found on them were copied by artists and artisans, thereby spreading similar imagery across the medieval world, such as Islamic calligraphy being depicted by Italian artists as pseudo-Kufic in trecento painting.[45] Furthermore, the commonalities

---

späten Mittelalters als Medien der Repräsentation, Gaben und Erinnerungsträger (Petersburg, Germany: Michael Imhoff Verlag, 2018).

45 Eva Hoffman, "Pathways of Portability: Islamic and Christian Interchange from the Tenth to the Twelfth Century," *Art History* 24, no. 1 (2001): 17–50. For more on Arabic script and/or pseudo-Arabic (known as pseudo-Kufic), see Isabelle Dolezalek, *Arabic Script on Christian Kings: Textile Inscriptions on Royal Garments from Norman Sicily* (Berlin: De Gruyter, 2017); Louise W. Mackie, *Symbols of Power: Luxury Textiles from Islamic Lands, 7th–21st Century* (New Haven, CT: Yale University Press, 2015); Mackie, "Toward an Understanding of Mamluk Silks: National and International Considerations," *Muqarnas* 2 (1984): 127–46; Mack, *Bazaar to Piazza*.

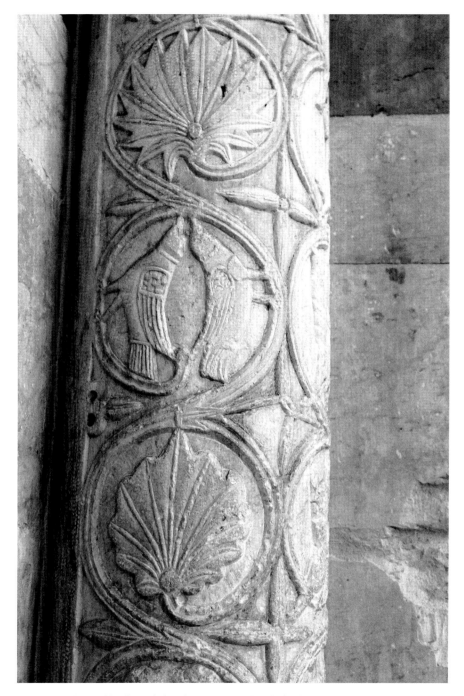

Fig. 2.11: Addorsed birds circled with vegetation, detail of colonnette attached to the compound pier between the central and southern arches of the west facade of Cathedral of San Martino, Lucca, Italy, mid-thirteenth century. Photo: Tania Kolarik.

between the various court cultures across the global Mediterranean were not limited to royal/imperial or ecclesiastical courts, but also included the "courts" assembled through the commune who used the term *palazzo* (palace) for their civic buildings. The communal leaders employed this established visual language of the courts to legitimize their rule within the Italian city-state. In her analysis of the late-thirteenth- and early-fourteenth-century frescoes within the communal buildings of San Gimignano, C. Jean Campbell argues that it was necessary for members of the communal governments to exhibit nobility and courtliness as qualifications for their place as the ruling class within medieval society.[46] The frescoes of the Sala del Consiglio, the main council chamber within the Palazzo Comunale of San Gimignano, convey Campbell's concept of a municipal government attempting to assert its courtliness, and thereby its right to rulership, with depictions of jousting knights above scenes of hunting with falcons and dogs. To push this concept further, I suggest that these images within San Gimignano's communal palace reflect the proposed effects of good government (such as the pursuits of jousting and hunting found at royal courts elsewhere in Europe) that the ruling men were trying to impress upon their commune. Similarly, in Ambrogio Lorenzetti's *Allegory of Good and Bad Government* (ca. 1338) within the Palazzo Pubblico of Siena, the good government of the city is supported by members of the countryside bringing in carts of goods, such as food and livestock. In turn, the city offers the infrastructure for manufactured products to be sold and then taken into the countryside, which represents the integral and important reciprocal relationship between the two entities under common civic rule. An effect of good government in both the city and country is conveyed through the depiction of noble members of the commune riding off into the country to hunt.[47] As a result, the use of secular hunting imagery on the facades of San Martino and San Michele in Lucca during the thirteenth century not only demonstrates its use before the fourteenth-century examples noted above within public communal spaces of Italian city-states, but also reflects prosperity and good leadership.

The power and control over nature that hunting and falconry symbolize are employed literally and metaphorically to promote the nobility's place at or near the top

---

46 Campbell, *The Game of Courting*, 198–200.

47 Judith B. Steinhoff, "Urban Images and Civic Identity in Medieval Sienese Painting," in *Art as Politics in Late Medieval and Renaissance Siena*, ed. Timothy B. Smith and Judith B. Steinhoff (Farnham, UK: Ashgate, 2012), 15–38, at 30–31; Diana Norman, *Painting in Late Medieval and Renaissance Siena, 1260–1555* (New Haven, CT: Yale University Press, 2003), 101; Chiara Frugoni, *Pietro and Ambrogio Lorenzetti*, trans. L. Pelletti (Florence: Scala Books, 1998). In a fourteenth-century example, the Pisan Camposanto's *Triumph of Death* fresco depicts a version of *The Three Living and Three Dead* with a group of twelve noblemen, dressed in colorful and patterned clothing, who while out hunting come across three dead bodies each in a different stage of decomposition. The fresco conveys the message of *memento mori* to the medieval audience, while the horrified noblemen's hunting intentions are made clear through the presence of falcons on the arms of two of the hunters and the three dogs who run alongside the party.

of medieval social structures. Jamie Sanecki suggests that the decision to include these secular scenes was a way to connect the canons and the commune office holders who were from the same strata of Lucchese nobility.[48] However, with the contemporaneous increase in mercantile middle-class members of the commune becoming part of the governing *popolo*, I argue that this imagery was a subtle means for the bishop and his cathedral canons, sourced from established noble families, to assert their inherent noble power over the two city centers and thereby the entire city and countryside. The choice of hunting imagery conveys what good governance of the city brings, and the location of this imagery on a church facade and not within a communal palace further exemplifies that prosperity and good governance derive from the bishop and his canons and not from the communal secular authorities. The means and visual language through which this was accomplished come directly from the extremely financially profitable textile industry that was evident throughout the city's markets, residents' clothing, and the building projects. Lisa Golombek has argued that certain characteristics of Islamic art and architecture are due to a "textile mentality" within the culture.[49] I suggest that this "textile mentality" is not limited to Lucca or to the Islamic world but is a wider global medieval textile mentality. While thirteenth-century Lucca is just one example within the larger medieval world, it represents a particular time and space where the economic climate of the city is intrinsically tied to the textile industry.

ASSERTING POWER THROUGH THE DESIGN OF TWO FACADES

The textile industry created changes to the existing economic climate of Lucca in the twelfth century, as those engaged with mercantile activities grew their wealth, increasing their power and influence within the municipal government. As the power dynamics began to change, the historic power broker of Lucca, the bishop, became less of an authority within the secular governance of the city, especially after the rec-ognition of Lucca as an independent commune in 1186. Before this date, the center of power within the city was located at the Cathedral of San Martino in the southeast corner of Lucca, and it was in this area of the city where the bishop and cathedral canons, who were mostly members of the Lucchese nobility, resided and ruled the city and its territories. Once Lucca became an independent commune, the center of the city's power shifted to the northwest of San Martino, as the communal municipal palace was constructed by 1197 on the north side of San Michele in Foro. This shift was, in a sense, a return to the historical core of the Roman city since the center of all Roman cities was the forum where the main streets intersected. This effectively created physical and legal separation between the civic rule of Lucca and the authority of the bishop and his canons. Additionally, by placing the site of communal government in

---

48 Sanecki, "Cathedral and Commune," 178.

49 Lisa Golombek, "The Draped Universe of Islam," in *Content and Context of Visual Arts in the Islamic World*, ed. Priscilla P. Soucek (University Park: Pennsylvania State University Press, 1988), 25–49, at 34.

the former Roman forum, the *popolo* could argue for their authority as being based upon the ideals of the Roman Republic. For example, the title of "consul" was given to members of the secular government and further shows the exhibition of *romanitas*, or "Roman-ness," that was prevalent throughout the Italian city-states.[50] The growing split between civic and religious authorities within the urban landscape of medieval Italian communes created several instances of rival city centers.[51]

Prior to the mid-twelfth century, Lucca's civic leaders were from the same noble families that filled the ranks of the cathedral canons. The growing influence and wealth of the Court of Merchants allowed members of the emerging mercantile elite—some from established noble families—to obtain positions within the communal government of the city and have a say in important decisions such as electing the *podestà*, the top civic leader. Violence between the nobility allied with the bishop and the *popolo* erupted over civil decisions, such as the riot in 1214 that led to the nobility fleeing the city. It was during this increasing upheaval to the existing power dynamic between the bishop and the municipal authorities that the two facades of San Martino and San Michele were constructed.[52]

Sanecki argues that the canons of San Martino would have had the most influence on the design of the facade and its sculptures.[53] This is based on the artisans working closely with the canons of the *Opera* of San Martino, the office in charge of the physical structure and renovations of the cathedral. This office was the main organization for paying and providing housing, alongside the canons, for the artisans working on the facade, thereby creating a climate for the exchange of ideas concerning design. There was also the inherent power dynamic where the artisans were being paid directly by the canons. Meanwhile, the money itself was raised and provided by the civil merchant-run *Opera* of Santa Croce, but the true patrons and designers of the facade were the canons who directly managed, fed, and conversed with the artisans.[54] In contrast, for the construction of the facade at San Michele, it is clear from the discussion of Lucca's liturgy by Charles Buchanan that the canons of San Michele would have bent

---

50   For more on the use of consuls in medieval Italy, see Chris Wickham, *Courts and Conflict in Twelfth-Century Tuscany* (Oxford: Oxford University Press, 2003); Thomas W. Blomquist and Duane J. Osheim, "The First Consuls at Lucca: 10 July 1119," in Blomquist, *Merchant Families*, 31–40.

51   A comparable example occurs in Florence where the center of power moved from the Duomo to the Palazzo Vecchio. Marvin Trachtenberg, *Dominion of the Eye: Urbanism, Art, and Power in Early Modern Florence* (Cambridge: Cambridge University Press, 1997).

52   Savigni, *Lucca*, 143. For a description of the riot of 1214 that was led by the consuls of the Court of Merchants, see Sercambi, *Le Croniche*, 1:15–16. For more on Giovanni Sercambi, see Duane J. Osheim, "Chronicles and Civic Life in Giovanni Sercambi's Lucca," in *Chronicling History: Chroniclers and Historians in Medieval and Renaissance Italy*, ed. Sharon Dale, Alison Williams Lewis, and Duane J. Oshem (University Park: Pennsylvania State University Press, 2007), 145–69; and Fabrizio Mari, "A Tale of Two Chroniclers: Ptolemy of Lucca and Giovanni Sercambi" (M.A. thesis, Durham University, 2008).

53   Sanecki, "Cathedral and Commune," 52–92, esp. 91–92.

54   Sanecki, "Cathedral and Commune," 92; Savigni, *Lucca*, 152–53. The *Opera* of Santa Croce assumed authority over the building projects in 1274.

to the wishes of the bishop and his canons headquartered at San Martino.[55] This leads to the question as to why these two churches had such similar facades constructed, especially with their relative proximity.

During the twelfth through the mid-thirteenth centuries the majority of churches in Lucca were under renovation or rebuilding.[56] I suggest that the design of these two facades was an attempt by the cathedral canons of San Martino to assert their dwindling power within both the main religious and civic spaces in Lucca. The visual connection through architecture was likely intended to be a reminder to those officials in the communal palace that the wealth that the textile industry provided was rooted in the spiritual religious leadership of the bishop and his church. This attempt to create a communal identity between the civic and ecclesiastical sectors of the city may also have acted to challenge the power of the reformist Lucchese canons of the Basilica of San Frediano who were bestowed with papal favor in the twelfth century and did not have to answer to the bishop of Lucca.[57] The location of San Frediano right inside the eleventh- to twelfth-century walls and next to the northern gate along the pilgrimage route of the Via Francigena further contributed to the desire of the bishop and cathedral canons to consolidate their power within the city proper.[58] It was in the bishop's best interest to have pilgrims give alms to his churches and not to the neighboring San Frediano, which he did not control. Further, the continuity in design between San Martino and San Michele (figs. 2.1 and 2.2) would have visually contrasted with the thirteenth-century Sicilio-Byzantine mosaic facade of the Basilica of San Frediano that was constructed by Sicilian mosaicists (fig. 2.12).[59] Additionally, the ongoing political rivalry between Pisa and Lucca, which preceded the Pisan military conquest and political rule of the commune during 1342–69, may have influenced the arcaded design of the two facades. The arcades of Pisa cathedral predated San Martino's facade renovation, which may have been an attempt to outdo Pisa.[60] Therefore, the decision

---

55 Charles Buchanan, "Spiritual and Spatial Authority in Medieval Lucca: Illuminated Manuscripts, Stational Liturgy and the Gregorian Reform," *Art History* 27, no. 5 (2004), 737–40.
56 Sanecki, "Cathedral and Commune," 51.
57 Buchanan, "Spiritual and Spatial Authority," 723–44.
58 San Frediano is not located within the Roman boundaries of the city and it is this proximity to the entrance to the city via the northern medieval road that was another source of concern regarding pilgrimage traffic in and out of the city. Additionally, the walk through the city between the Cathedral of San Martino and the Basilica of San Frediano only takes around 10 to 15 minutes.
59 Savigni, *Lucca*, 174–77; Romano Silva, *La Basilica di San Frediano in Lucca: Urbanistica, architettura, arredo* (Lucca: M. Pacini Fazzi, 1985).
60 The correspondences between arcaded facades of Pisa and Lucca have been extensively discussed, with many scholars making a claim for Lucca's inferiority as a Pisan derivative. See Mario Salmi, *L'architettura romanica in Toscana* (Milan: Bestetti e Tumminelli, 1926); Pietro Toesca, *Storia dell'arte italiana: I. Il medioevo* (Turin, Italy: Unione Tipografico-Editrice Torinese, 1927); Eugenio Luporini, "Nota introduttiva all'architettura romanica Lucchese," *Belle arti* 1 (1946–48): 311–24; Carlo L. Ragghianti, "Architettura Lucchese e architettura pisana," *Critica d'arte* 8 (1949): 168–72; Kopp, *Die Skulpturen der Fassade*, 9–12, 21–29. For more information about Pisan rule over Lucca in the fourteenth century,

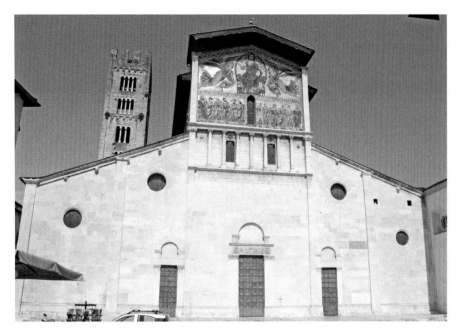

Fig. 2.12: Facade, Basilica of San Frediano, Lucca, Italy, thirteenth century. Photo: Myrabella, Creative Commons license BY-SA 3.0, via Wikimedia Commons, cropped from original.

to employ textile motifs to clothe the facades of San Martino and San Michele worked to visually mark the implied connection between the bishop and cathedral canons and the communal government within the city similar to the ways in which clothing is used to identify individuals of a certain rank or profession.

CLOTHING AND CITY AS IDENTITY

Textiles and clothing conveyed several nonverbal messages about the social position of the individual within medieval society. However, as anthropologist Mary Douglas has discussed, the body is symbolic of the larger social whole.[61] If we substitute the

---

see Christine Meek, *The Commune of Lucca Under Pisan Rule, 1342–1369* (Cambridge, MA: Mediaeval Academy of America, 1980); Louis Green, *Lucca Under Many Masters: A Fourteenth-Century Italian Commune in Crisis (1328–1342)* (Florence: L. S. Olschki, 1995).

61 Mary Douglas, *Natural Symbols: Explorations in Cosmology*, 2nd ed. (London: Routledge, 1996), 69–87. For more on how society is shaped by class structures, see Pierre Bourdieu, "Cultural Reproduction and Social Reproduction," in *Knowledge, Education, and Cultural Change: Papers in the Sociology of Education*, ed. Richard Brown (London: Tavistock, 1973), 71–112.

human body for the physical body of a church,[62] then the appearance of the church can be reflective of society at large, and in this case the society of Lucca. In her book on Parma's communal and episcopal piazzas, Areli Marina contends that the social body of the city was identified with the physical form, especially the public buildings.[63] Therefore, by having these two Lucchese church facades constructed in this particular style across the two main public spaces of the city, the identity of the commune is front and center in a citizen's civil and religious life. This is further corroborated by the fact that these two public spaces were major banking and market centers necessary for all members of the population. The piazza of San Martino was the home of Lucca's bankers who would change money in their market stalls around the edges of the piazza. In addition to the money changers, spice dealers were also present, as evidenced by the oath for spice dealers and money changers to perform their respective trades honestly that was inscribed on the facade in 1111.[64] Textiles would have been seen in market stalls of both piazzas, though with the presence of other professions around San Martino textile merchants may have congregated elsewhere, such as San Michele. A visual example of what these textile markets would have been like within the medieval Italian city can be seen in the illuminated frontispiece of the register of Bologna's cloth merchants' guild, dated 1411, that shows the market in the piazza di Porta Ravegnana in Bologna. Market stalls line the perimeter of the piazza, offering a colorful variety of textiles to purchase and clothing to try on.[65] As one of the cities that benefited from an influx of Lucca's fleeing textile artisans in the preceding century, Bologna's market offers a glimpse as to what could have been experienced in Lucca during the thirteenth century. Furthermore, the juxtaposition of the variety of textiles being sold in the piazzas and the backdrop of the facades of San Martino and San Michele would have further enhanced the communal textile identity of the Lucchese.

For those of the upper echelons of society—royalty, nobility, clergy, and increasingly the wealthy mercantile middle class—their clothing was not only made of some of the best imported materials but also decorated with woven and/or embroidered symbols of powerful animals like lions or mythical beasts such as griffins that further conveyed their societal position. In addition to the symbolism of powerful animals, the act of weaving or embroidering figures of any kind would immediately increase the price of the textile since it would require more materials and labor. These power-

---

62 Ann W. Astell, *The Song of Songs in the Middle Ages* (Ithaca, NY: Cornell University Press, 1990), 15; Line Cecilie Engh, "Religion: Theology, Symbolism, and Sacrament in Medieval Marriage," in *A Cultural History of Marriage in the Medieval Age*, ed. Joanne M. Ferraro and Frederik Pedersen (London: Bloomsbury Academic, 2020), 37–56.

63 Marina, *The Italian Piazza Transformed*, 128.

64 Ricardo Ambrosini, "Le iscrizioni del Duomo e della Curia," in his *San Martino di Lucca: Gli arredi della cattedrale* (Lucca: Istituto Storico Lucchese, 1999), 7–24; and Sanecki, "Cathedral and Commune," 91. Sanecki also mentions apothecaries having market stalls in the piazza around San Martino beginning in the twelfth century.

65 Bologna, Museo Civico Medievale, MS 641, 1r (frontispiece), reproduced in Trinita Kennedy, ed., *Medieval Bologna: Art for a University City* (London: Paul Holberton Publishing, 2021), fig. 71.

ful symbols can be found throughout surviving medieval clothing contained within royal and clerical treasuries, such as the *pellote* and tunic of Fernando de la Cerda, ca. 1275, which are covered with the Castilian coat of arms that depicts both lions and castles.[66] The facades of San Martino and San Michele in Foro are filled with symbols of power, such as lions, griffins, panthers, and dragons, among others.[67] The correlations between the clothing of powerful figures in the city and the facades would not have been easily missed and only strengthened these motifs as identifiers of individual and institutional prestige.

The power of religious institutions in Lucca was also reinforced by the number of textiles and vestments that were owned by the various churches around the city, including the cathedral. An inventory from February 28, 1239, contains several descriptions of liturgical vestments and textiles within the Cathedral of San Martino, such as a green and vermilion (bright red) alb of Lucchese samite.[68] However, unlike the previously mentioned papal inventory of Clement V, the 1239 treasury inventory from San Martino does not list any figural motifs, only providing color and type of garment with an occasional origin of manufacture.[69] In the Dominican 1264 inventory from the church of San Romano in Lucca, several silk vestments, hangings, and liturgical textiles are listed among the objects held in the church's sacristy. There were four altar cloths, and among the vestments there were multiple sets for the priest, deacon, and subdeacon, including one with gold eagles (or eagles woven on a gold background) and another of red samite.[70] Also, some of the vestments had been transferred to the Dominicans from the Benedictines in 1237, when they had handed over the church. Joanna Cannon attributes the large number of silk vestments and liturgical textiles in the inventory to the silk industry within Lucca.[71] I suggest that the wealth of litur-

---

66 Kristin Böse, "Cultures Re-Shaped: Textiles from the Castilian Royal Tombs in Santa María de las Huelgas in Burgos," in *Dressing the Part: Textiles as Propaganda in the Middle Ages*, ed. Kate Dimitrova and Margaret Goehring (Turnhout, Belgium: Brepols, 2014).

67 Mackie, *Symbols of Power*, 180.

68 "Inventario del tesoro della sagristia," 121. The specific inscription is "… una verde et alia vermilia de sciamito Luchese …." According to Del Punta and Rosati (*Lucca una città di seta*, 20), this is the first documented use of the term *Luchese* to describe an item made from silk produced within Lucca.

69 As stated above, it is not until the fourteenth-century cathedral inventories that descriptions of figural motifs are included, which does not mean that they were not there originally, just that it was not deemed important or necessary to record previously. See Guidi and Pellegrinetti, *Inventari del Vescovato*, 191–213; Del Punta and Rosati, *Lucca una città di seta*, 42.

70 Federigo Vincenzo Di Poggio, "Monumentorum Variorium Monitum: Inventarium Sacristiæ," in *Stephani Baluzii Tutelensis Miscellanea novo ordine digesta et non paucis ineditis monumentis*, vol. 4, ed. Étienne Baluze (Lucca: 1764), 600–1. These mentions in the inventory are transcribed by Di Poggio as "Unum de auro ad aglas; Unum de Samito (*a*) rubeo."

71 Joanna Cannon, *Religious Poverty, Visual Riches: Art in the Dominican Churches of Central Italy in the Thirteenth and Fourteenth Centuries* (New Haven, CT: Yale University Press, 2013), 113–15.

gical textiles within San Romano, which was a considerably smaller church than San Martino or San Michele, should be indicative of the richness of textiles owned by all of Lucca's churches in the thirteenth century.

Between attendance at regular Mass services, feast days, and processions, the medieval viewer would have been regularly exposed to richly embroidered silk vestments made in Lucca and those that were imported. For example, on the feast of the Appearance of St. Michael on May 8, the canons from San Martino processed to San Michele to hold their divine offices before the official feast day and liturgical services.[72] This would have placed luxury textiles worn by members of the clergy in direct contrast to the facades of both churches. Additionally, there is also the lavish clothing of the laity that would have been on display during festivals or secular wedding processions. As Christine Meek describes in her discussion of clothing distrained for debts in the 1370 Court of Merchants records, some of the clothing items that were held for unpaid debts were likely not for everyday wear but instead worn during "high days and holidays."[73] For example, the woman's tunic with forty-five "gilded silver buttons on the sleeves" that was obtained from Bartolomeo Andree of Vinci probably belonged to his wife and was likely one of these special occasion garments.[74] Therefore, there was an intentionality demonstrated both by the clergy and the prominent and wealthy citizens of Lucca when they clothed themselves in luxury garments. This further distinguished their identity, wealth, and importance from the commoners of the city and countryside, especially on days where they could see and be seen by the greater community such as during liturgical festivals.

The presence of textile-influenced images on the facades of San Martino and San Michele conveyed the communal identity of the city as one where the textiles were the source of economic prosperity. This communal identity was not just meant to be communicated to the local public, but also to the plethora of pilgrims who traveled along the Via Francigena and stopped to view the *Volto Santo* in the Cathedral of San Martino on their way to Rome. The *Volto Santo*, a sculpture attributed to Nicodemus (one of the men who helped bring Christ down from the cross), was described as being able to perform miracles for those who visited and prayed before it. This important stop on the pilgrimage route would have provided many people with an opportunity to view San Martino's facade, among the many other churches in Lucca, from the thirteenth century onward.[75] Additionally, due to the prosperous city's prestige as a center of textile activity, demonstrated through its marketplaces and the clothing of its inhabitants, it is unlikely that pilgrims, of whatever social class, could have missed

---

72 Brand, "The Vigils of Medieval Tuscany," 52–53.
73 Christine Meek, "Clothing Distrained for Debt in the Court of Merchants of Lucca in the Late Fourteenth Century," *Medieval Clothing and Textiles* 10 (2014): 114.
74 Meek, "Clothing Distrained for Debt," 118.
75 Blomquist, "The Dawn of Banking," 54.

the Lucchese textile mentality and textile identity that manifested itself on the facades of the Cathedral of San Martino and the church of San Michele in Foro.

CONCLUSION

Interwoven into Lucca's thirteenth-century intarsia facades of the Cathedral of San Martino and the church of San Michele in Foro are multiple layers of political and economic realities that influenced the design and execution. Sociopolitical changes during the twelfth and thirteenth centuries contributed to the bishop and cathedral canons' attempt to assert their power, both religious and secular, by drawing upon the role textiles played within the economy and conspicuous display of wealth in medieval Lucca. Members of the commune, which was made up of officials who profited from the textile industry, were reminded of their trade and source of wealth through the facades of what would have been some of the most visited churches for these individuals. This prompt would have had even greater weight since the luxurious clothing worn by members of the communal government and the clergy, especially during special occasions, would have been juxtaposed with one or both facades, thereby creating reflections of a shared communal woven identity.

Clothing the City's Martyrs: Weaving and Spinning in Late Medieval Cologne and Devotion to the Cult of the Eleven Thousand Virgins

Claire W. Kilgore[1]

A young woman clasps her hands in prayer, embodying piety and an elegant symmetry that displays her fashionable gown, made from a green-and-gold patterned silk with tight-fitted, set-in sleeves embellished with buttons from above the elbow to the wrist, as well as a red band of trim decorated with gold floral swirls along the neckline. However, the body wearing these garments is crafted of polychromed walnut, not flesh and blood. She represents one of the Virgin Martyrs of Cologne and served as a reliquary container for bones associated with the cult (fig. 3.1). The sculpture was produced in the mid-fourteenth century and is now in the collection of the Schnütgen Museum in Cologne, where it is identified with the record A 974.[2] It is one of hundreds of wooden reliquary busts made for the relics of Cologne's Virgin Martyrs, although

1 Thank you to the many friends and colleagues who have offered feedback, read drafts, and listened to my enthusiasm for the Virgin Martyrs' fashion and fabrics, especially Tania Kolarik, Abby Armstrong Check, Mya Frieze, and Scott Montgomery. I also extend my gratitude to the three anonymous reviewers for their thoughtful suggestions and critiques. This paper began through the happy overlapping of very different seminars, one on medieval art and death taught by Professor Thomas E. A. Dale, and another on Chinese textiles taught by Professor Yuhang Li, at the University of Wisconsin–Madison during my doctoral coursework. I had the opportunity to further refine my thinking on the topic at a DISTAFF-organized session presented at the 2021 International Medieval Congress at Leeds. Research funding provided by the UW–Madison Graduate School, the Department of Art History, and the Program in Medieval Studies enabled me to conduct fieldwork in Cologne, including visiting the Virgin Martyr busts and their churches.
2 The bust is listed as part of a private collection in Oskar Karpa, *Kölnische Reliquien- büsten: Der gotischen Zeit aus dem Ursulakreis (von ca. 1300–bis ca. 1450)* (Düsseldorf: L. Schwann, 1934). It was published in 1931 in an inventory of works belonging to Dr. Richard von Schnitzler (1855–1938), a Cologne banker; see Otto H. Förster, ed. *Die Sammlung Dr. Richard von Schnitzler* (Munich: F. Bruckmann AG, 1931), 45, 81. The Schnütgen Museum acquired it in 1950.

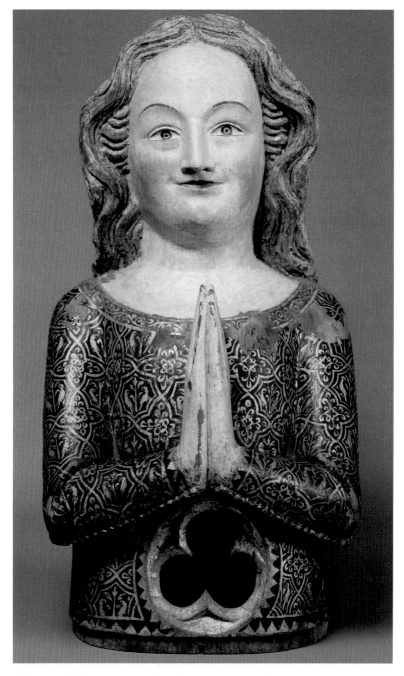

Fig. 3.1: Half-figure reliquary bust of a Virgin Martyr wearing green and gold, Cologne, second quarter of the fourteenth century (Cologne, Museum Schnütgen, inv. no. A 974). Polychromed walnut, 51 centimeters tall. Photo: Copyright © Rheinisches Bildarchiv Köln, by permission.

the half-length torso with arms and hands is a more unusual form. The majority of busts extend only to the shoulders.[3]

The Virgin Martyrs of Cologne did not always number eleven thousand or follow a leader named Ursula.[4] The canonical number of eleven thousand virgin martyrs and the designation of St. Ursula as their leader gained acceptance in the centuries after their mid-fourth-century martyrdom near Cologne. The earliest descriptions of the massacre of an unknown number of virgin martyrs came from a dedicatory plaque installed in the early fifth century by a devotee named Clematius who restored the basilica dedicated to their martyrdom.[5] By the eighth century, the Virgin Martyrs numbered eleven thousand, according to the earliest surviving devotional office which describes a mass and oration for their October 21 feast day.[6] By the eleventh century, their hagiography had become more detailed, with the primary Virgin Martyr understood to be a princess from pagan Britannia named Ursula. While her father intended her to marry a pagan prince, Ursula desired to remain a pious virgin, betrothed to Christ. Seeking resolution of this conflict, she embarked on a pilgrimage to Rome, accompanied by ten fellow virgin companions and their additional entourages, totaling eleven thousand. Their journey to Rome followed the Rhine through Cologne, where an angel delivered the message that their group would be martyred on their return journey. After completing pilgrimage in Rome, including receiving the sacrament of baptism, Ursula and her companions began their journey back to Britannia. Near Cologne, they were martyred by the Huns after refusing to abandon their vows of chastity and pious virginity. When the Huns subsequently besieged Cologne, they were stopped by a heavenly army led by Ursula and her fellow Holy Virgins. In gratitude for this intercession, the citizens of Cologne buried the martyrs outside the city walls and recognized the Holy Virgins as their civic protectors.

Reliquaries, including the half-length bust reliquary Schnütgen A 974, were constructed to house the relics of the Virgin Martyrs in the centuries after the unearthing of a cache of bones in what became known as the *Ager Ursulanus* (Field of Ursula) during expansions of the city walls in 1106.[7] These bodily fragments provided the

---

3 Scott B. Montgomery, *St. Ursula and the Eleven Thousand Virgins of Cologne: Relics, Reliquaries and the Visual Culture of Group Sanctity in Late Medieval Europe* (Oxford: Peter Lang, 2010), 59–65. Many busts remained in Cologne or at monastic institutions in the surrounding region.

4 For example, a sermon from 922 identifies the British princess who led the band of martyrs as Pinnosa. As Montgomery discusses, the translation of St. Pinnosa's relics from Cologne to Essen in the mid-tenth century might explain the shift from Pinnosa to Ursula as the leader of the Cologne Virgin Martyrs and a way to keep the focus of the cult on Cologne, not Essen. See Montgomery, *St. Ursula*, 13–14.

5 The earliest reference to the martyrdom of the Holy Virgins is the early-fifth-century Clematius inscription; for original text and translation, see Montgomery, *St. Ursula*, 9–11. See also Jacobus de Voragine, *The Golden Legend: Readings on the Saints*, trans. William Granger Ryan, 2 vols. (Princeton, NJ: Princeton University Press, 1993), 2:256–60.

6 Montgomery, *St. Ursula*, 11–15.

7 Montgomery, *St. Ursula*, 19–25. In the case of the half-length bust reliquary Schnütgen A 974 (fig. 3.1), the relics were likely displayed in the trefoil cavity in the abdomen or stored

source of the Virgin Martyrs' intimate connection to God and the saints in heaven, along with the intercessory powers sought by their earthly devotees.[8] While there are many virgin martyr saints in medieval Christianity, the eleven thousand virgins existed as a collective grouping, separate from other virgin martyr saints such as St. Agatha or St. Barbara.[9]

Familiar and recognizable details of fourteenth-century dress and fashion help frame the green-and-gold-dressed reliquary bust's visualization of intercessory power in tangible terms for the earthly viewer. Although the materiality of medieval metalwork reliquary busts has been extensively studied by art historians, such as Cynthia Hahn, the textile details simulated on the surface of reliquary busts have generally been ignored.[10] While I use Schnütgen A 974 as my main exemplar in this article, my argument extrapolates to the larger corpus of Cologne's Virgin Martyr bust reliquaries. I contend that the bust reliquaries should be considered from the perspective of textiles, including those used to wrap the cult's relics and the simulated polychrome versions that clothe the surfaces of the wooden reliquary busts. I argue that the depiction of contemporary fashions and textile motifs on the reliquary busts provided a potentially meaningful connection between the sanctified Virgin Martyrs and the female-dominated textile industries of Cologne, namely silk weaving and gold spinning.[11] Furthermore, these reliquaries likely encouraged a participatory interac-

---

in the now-missing pedestal. Other Virgin Martyr of Cologne reliquary busts, especially ones that do not have a full torso, often contained relics in a cavity in the head of the bust, accessed via a lid on the crown of the head.

8 Peter Brown, *The Cult of the Saints: Its Rise and Function in Latin Christianity* (Chicago: University of Chicago Press, 2014), 3–4, 78–80, 88–92.

9 For the purposes of this paper, the terms Virgin Martyrs and Holy Virgins are used exclusively to refer to the Virgin Martyrs of Cologne, whether known by a specific name such as Ursula, Pinnosa, or Cordula, or an anonymous member of their entourage. On the names of Cologne's Virgin Martyrs, see Scott B. Montgomery, "What's in a Name? Navigating Nomenclature in the Cult of St. Ursula and the Eleven Thousand Virgins," in *The Cult of St. Ursula and the 11,000 Virgins*, ed. Jane Cartwright (Cardiff: University of Wales Press, 2016), 1–11. It was not essential that every Virgin Martyr have a distinct name. An identifying tag attached to a relic in the collection of the Aachen Cathedral Treasury only specifies that it comes from one of the Eleven Thousand Virgins whose names are known only to Christ: "undecim milium virginum aliorumque, quorum nomina colligit Christi scientia"; Montgomery, *St. Ursula*, 38.

10 Cynthia Hahn, *Strange Beauty: Issues in the Making and Meaning of Reliquaries, 400–circa 1204* (University Park: Pennsylvania State University Press, 2012), 117–34. Hahn writes extensively about bust reliquaries, although many of these examples end at the neck, and thus do not require consideration of details of dress present on the upper torso. See also Martina Bagnoli, "The Stuff of Heaven: Materials and Craftsmanship in Medieval Reliquaries," in *Treasures from Heaven: Saints, Relics, and Devotion in Medieval Europe*, ed. Martina Bagnoli et al. (New Haven, CT: Yale University Press, 2011), 137–48; Scott B. Montgomery, "Mittite capud meum ... ad matrem meam ut osculetur eum: The Form and Meaning of the Reliquary Bust of Saint Just," *Gesta* 36, no. 1 (1997): 48–64.

11 The type of weaving used to produce silk in Cologne is not easily answered in the archival sources and merits a more specific study singularly focused on the topic than this essay can satisfactorily provide. Evidence points to tablet weaving, especially since the city

tion with the elite women able to purchase and wear similar garments as well as the women involved in the production of materially similar items, their raw materials, or semi-finished components.

In the extensive literature on the cult of St. Ursula and the Eleven Thousand Virgins, few scholars have commented upon the role of clothing beyond brief re-marks noting that the youthful and beautiful Virgin Martyrs are depicted wearing luxurious, fashionable, and contemporary dress.[12] For example, Anton Legner ob-serves that the reliquary busts appeared to wear the latest fashions with their costly Italian silks, tightly buttoned sleeves and, in some examples, frilled *kruseler* veils (fig. 3.2).[13] However, he restricts his observations to the idea that these earthly fashions reinforced the terrestrial, even ordinary, presence of the saint who interceded on behalf of the devotee in heaven.[14] Joan Holladay connects the lifelike polychromy, fashionable clothing, and headgear of the Virgin Martyr busts with the growing be-guine populations in mid-fourteenth-century Cologne. Beguines were lay women seeking a pious, religious life although without the restrictions of rule, dress, and male authority imposed on the traditional established monastic orders.[15] Despite forming

---

specialized in smaller, narrow-ware goods such as decorative trims and braids (*borten*) as well as pouches and purses (for example, the reliquary *bursa* discussed later in this article). However, this does not rule out larger vertical or horizontal looms from con-sideration as potential tools used in the city's silk-weaving industry. As scholars have noted, Cologne did, alongside Cyprus and southern Italy, produce large volumes of the lower-quality silk *cendal* that appeared in Parisian markets. Sharon Farmer, *The Silk In-dustries of Medieval Paris: Artisanal Migration, Technological Innovation, and Gendered Experience* (Philadelphia: University of Pennsylvania Press, 2017), 88. See also Florence M. Edler, "The Silk Trade of Lucca During the Thirteenth and Fourteenth Centuries" (Ph.D. diss., University of Chicago, 1930), 21–22.

12 On the cult of St. Ursula broadly, see Frank Günter Zehnder, *Sankt Ursula: Legende, Ver-ehrung, Bilderwelt* (Cologne: Wienand, 1985).

13 Anton Legner, *Kölner Heilige und Heiligtümer: Ein Jahrtausend europäischer Reliquien-kultur* (Cologne: Greven, 2003), 70. Legner specifically uses the adjective "Italian" in his discussion. On Lucca and silk, see Ignazio del Punta and Maria Ludovica Rosati, *Lucca una città di seta: Produzione, commercio e diffusione dei tessuti lucchesi nel tardo medieoevo* (Lucca: Maria Pacini Fazzi, 2017). On frilled veils, see Isis Sturtewagen, "Unveiling Social Fashion Patterns: A Case Study of Frilled Veils in the Low Countries (1200–1500)," *Medi-eval Clothing and Textiles* 7 (2011): 33–64.

14 Legner, *Kölner Heilige*, 70; Elisabeth Jägers, "Zur Polychromie der Kölner Skulptur vom 12. bis zum Ende des 14. Jahrhunderts," in *Schnütgen-Museum: Die Holzskulpturen des Mit-telalters (1000–1400)*, ed. Ulrike Bergmann (Cologne: Stadt Köln & Schnütgen-Museum, 1989), 85–106, note § "Gemalte Muster: Fellmuster—Textile Muster," 98–99. Scholars do discuss the elaborate textiles used to wrap the skull relics associated with the cult, although not in connection to the polychromy and sculpted details of dress incorporated into the reliquary busts. Montgomery, *St. Ursula*, 79; Gudrun Sporbeck, "Die frühen Kölner Borten und ihre Genese," in *Kölner Bortenweberei im Mittelalter: Corpus Kölner Borten, Mit ei-nem Beitrag und textiltechnischen Analysen von Monika Nürnberg*, ed. Marita Bombek and Gudrun Sporbeck (Regensburg, Germany: Schnell & Steiner, 2012), 39–58.

15 Joan A. Holladay, "Relics, Reliquaries, and Religious Women: Visualizing the Holy Vir-gins of Cologne," *Studies in Iconography* 18 (1997): 67–118, esp. 70–71. According to

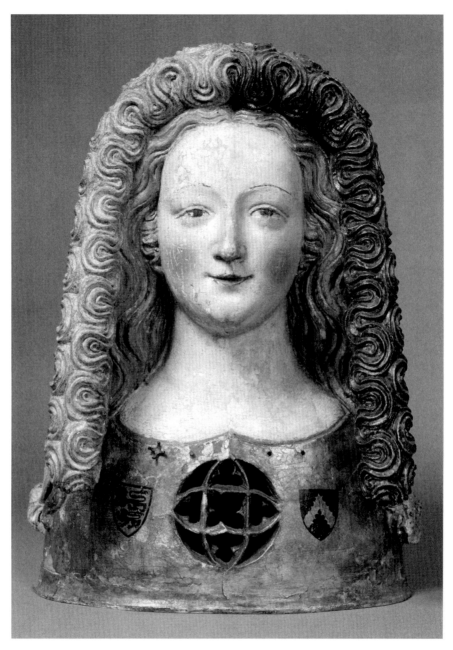

Fig. 3.2: Reliquary bust of a Virgin Martyr with *kruseler* veil, Cologne, around 1350 (Cologne, Museum Schnütgen, inv. no. A 97). Polychromed walnut, 44 centimeters tall. Photo: Copyright © Rheinisches Bildarchiv Köln, by permission.

more informal and flexible communities, beguines set themselves apart through their piety and charity as well as through their dress, typically wearing simple and plain materials that resembled monastic habits.[16] According to Holladay, Cologne women who might one day consider joining a beguinage and had not yet forsaken their fashionable attire were a likely audience of the Virgin Martyr busts.[17] She argues that the reliquary busts of the Virgin Martyrs of Cologne reminded viewers of the piety of Ursula and her fellow Virgin Martyrs, especially their obedience to male and clerical authority as well as the city's long history of "local women whose lives brought honor to both their families and the city."[18] Holladay focuses on the behavioral relationship modeled by the saints to their devotees, but she does not specifically discuss textiles or details of dress beyond noting that the Virgin Martyr busts were relatable to the young women of Cologne because of their fashionable nature.[19] Scott B. Montgomery notes the elaborate textile wrappings made for the relics, arguing that the inclusion of *nonnenarbeit*, or nuns' work, in the decoration and protection of the relics served as evidence of the close connection between the cult and religious women. But this is not the primary focus of his study, and he does not consider the polychrome decoration of the busts themselves, only the physical textiles that wrapped the cult's relics.[20]

Similarly, discussions of medieval Cologne's important textile economies largely ignore extant pieces, whether surviving textiles or depictions of them.[21] Historians, such as Bruno Kuske, Margret Wensky, and Martha C. Howell, have primarily relied on written sources, especially descriptions relating to the city's guilds and the activities of their members, such as import and export data and tax records.[22] Cologne's textile economies encompassed a wide variety of products and materials, ranging from wool,

---

Holladay, numerous houses of beguines, both large and small, existed for women in Cologne seeking a religious lifestyle in addition to several orders of canonesses, eleven other monastic orders, and two mendicant orders.

16 Alejandra Concha Sahli, "Habit Envy: Extra-Religious Groups, Attire, and the Search for Legitimation Outside the Institutionalised Religious Orders," *Medieval Clothing and Textiles* 15 (2019): 137–56.

17 Holladay, "Relics, Reliquaries, and Religious Women," 103.

18 Holladay, "Relics, Reliquaries, and Religious Women," 103.

19 Holladay, "Relics, Reliquaries, and Religious Women," 67–118, esp. 70–71, 94, 103.

20 Montgomery, *St. Ursula*, 79. Montgomery focuses on the relationship between bones, the substance of the cult's relics, and the production of its visual culture in Cologne and related practices of devotion, especially concerning the cohesive, group identification of the Virgin Martyrs as intercessors.

21 I use "textile economies" here to refer to the production and trade of in-progress and completed textiles as well as their raw materials.

22 Bruno Kuske, *Köln, Der Rhein und das Reich* (Cologne: Böhlau, 1956), 1–48, 138–76; Margret Wensky, *Die Stellung der Frau in der stadtkölnischen Wirtschaft im Spätmittelalter* (Cologne: Böhlau, 1980), 61–186; Margret Wensky, "Women's Guilds in Cologne in the Later Middle Ages," *Journal of European Economic History* 11, no. 3 (1982): 631–50; Martha C. Howell, *Women, Production, and Patriarchy in Late Medieval Cities* (Chicago: University of Chicago Press, 1988), 95–160.

leather, and linen to silk and gold.[23] Notably, exclusively female guilds were intimately involved in the spinning and weaving of silk and gold.[24] The gendered identity of these guilds is complex, with many female-specific guilds having close overlaps, through materials as well as marriage, with affiliated crafts produced by male guilds, such as gold beating.[25] Gendered overlaps also appeared through the relationship of female makers and their merchant husbands.[26] Despite these complexities regarding gendered labor in late medieval Cologne, textile work remained connected in the medieval imagination with "women's work." This gendering of work appeared in iconographies of the labors of Adam and Eve after their eviction from the garden of Eden, where Adam is shown tilling the earth while Eve spins using a distaff.[27] Another major example is the Virgin Mary, who modeled these tasks through her childhood labor in the Jewish Temple, where she contributed to the spinning and weaving of the temple veil. These actions were frequently visualized in medieval devotional art and included in anthologies

23 For more on these industries, see Wensky, *Die Stellung*, and Howell, *Women, Production, and Patriarchy*.

24 Wensky, "Women's Guilds," 632–45; Wensky, *Die Stellung*, 37–44, 61–70, 72–183; Howell, *Women, Production, and Patriarchy*, 124–60; Sporbeck, "Die frühen Kölner Borten," 52–55. The guilds for gold spinners and yarn makers were founded in 1397, with the silk guild (*seideamt*) appearing in 1437. The specific trade names and their German equivalents, with Latin if applicable, are outlined here: silk makers (*seideweberinnen* or *seidemacherinnen*; also, *cindatores* beginning in 1252), silk spinners (*seidespinnerinnen*), gold spinners (*goldspinneren* or *filatrices*), yarn makers (*garnmacherinnen*). While the guild name *goldspinneren* specifies gold, they also produced silver and other metal-wrapped threads. The yarn makers produced a blue-dyed linen yarn (*coelsch yarn / fil de Cologne / collen threden*) frequently exported to England and the Netherlands; see Wensky, "Women's Guilds," 632. As Howell notes, the silk spinners gained guild status rather late, in 1456, and "possessed none of the attributes associated with high-status work because they were piece workers in the employ of silk mistresses" (124). The guild for silk embroidery (*wappensticker*) was founded in the mid-fourteenth century and notably was not monopolized by women. By 1397, both men and women were able to have full membership and training rights in the guild. Howell hypothesizes that the guild name of *wappensticker*, referring to coats of arms (*wappen*), perhaps indicated that men specialized in that aspect of embroidering while women specialized in embroidered *borten* and liturgical commissions (131–32 n. 34). Notably, a fifteenth-century *borte* contains an inscription identifying a female silk maker, either as maker or perhaps as commissioning patron of the *borte*: "Byt vur Katheria syde-mechers"; Wensky, *Die Stellung*, 94.

25 Howell, *Women, Production, and Patriarchy*, 124–60; Wensky, "Women's Guilds," 633–50. Note that the *seideamt* had a board comprising two women and two men who were connected by marriage to female silk makers. Further complicating gendered guilds were the existence of widow and widower's rights; Howell, 133–37.

26 Wensky, "Women's Guilds," 638–48. Unmarried female silk makers also occasionally appear in the role of merchants in tax records: for example, the sisters Fygen and Sewis van Bercham in the second half of the fifteenth century; Wensky, "Women's Guilds," 647 n. 50.

27 Sarah Randles, "'When Adam delved and Eve span': Gender and Textile Production in the Middle Ages," in *Women and Work in Premodern Europe: Experiences, Relationships and Cultural Representation, c. 1100–1800*, ed. Merridee L. Bailey, Tania M. Colwell, and Julie Hotchin (New York: Routledge, 2018), 71–102.

of devotional texts, for example Jacobus de Voragine's *Golden Legend*.[28] The Virgin Mary's association with the tasks of weaving and spinning enhanced their medieval perception as virtuous and diligent actions for pious women.

Methodologically, this paper echoes Cordelia Warr's understanding of clothing, accessories, and fashion as communicators within medieval society, functioning as a fluid pathway not only between earthly geographies but also between the terrestrial and the otherworldly, mortal and immortal.[29] I also draw on theories of material culture and lived religion in order to contextualize the reception of the Virgin Martyr reliquary busts within the economic and religious landscapes of medieval Cologne and the devotional practices of the city's inhabitants.[30] As theorized by David Morgan, material religion reframes religious practice in terms of objects and how things actively facilitate devotion through their material characteristics.[31] Additionally, as Caroline Walker Bynum specifically argues within the context of the Christian Middle Ages, materiality proved crucial to sacred experience and religious devotion.[32] Reception theory further allows for the contextualization of viewers', especially female viewers', recognition of and potential reaction to the appearance of simulated textiles on the surfaces of Cologne's Virgin Martyr reliquary busts that reference the materiality of silk and gold.[33] By considering the audience of the reliquary busts and their surrounding material environment, we better understand the people of medieval Cologne's perception of the cult of the Virgin Martyrs and the interwoven connections to the city's local textile industries.

28 Note the prominence of spinning in a panel of Mary and Elizabeth with their children from an early-fifteenth-century winged altarpiece, now in the Germanisches National-museum in Nuremberg (Gm 1087); Voragine, *The Golden Legend*, 2:149–58. For more on Marian devotional texts discussing her early life in early Christian and medieval religion, see Lily C. Vuong, *The Protevangelium of James* (Eugene, OR: Cascade Books, 2019), and Ronald F. Hock, *The Infancy Gospels of James and Thomas* (Santa Rosa, CA: Polebridge Press, 1995).

29 Cordelia Warr, *Dressing for Heaven: Religious Clothing in Italy, 1215–1545* (Manchester: Manchester University Press, 2010), 4–5.

30 Birgit Meyer, "Introduction: Media and the Senses in the Making of Religious Experi-ence," *Material Religion* 4 (2008): 124–35; David Morgan, *The Thing About Religion: An Introduction to the Material Study of Religions* (Chapel Hill: University of North Carolina Press, 2021), 3–22; David Morgan, "The Material Culture of Lived Religion: Visuality and Embodiment," in *Mind and Matter: Selected Papers of Nordik 2009 Conference for Art Historians*, ed. Johanna Vakkari (Helsinki: Society of Art History, 2010), 14–31; Caroline Walker Bynum, *Christian Materiality: An Essay on Religion in Late Medieval Europe* (New York: Zone Books, 2011).

31 Morgan, *The Thing About Religion*, 6–7, 19–23. Morgan subdivides agency into six differ-ent types: external, ritual, mimetic, inherent, instrumental, and aesthetic.

32 Bynum, *Christian Materiality*, 19–25.

33 On reception theory broadly, see Michael Baxandall, *Painting and Experience in Fifteenth-Century Italy* (Oxford: Oxford University Press, 1988), and Hans Robert Jauss, *Toward an Aesthetic of Reception* (Minneapolis: Minnesota University Press, 1982).

FASHIONING BUSINESS AND PIETY IN MEDIEVAL COLOGNE

Fourteenth-century Cologne occupied a prominent position within the surrounding European landscape, facilitated not only by its membership in the Hanseatic League and location on the Rhine River but also by its numerous churches and their prestigious collections of relics.[34] The city famously received the relics of the Three Magi in 1164, translated from Milan to Cologne after Emperor Frederick Barbarossa gave the precious remains to Rainald of Dassel, archbishop of Cologne. Upon arrival in Cologne, these relics found in their new earthly home another collective grouping of relics: those of St. Ursula and her eleven thousand Virgin Martyrs.[35] Like the Magi, pilgrims from the East who traveled to visit the infant Christ, St. Ursula and her Virgin Martyrs modeled pilgrimage as a devotional practice. Following the initial unearthing of the relic cache in 1106, devotion to the cult significantly expanded, and new reliquaries were constructed and then distributed throughout the city's churches. The discovery of the Virgin Martyr relics and renewed prominence of their cult also resulted in the expansion of their titular church, with the addition of a reliquary-like Rayonnant Gothic–style choir in the thirteenth century with embedded relic niches beneath the stained-glass windows.[36] In the Middle Ages, the church now known as St. Ursula's was generally known as the Church of the Virgin Martyrs or the Holy Virgins. The identification as St. Ursula's is a post-medieval development.[37] While the Church of the Holy Virgins commemorated the location of their martyrdom, it was not the only location of their relics or reliquary busts in medieval Cologne.

The wooden bust reliquaries of the Virgin Martyrs, primarily produced between the late thirteenth and mid-fifteenth centuries, adopted the form of strikingly lifelike bodies with youthfully flushed cheeks, softly curving hair, and fashionable, contemporary forms of dress. While the relic cache was initially discovered in 1106, more relics continued to be discovered throughout the twelfth century. Not all relics were immediately placed in reliquaries. Many were stored in sacred furniture or wrapped in textiles or placed within church altars and walls. The majority of the bust reliquaries were produced during the fourteenth century and the first half of the fifteenth century, and their fashions reflect the dates of their manufacture.[38] This style of reliquary is in contrast to other thirteenth- and fourteenth-century reliquaries that imitated architectural forms, such as the elaborate metalwork shrine for the relics of the Three Magi in Cologne Cathedral.[39] According to Scott B. Montgomery, the similarly smiling faces

---

34 Howell, *Women, Production, and Patriarchy*, 99–105; Legner, *Kölner Heilige*, 7–15. Wine, textiles, and metalwork were major industries.

35 Legner, *Kölner Heilige*, 186–97.

36 Montgomery, *St. Ursula*, 19–20, 51–53.

37 Montgomery, *St. Ursula*, 47.

38 Montgomery, *St. Ursula*, 19–31, 62–63.

39 On the Shrine of the Three Kings, see Lisa Victoria Ciresi, "A Liturgical Study of the Shrine of the Three Kings in Cologne," in *Objects, Images, and the Word: Art in the Service of the Liturgy*, ed. Colum Hourihane (Princeton, NJ: Princeton University Press, 2003), 202–30.

of the Virgin Martyr reliquary busts reflected continuity, with the grouping of busts serving to "not only flesh-out the relics, but also the notion of corporate solidarity, as they band together and appear as one—a band of sisters."[40] This liveliness was observed by devotees of the Virgin Martyrs. The description of one fourteenth-century miracle at the Cistercian Abbey of Esrom in Denmark recounted that a grouping of Virgin Martyr busts placed on the main altar sang a response to the *Te Deum* during the Christmas Eve liturgy.[41] Textiles represented another major method of containment for the cult's relics, wrapping the bones and skulls of the martyrs whether they were stored within the reliquary busts, on shelves, or in other sacred furniture.[42] These fabric wrappings contributed another layer to the liveliness of the Virgin Martyrs, serving as a reminder of their original bodies that were also once clothed in textiles as well as adding a warmth and softness to the hard and stark materialities of the relic bones and skulls.

The visual display of the relics of the thousands of Virgin Martyrs communicated the power, prestige, and holiness of Cologne.[43] Virgin Martyr relics and their identifying bust reliquary containers spread throughout Europe, documented by their inclusion in many church and monastery inventories.[44] Montgomery notes that in addition to the spread of the cult due to its increasing popularity and the European relic trade between religious institutions, the city of Cologne itself participated in the distribution of relics of the Holy Virgins as a form of civic gifting.[45] As the location of St. Ursula and her Virgin companions' martyrdom, the city of Cologne acquired a reputation as a place of pilgrimage and repository of relics, including those of many other prestigious Christian saints.[46] The gifting of Virgin Martyr relics to locations outside of Cologne functioned as a form of advertising. The practice affirmed the importance of Cologne as the place where the Virgins were martyred and drew attention to the city's other, less circulated relics, such as those of the Three Magi, which permanently reside in the cathedral there.

40 Montgomery, *St. Ursula*, 67–69. German scholarship terms these reliquaries *Ursulabüste*. While this identification of the reliquary busts of the Virgin Martyrs takes the name from the leader of their group, these reliquary busts do not identify a singular "Ursula" but instead her many companions, some identified with names, some anonymous. Montgomery, *St. Ursula*, 9–16; Montgomery, "What's in a Name?" 1–11.

41 Montgomery, *St. Ursula*, 29.

42 Legner, *Kölner Heilige*, 100. Many of these surviving skull-wrappers are post-medieval.

43 The Virgin Martyrs also provided protection for the city. According to civic legend, the Virgin Martyrs appeared, alongside the male martyr group of St. Gereon and the Theban Legion, on the city's besieged walls to lend aid in October 1268 when the city walls were breached by Archbishop Engelbert II von Falkenstein (r. 1261–74). See Scott B. Montgomery, "Bones and Stones: Imaging Sacred Defense in Medieval Cologne," in *Push Me, Pull You: Imaginative, Emotional, Physical, and Spatial Interaction in Late Medieval and Renaissance Art*, vol. 1, ed. Sarah Blick and Laura D. Gelfand (Leiden, Netherlands: Brill, 2011), 569–74.

44 Montgomery, *St. Ursula*, 24–32.

45 Montgomery, *St. Ursula*, 27.

46 Holladay, "Relics, Reliquaries, and Religious Women," 80.

While relics and the business of pilgrimage formed one facet of the economy of medieval Cologne, the city was renowned for its many other industries, including textiles. Local production and the intermediary actions of import and export contributed to the city's economic well-being and international reputation as well as its civic pride and prestige. The overlap of economies of trade and piety should not be overlooked. For example, visiting merchants and craftspeople could transact their business, and while they were there, complete a pilgrimage as well by visiting Cologne's many relics and churches or witnessing religious processions. Similarly, pilgrims and devotees to the city's saints encountered the markets and merchandise, perhaps taking advantage of the chance to purchase goods or souvenirs. In addition to those visiting Cologne from elsewhere, the city's inhabitants provided an important local audience for its intersecting economies of trade and religion.

As both Martha C. Howell and Margret Wensky have shown, women played an important role in the city's textile economies.[47] Medieval Cologne's female-specific guilds for yarn making, gold thread spinning, and silk throwing and weaving were unique among German cities in this respect and comparable to Paris, which had similar gender-specific textile organizations.[48] Cologne specialized in smaller, luxury goods including half-silk (*halbseide*) narrow ware, silk-embroidered goods, and similar items, which were typically produced by women.[49] Used in the production

47 Howell and Wensky both highlight the silk-making, yarn-making, and gold-spinning industries. Howell, *Women, Production, and Patriarchy*, 124–60; Wensky, "Women's Guilds," 631–50; Wensky, *Die Stellung*, 61–77, 83–112. Note Howell's discussion of the larger economic landscape and the role of the family unit in the imports, exports, and craft activity.

48 Wensky, "Women's Guilds," 631; Howell, *Women, Production, and Patriarchy*, 124–29. Specifically, Howell argues that "Three of the guilds—the yarn makers (*Garnmacherinnen*), the gold spinners (*Goldspinnerinnen*), and the silk makers (*Seideweberinnen*)— produced high-quality export goods of great value to the city's economy and, with only a few exceptions, the women of these guilds did so as independent, highly skilled artisans with their own shops, their own apprentices, and their own materials." While the guilds were generally founded at the end of the fourteenth century, embroidery, weaving, spinning, and gold spinning had a long legacy as women's work, especially for elite women. For similar gendered guilds in Paris, see Farmer, *Silk Industries*.

49 Records indicate that Cologne also produced lower-quality *cendal* silk, likely woven on a full-sized loom by men, that was exported to other markets, including Paris, from the mid-thirteenth century onwards. Makers of *cendal*, termed *cindator* or *cindatores*, begin to appear in Cologne's parish registers starting in the mid-twelfth century. See Wensky, *Die Stellung*, 87; Edler, "Silk Trade of Lucca," 21–22; Farmer, *Silk Industries*, 88–90 n. 62. Regarding narrow ware and similar objects, see Wensky, *Die Stellung*, 83–96; Farmer, *Silk Industries*, 88; Sophie Desrosiers, *Soieries et autres textiles de l'Antiquité au XVIe siècle* (Paris: Musée National du Moyen Âge, 2004), 258–62; Bombek and Sporbeck, *Kölner Bortenweberei*. Typical examples of Cologne silk work include fragments no. 09.50.1263 and no. 09.50.922 in the Metropolitan Museum of Art, New York, both part of the large textile bequest of German textile collector and pattern designer Friedrich Fischbach. Other fragments from his collection that are identified as German and are potentially but not necessarily from Cologne include nos. 09.50.1270 and 09.50.1271.

of gold-wrapped threads, Cologne spun gold was a valued commodity.[50] Notably, it bypassed the city of Lucca's restrictive raw material guidelines imposed on the silk-making industry in the last quarter of the fourteenth century.[51] In addition to Cologne's prominent role in the production of metal-wrapped threads, the city was also renowned for its production of woven and embroidered borders or braids (*borten*) that wrapped relics and adorned liturgical garments, on which they were applied similarly to orphrey panels.[52] It is difficult to definitively ascertain the precise origins of individual textiles, particularly given that certain raw materials or half-finished goods were imported to Cologne, completed in the city, and then sold as Cologne-manufactured items. This identification conundrum can be broadly applied to textiles associated with other centers of production as well.[53] While economic historians such as Howell and Wensky have studied the role of textiles in late medieval Cologne and art historians have noted their presence within the city's church treasuries and collections of liturgical accouterments, these two elements have not been sufficiently connected through the framework of gender, labor, and fashion.[54] Connecting the textile motifs on the reliquary busts and the textiles wrapping the physical relics with the varied textiles produced by the city's female artisans highlights

50 The gold thread product is referred to in historical sources by the terms *oro di Cologna*, *kolzgolt*, or *koltzgolt*; Wensky, *Die Stellung*, 72–82. On other forms of gold thread and other medieval centers of production, see David Jacoby, "Cypriot Gold Thread in Late Medieval Silk Weaving and Embroidery," in *Deeds Done Beyond the Sea: Essays on William of Tyre, Cyprus and the Military Orders Presented to Peter Edbury*, ed. Susan B. Edgington and Helen J. Nicholson (New York, Routledge, 2016), 101–14; Margarete Braun-Ronsdorf, "Gold and Silver Fabrics from Medieval to Modern Times," *CIBA Review* 3 (196): 2–16.

51 This guideline prohibited the use of non-locally sourced materials in Lucca's silk industry, except for Cologne gold and silver threads that were specifically prescribed in the production of certain brocades. Cologne-produced gold and silver threads were allowed via Lucca statute in 1376 and specifically required in the production of "imperiali" and "raccanati" brocades per an additional statute issued June 21, 1382. Wensky, "Women's Guilds," 638; Walter Endrei and Wolfgang von Stromer, "Textiltechnische und hydraulische Erfindungen und ihre Innovatoren in Mitteleuropa im 14./15. Jahrhundert," *Technikgeschichte* 41 (1974): 107.

52 Wensky, "Women's Guilds," 632, 635–38; Marita Bombek, "Kölner Borten, Kölner Garn, Kölner Gold in der mittelalterlichen Textilwirtschaft der Stadt Köln," in Bombek and Sporbeck, *Kölner Bortenweberei*, 17–20.

53 David Jacoby, "Silk Economics and Cross-Cultural Artistic Interaction: Byzantium, the Muslim World, and the Christian West," *Dumbarton Oaks Papers* 58 (2004): 197–240.

54 For the role of textiles in religious devotion in medieval Cologne, see Legner, *Kölner Heilige*, and Anton Legner, ed., *Ornamenta Ecclesiae: Kunst und Künstler der Romanik in Köln*, vol. 2: *Katalog der Ausstellung des Schnütgen-Museums in der Josef-Haubrich-Kunsthalle* (Cologne: Schnütgen-Museum der Köln, 1985).

the importance of the materials and their makers within the context of devotion to the cult of St. Ursula and the Virgin Martyrs in medieval Cologne.

MATERIAL CULTURE AND DEVOTION TO THE CULT OF THE VIRGIN MARTYRS

A rich and diverse range of material culture, including textiles, paintings, sculpture, stained glass, and metalwork, accompanied the rituals and liturgies of medieval Christianity.[55] Cologne's Virgin Martyr reliquary busts formed one facet of this sumptuously sensory backdrop to Christian devotional practice. Although the reliquary busts of the Virgin Martyrs were associated with their leader St. Ursula, they could be found throughout medieval Cologne's churches and convents and were not restricted to their titular church.[56] Churches such as St. Kunibert and St. Gereon continue to possess large quantities of Virgin Martyr bust reliquaries, including objects absorbed from the holdings of now closed churches, convents, and monasteries.[57] Modern viewers often encounter the art and furnishings of medieval Cologne's churches as fragments, juxtaposed with post-medieval additions, or dispersed to both local and distant museum collections. However, for the city's fourteenth- and fifteenth-century inhabitants, the reliquary busts, textiles, and altarpieces adorning the city's churches worked together to provide a multimedia and multisensorial interaction with the sacred. These material objects could have combined to display multiple references to a particular intercessor, especially through garments that when worn may have been placed in visual juxtaposition with objects such as the reliquary busts. One possible example of this is a mid-fifteenth-century *borte* panel (fig. 3.3) that displays *Ursulaschutzmantelheilige* (Ursula as the mantle of mercy) iconography, in which St. Ursula protectively gathers together her fellow Virgin Martyrs under her cloak, demonstrating actions of care and intercession.[58] A priest likely wore a garment embellished with this panel while celebrating liturgies for the Virgin Martyrs' feast day on October 21, when it would

---

55 Many examples of these objects specific to Cologne are published in Legner, *Kölner Heilige* and *Ornamenta Ecclesiae*.

56 Montgomery, *St. Ursula*, 47.

57 Ulrike Bergmann, "Die gotischen Reliquienbüsten in St. Kunibert," *Colonia Romanica: Jahrbuch des Fördervereins Romanische Kirchen Köln e. V.* 7 (1992): 131–46, at 131. Not all of the Virgin Martyr relics and reliquaries remained under ecclesiastical control. Many left their religious context in the nineteenth century, ending up in private collections and museums when many religious institutions were dissolved and their objects sold.

58 Following the German convention of compound words, this iconographic designation combines the saint's name, Ursula, with the Madonna of Mercy gesture known as *schutzmantel* (protective mantle) and the word for saint (*heilige*). The mid-fifteenth-century embroidered panel was at some point removed from its original medieval garment. It was re-applied, including being trimmed as needed, to a baroque-era chasuble in the mid-nineteenth century. Bombek and Sporbeck, *Kölner Bortenweberei*, 209–11.

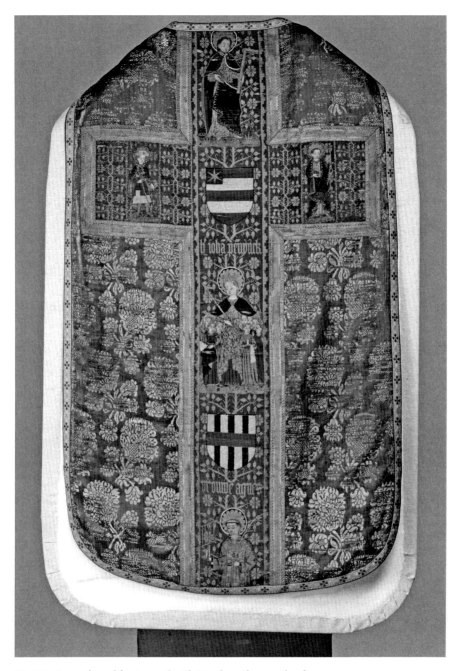

Fig. 3.3: Cross-shaped *borte* panel with Ursula as the mantle of mercy
(*Ursulaschutzmantelheilige*) and heraldic shields, Cologne, ca. 1470, applied in the mid-
nineteenth century to the baroque chasuble of Johann Penninck at St. Cecilia's Church,
Cologne (Cologne, Museum Schnütgen, inv. no. P 864). Photo: Copyright © Rheinisches
Bildarchiv Köln, by permission.

have been seen in proximity with their reliquary busts.[59] Not restricted to the interiors of sacred spaces, the textile-clad bodies of clergy, relics, and reliquaries also appeared throughout the city via liturgical processions associated with the Virgin Martyrs.[60]

In addition to the image of St. Ursula sheltering martyrs under her cloak, the cross-shaped *borte* panel features four other standing saints and two heraldic shields, one at the center crossing above the protective *Ursulaschutzmantelheilige* and another directly below.[61] Both shields have inscriptions underneath identifying their patrons. The center crossing shield portrays a white or silver field with three red transverse stripes, and in the upper left, a six-pointed gold star on a blue field. The inscription beneath reads "*h' johan pennynck*," referring to Herr Johann Pennynck (d. 1474/79), a Cologne patrician and city councilor belonging to the wool-weavers' guild (*windeck gaffel*). Beneath the figure of St. Ursula is the shield of his wife Agnes, featuring a white background with three vertical blue bars overlaid with a transverse red stripe.[62] These details reveal the local textile connections and ongoing patronage and recognition of the cult of the Virgin Martyrs. Similarly, the depiction of St. Ursula via the *schutzmantelheilige* iconography conveys the layered ways the saint and her companions appear within Cologne's material culture.

It is important to note that a mismatch exists between the physical textiles circulating within the markets and sacred spaces of medieval Cologne and the depicted tactile surfaces of the Virgin Martyr busts. They are dressed not in literal fabric, in which observers could discern texture or weave structure, but through the artistic interpretive lens of a painter or other craftsperson. Some busts also feature punchwork (*punzierung*) ornamentation, adding traces of texture (see fig. 3.10). The surface patterning replicated the exotic figured silks imported from the Middle East and Asia and imitated by European workshops, including those in Lucca and other Italian cities. The craftspeople producing the reliquary busts were likely not connected with the female-dominated trades of silk narrow-ware weaving and silk or gold thread spinning but rather the male-dominated trades of painting and sculpting. These artists may have been visually and perhaps even haptically familiar with luxury textiles. Artists frequently painted

---

59 Montgomery, "Bones and Stones," 588. The Virgin Martyrs' feast day was a major liturgical celebration in the diocese of Cologne, designated as an official and obligatory event in 1305 by Archbishop Heinrich von Virneburg. Note also the mid-sixteenth-century altar frontal with *Ursulaschutzmantelheilige* from St. Gereon's Church, Cologne (Rheinische Bildarchiv 05171729). On liturgical clothing, see Maureen C. Miller, *Clothing the Clergy: Virtue and Power in Medieval Europe, c. 800–1200* (Ithaca, NY: Cornell University Press, 2014).

60 Bergmann, "Die gotischen Reliquienbüsten," 132. Noting the presence of labels identifying which busts belong to which church treasuries, Bergmann suggests that the Virgin Martyr reliquary busts were carried in religious processions throughout medieval Cologne.

61 On the provenance of this *borte* and its other known fragments, see Bombek and Sporbeck, *Kölner Bortenweberei*, 209–11. In the same volume, note the ends of a maniple which combines silk embroidery and half-silk weaving and features Ursula as *schutzmantelheilige* and St. Gereon, 105–06, and the picture of the reverse side of the embroidery, 70.

62 The text under the lower shield reads *vrouwe agnes*.

depictions of luxurious silks and velvets, both as worn garments or as props such as background curtains, bedding, and cushions.[63] Lisa Monnas has raised important questions about how artists gained familiarity with luxury textiles, noting issues of access, especially regarding affordability and sumptuary legislation.[64] One major source of access may have been the observation of liturgical textiles, as the most valuable and sumptuous examples were displayed during services and processions for major feast days. Records also indicate that medieval artists' workshops received commissions to paint imitations of luxury textiles on cheaper materials, simulating cloth of gold on canvas or an elaborate patterned silk on plain silk, for example.[65] Painters' workshops innovated to create or modify fictive patterns, perhaps using stencils or stamps to imitate woven designs as well as translating details onto the painted surface using gold tooling techniques.[66] Other alterations by the artist included modifying the quality of the depicted textiles incorporated into a painting or sculpture based on the needs and wishes of the patrons, for example adding the illusion of gold threads and other details not found in surviving similar textiles that likely served as artistic models.[67] The artists producing the Cologne Virgin Martyr busts were engaged in a process of translation from actual to fictive textile.[68] The Virgin Martyr bust surfaces displayed a

63 For example, note the so-called *Dombild Altarpiece*, sometimes known as the *Altarpiece of the Patron Saints of Cologne*, attributed to local artist Stefan Lochner around 1440. Originally painted for the St. Maria in Jerusalem Chapel for Cologne's city council, it was moved to Cologne Cathedral (the source of the name *Dombild*, or cathedral painting) in 1810, where it is currently located in the Marienkapelle (Marian chapel), south of the choir. Other recognizable luxury textiles appear in the *Life of Mary* panels painted around 1480 by the Master of the Life of Mary (Cologne) for the church of St. Ursula. Its panels are now split between the National Gallery (London) and the Alte Pinakothek (Munich).

64 Lisa Monnas, *Merchants, Princes and Painters: Silk Fabrics in Italian and Northern Paintings, 1300–1550* (New Haven, CT: Yale University Press, 2008), 23–40.

65 Monnas, *Merchants, Princes and Painters*, 23, 38–39. Monnas cites examples from Italy, specifically Florence, as well as France and England, indicating that this was a widespread practice, especially for poorer and more rural parish churches lacking the resources to invest in luxury altar frontals and vestments.

66 For example, *sgraffito*, a term describing the scratching away of paint applied on top of gold leaf, thus creating a gold pattern, or *pressbrokat* (tin relief) to create three-dimensional details, useful for capturing details such velvet pile, using molded tin foil. Monnas, *Merchants, Princes and Painters*, 88–93, 305; Pamela Betts and Glenn Gates, "Dressed in Tin: Analysis of the Textiles in the *Abduction of Helen* Series," *Journal of the Walters Art Museum* 74, online at https://journal.thewalters.org/volume/74/essay/pressbrokat (accessed Oct. 9, 2024).

67 Monnas, *Merchants, Princes and Painters*, 67–95, esp. 88–93, and the discussion of painted textiles in Giovanni del Biondo's *St. Catherine of Alexandria with a Donor* (early fifteenth century, Museo dell'Opera del Duomo, Florence) versus a surviving lampas fragment in London's Victoria and Albert Museum (inv. no. 7084-1860).

68 This process of translation appears frequently in medieval visual arts, especially in two-dimensional arts (e.g. panel painting, wall frescoes, and manuscript illumination) starting in the mid-fourteenth century and flourishing throughout the fifteenth century. Textiles are depicted as worn on bodies and as interior decorations (e.g. cloths of honor, curtains, and pillows). While portrayed and often treated in scholarship as examples of

recognizable surface and simulated materiality within which the members of Cologne's female gold and silk work guilds might recognize the components of their craft.

The multisensory and layered textile-centric associations between the surfaces of the Virgin Martyr busts and textile-producing craftswomen would have been further enhanced by the juxtaposition of the busts with the textile-clad bodies of the clergy and relics nearby.[69] Public liturgical processions visually reinforced the saints' protective power over the city and displayed the materiality and substance of the reliquary containers. Members of the clergy participating in these processional displays of the reliquary busts and their relics likely wore garments produced with similarly embellished silks and trims, both imported and locally produced. This crafted visual and sensorial continuity. For example, a woven stole (fig. 3.4) made in Cologne in the early fourteenth century and now in the cathedral treasury at nearby Münster features Virgin Martyr reliquary busts interspersed with heraldic shields, a noteworthy departure from the more prevalent (at least in extant liturgical textiles) *Ursulaschutzmantelheilige* iconography.[70] This self-referential imagery speaks both to the recognizable iconography of the reliquary bust within the cult of the Virgin Martyrs and to the contributions of the local textile industry and its makers as important patrons of and contributors to the city's church treasuries and export markets. Furthermore, the visual juxtaposition of clergy (wearing luxury textiles incorporating both locally produced and imported materials) carrying the Virgin Martyr reliquary busts ("wearing" painted representations of rich textiles) communicated the city's spiritual power and material wealth.

The luxury textiles recreated on the Virgin Martyr busts and circulating through the city's markets were more than beautiful or sensorially desirable objects. Imported figured silks also proved inspirational for the design of local textiles in some instances. Gudrun Sporbeck notes the existence of a thirteenth-century cable-stitched embroidery using colored silk thread and probably made in Cologne, preserved through its incorporation into a late Gothic dalmatic belonging to the parish church of St. Peter and Paul in Grieth, a Hanseatic town on the Rhine near Kalkar.[71] In addition to typical star-shaped rosettes, the embroidery also references an imperial quadriga rider, imagery which may have been borrowed from imported Syrian silks of the eighth century.[72] The devotional use of textiles appeared throughout the Middle Ages

---

"real" medieval textiles, these representations should be critically considered through the lens of artistic invention and modification, not as literal documentary evidence.

69 Here, I have found Tania Kolarik's methodology of textility useful, where "textility functions to 'make' an *art object* (painting, fresco, work of architecture, sculpture, etc.) 'woven' or textilic (textile-like) through its materials, reproduction of a textile aesthetic, and/or metaphorical description." My thanks to Tania for sharing the text of her paper presented in June 2024 at the 36th Comité International d'Histoire de l'Art World Congress in Lyon.

70 Sporbeck, "Die frühen Kölner Borten," 39–58, esp. 55–56.

71 Although Sporbeck does not provide a more specific date than "late Gothic," it is likely that this refers to the fifteenth century or perhaps the later fourteenth century.

72 Sporbeck, "Die frühen Kölner Borten," 52.

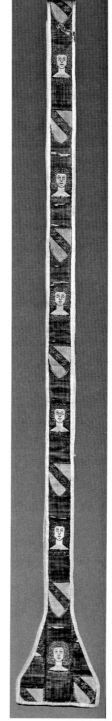
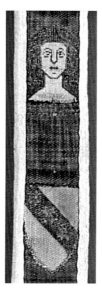

Fig. 3.4: Woven stole with Virgin Martyr busts and heraldic shields (*wappen*) with enlarged detail at right, likely made in Cologne during the fourteenth century (Cologne, Münster Cathedral Treasury). Silk, linen, and gold. Photo: Courtesy of Stephan Kube/SQB.

in Christian contexts.[73] Notably, these textiles did not need to have a Christian origin or motifs. Functioning as visualizations of wealth and power and easily transportable through the "pathways of portability" available in the global Mediterranean, Islamic and Eastern textiles covered and enshrined Christian relics.[74] Not confined to the religious sphere, the patterns of textiles brought from Byzantium, Persia, and China also influenced the appearance of European-produced fabrics and contributed to the shared, secular Mediterranean court culture that circulated through networks of trade.[75] The presence of imported items in medieval Cologne made the city's wealth and power visible and also served as models for artistic production, not only for the reliquary bust surfaces but also for textiles.

Many of the textile items produced in late medieval Cologne were used for religious purposes, either made as donations by pious patrons or commissioned by ecclesiastical leaders for institutions both near and far.[76] An example of this is a late-fourteenth or early-fifteenth-century woven linen bag (fig. 3.5) embroidered in geometric motifs with silk and metal-wrapped threads. Perhaps made by a local nun or beguine, this object is identified by Anton Legner, an art historian and specialist in medieval Cologne, as a *bursa* or reliquary pouch.[77] Another religious use of Cologne's textile output was as skull wrappings. Unfortunately, many of the textile-wrapped skull relics in the city of Cologne have had their wrappings replaced. At the Cistercian Abbey Church of Marienfeld, approximately 170 kilometers northeast of Cologne, a collection of forty

73 Textiles also have the potential to become relics in their own right, for example the tunic of the Virgin at Chartres Cathedral, in addition to appearing extensively in religious ritual through worn vestments, altar frontals, etc. For examples found in Cologne church treasuries, see Legner, *Ornamenta Ecclesiae*, vols. 1–3.

74 Eva Hoffman, "Pathways of Portability: Islamic and Christian Interchange from the Tenth to the Twelfth Century," *Art History* 24 (2001): 17–50.

75 Janet Snyder, "Cloth from the Promised Land: Appropriated Islamic *Tiraz* in Twelfth-Century French Sculpture," in *Medieval Fabrications: Dress, Textiles, Clothwork, and Other Cultural Imaginings*, ed. E. Jane Burns (New York: Palgrave Macmillan, 2004), 147–64; Del Punta and Rosati, *Lucca una città di seta*; Louise W. Mackie, *Symbols of Power: Luxury Textiles from Islamic Lands, 7th–21st Century* (New Haven, CT: Yale University Press, 2015).

76 Sporbeck, "Die frühen Kölner Borten," 44. Cologne *borten* appear throughout the Hanse as far as Danzig (Gdańsk) as well as in Scandinavia and the Baltics and were valued import items in other geographic areas as well.

77 Legner, *Kölner Heilige*, 80–85. The devotional textile work done by nuns and beguines is well documented. See Montgomery's comment on *nonnenarbeit*, *St. Ursula*, 79; June L. Mecham, *Sacred Communities, Shared Devotions: Gender, Material Culture, and Monasticism in Late Medieval Germany*, ed. Alison I. Beach, Constance H. Berman, and Lisa M. Bitel (Turnhout, Belgium: Brepols, 2014); Bevin Butler, "Crafting Agency in Needle and Thread: 'Nuns' Work' and Textile Production in Late Medieval Monasteries" (Ph.D. diss., Arizona State University, 2021). In Cologne, the quantity of religious textiles made by secular women versus religious or religiously affiliated women is less clear. It is likely that nuns and beguines sourced some of their materials, including gold-wrapped thread and woven *borten*, from secular makers in the city, in addition to using imported foreign silks.

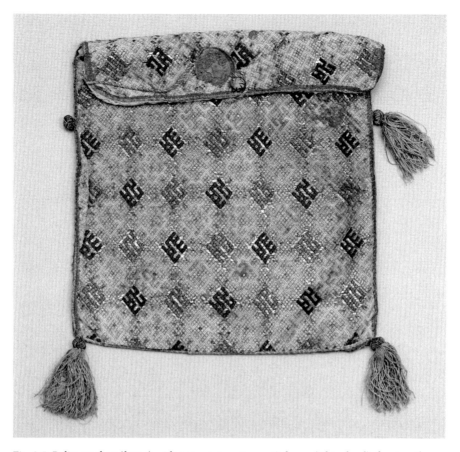

Fig. 3.5: Reliquary bag (*bursa*) with geometric patterns, Cologne (Rhineland), fourteenth or fifteenth century (Cologne, Museum Schnütgen, inv. no. P 870). Linen, silk, and gold-wrapped thread, woven and embroidered, 22.2 by 20.9 centimeters. Photo: Copyright © Rheinisches Bildarchiv Köln, by permission.

relic skulls, many associated with Cologne's cult of the Virgin Martyrs, have maintained their original thirteenth- and fourteenth-century wrappings. New textile covers were added on top of the existing fabric, thus preserving the original medieval fabrics, many of which were made in or imported via Cologne. The oldest example, from the first half of the thirteenth century, features a strikingly delicate geometric-patterned net of filet-work and pearl embroidery over a red silk wrapper.[78] Another skull (fig. 3.6) combines Cologne-produced and imported textiles in a multilayered wrapping, highlighting four distinct textiles added during the thirteenth through fifteenth centuries. They include a late-thirteenth-century Cologne-made *borte*, a filet-work silk with

78 Sporbeck, "Die frühen Kölner Borten," 54.

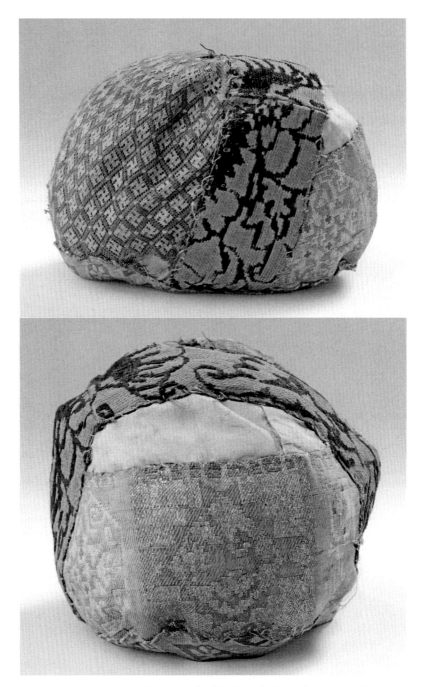

Fig. 3.6: Two views of a textile-wrapped skull relic with filet embroidery, Cologne, thirteenth to fifteenth century (Marienfeld, Germany, Cistercian Abbey Church of Mariä Himmelfahrt). Woven gold brocade and silk. Photo: Courtesy of Stephan Kube/SQB.

green-and-gold geometric patterns, a flower- and cube-patterned silk that Sporbeck identifies as possibly Spanish or potentially from Cologne, and a strip of fifteenth-century Florentine gold brocade with blue pile.[79] By participating in the creation of these textiles and materials exported for their creation elsewhere, the city's silk weavers and gold spinners contributed to the wealth of their city and the protection of its sacred treasures, working to clothe the bodies of the city's saints and clergy.

MODELS OF PIETY, FASHION, AND FAMILY

The Virgin Martyr reliquary busts are dressed as fashionable contemporary women, their style indicated by two-dimensional surface decoration emulating luxurious silks and three-dimensional sculpted details ranging from buttons to headgear.[80] As noted by Stella Mary Newton, the new sewing technology allowing set-in, narrow sleeves separate from the body of a garment is one of the major fashion innovations of the mid-fourteenth century, while elaborately frilled or crimped *kruseler* veils flourished

---

79 Sporbeck, "Die frühen Kölner Borten," 55. Per Sporbeck, other textiles used at Marienfeld include fourteenth-century Italian diaper weaves with patterns including paired parrots or staggered lilies, whose influence can be seen in later Cologne *borten*. A similar floral-patterned medieval German silk textile, potentially from Cologne, is at the Metropolitan Museum of Art, New York, inv. no. 09.50.1270.

80 Legner, *Kölner Heilige*, 70. On surviving examples of female clothing, see Elizabeth Coatsworth and Gale R. Owen-Crocker, *Clothing the Past: Surviving Garments from Early Medieval to Early Modern Western Europe* (Leiden, Netherlands: Brill, 2018). On fashion, see Maria Giuseppina Muzzarelli, *Guardaroba medievale: Vesti e società dal XIII al XVI secolo* (Bologna: Il Mulino, 1999); Françoise Piponnier and Perrine Mane, *Dress in the Middle Ages*, trans. Caroline Beamish (New Haven, CT: Yale University Press, 1997). Object descriptions routinely associate reliquary bust Schnütgen A 974 with Lucchese textiles, identifying the pattern and appearance of the polychrome with contemporary mid-fourteenth-century Italian silks. Some of these entries further associate the origin of the bust with Italy based on its surface decoration, despite the fact that busts known to be produced in Italy do not have similar polychrome ornamentation. This assumption also ignores the role of trade in distributing textiles around the global Mediterranean; the indexical function of textiles as symbols of luxury, wealth, and trade; and Cologne's participation in the textile industry through the distribution of finished silks and the production of materials involved in Lucchese silk weaving. For example, note the object description stating "the youthful companion of the saint [meaning a companion of St. Ursula] wears a robe with a 'Lucchese' silk pattern (rendered in green lustre-paint on silver and brush gilding). This treatment of the robe has led to the assumption that the bust comes from Italy." ["die jugendliche Begleiterin der Heiligen trägt ein Gewand mit 'lucchesischem' Seidenmuster (Grüne Lüsterfarbe auf Silber und Pinselvergoldung). Diese Gewandbehandlung hat zu der Vermutung geführt, die Büste stamme aus Italien."] Frank Günter Zehnder, "15. Reliquienbüste," in *Die Hl. Ursula und ihre Elftausend Jungfrauen: Wallraf-Richartz-Museum, Köln 6. Juli bis 3. September 1978*, ed. Gerhard Bott (Cologne: Museen der Stadt Köln, 1978), 54. For Italian busts, see the examples in Montgomery, *St. Ursula*, 73–75, esp. figs. 14 and 15.

between the mid-fourteenth and early fifteenth centuries.[81] These details can be seen widely in a range of media produced contemporaneously with the Cologne Virgin Martyr busts, ranging from manuscript illuminations to panel paintings.[82] Fashions of this period were in part facilitated by the court culture associated with Charles IV (1316–78), Holy Roman Emperor and King of Bohemia.[83] The vibrantly colored, textile-patterned surface of Schnütgen A 974 (fig. 3.1) places her among her lay peers, unconstrained by codes of religious dress governing the nuns and beguines of the city.[84] The luxurious textile-simulating surfaces of the other reliquary busts also reinforce the noble status of the Virgin Martyrs.[85] An Italian silk fragment dated to the second quarter of the fourteenth century, now in the collection of the Cleveland Museum of Art, shows the close visual relationship between the reliquary bust surface patterns and textiles produced during the same era (fig. 3.7). The fragment features vegetal swirls and paired birds in tan, faded from the original red, on a green background. This is similar to the pattern depicted on the gown of Schnütgen A 974.[86] The lustrous materiality of metallic thread in silks woven with gold- or silver-wrapped threads added both shimmering aesthetic qualities and weight from the heft of the metallic thread felt by the wearer or handler of the textile. For the medieval devotee

81 Stella Mary Newton, *Fashion in the Age of the Black Prince: A Study of the Years 1340–1365* (Woodbridge, UK: Boydell, 1980), 3–5, 86–109.

82 For example, note the woman with narrow sleeves and a frilled *kruseler* veil on fol. 7r of the Velislav Bible (Prague, National Library of the Czech Republic, MS XXIII C 124), illuminated in Bohemia in the mid-fourteenth century. Digitized at https://new.manu-scriptorium.com/en/velislav-bible (accessed Oct. 9, 2024).

83 On the artistic influence of Charles IV, see Barbara Drake Boehm and Jiří Fajt, eds., *Prague, the Crown of Bohemia 1347–1437* (New York: Metropolitan Museum of Art, 2005).

84 On Cologne's beguines and religious women, see Holladay, "Relics, Reliquaries, and Religious Women," 89–96. Significantly, reliquary bust Schnütgen A 974 survives with most of its medieval polychromy intact. For an overview of polychrome and technical analysis, especially for objects from twelfth- through fourteenth-century Cologne, see Jägers, "Zur Polychromie," 85–105. Further complicating the study of the polychromed and gilded surfaces of Cologne's medieval reliquary busts is the destruction sustained via age, poor restoration work, and World War II. Pre-war and pre-restoration archival photographs offer some glimpses of original, medieval surfaces. Objects that maintain the majority of their original polychrome decoration in combination with representative fragments that can be extrapolated across larger surface areas allow a glimpse into the types of surfaces popular in the fourteenth and fifteenth centuries.

85 Note that according to Virgin Martyr hagiography, St. Ursula was a princess, the daughter of a British king.

86 Anne E. Wardwell, "Flight of the Phoenix: Crosscurrents in Late Thirteenth- to Fourteenth-Century Silk Patterns and Motifs," *The Bulletin of the Cleveland Museum of Art* 74 (1987): 23. Similar fragments are also in the Schnütgen Museum. Bird motifs also appear in textiles known to have been produced in Cologne, including a *borte* produced around 1400, now in the collection of the Schnütgen Museum, which prominently features paired birds. Sporbeck, "Die frühen Kölner Borten," 50.

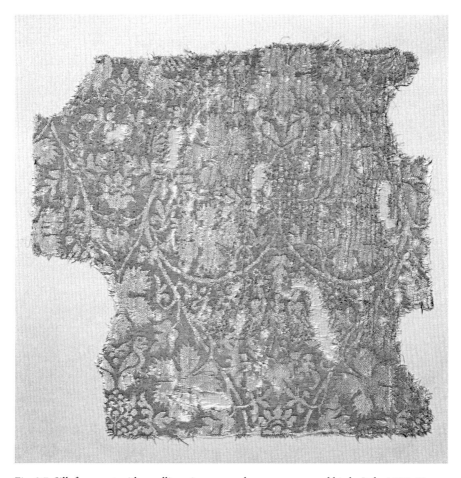

Fig. 3.7: Silk fragment with scrolling vines, grape leaves, grapes, and birds, Italy, 1325–50 (Cleveland Museum of Art, Florence and Charles Abel Oriental Rug Collection by exchange 1971.75). Lampas silk, 24.1 by 25.4 centimeters. Photo: Open access, courtesy of the Cleveland Museum of Art.

gazing at the Virgin Martyr reliquary busts, these sensorial qualities contributed to their perception of the object.

Virgin Martyr reliquary busts depict several variations of the saintly body, including some with arms posed in gestures of prayer, such as that shown in Schnütgen A 974. This gesture indicated piety and proper devotional behavior while emphasizing the fashionable style of the Virgin Martyr reliquary bust, with lavish rows of buttons bordering each arm. Originally functional in that they were needed to secure the tightly fitted sleeves popular in the fourteenth century, buttons transformed into symbols of fashion and status when applied in excess as ornamentation.[87] Furthermore, the buttons of the half-length busts appeared in three dimensions, physically sculpted on the reliquary busts. This tactility is not unique to Schnütgen A 974. It appears in another fourteenth-century half-torso bust associated with the Goldene Kammer (Golden Chamber) in the church of St. Ursula, represented as the leftmost line drawing in figure 3.8.[88] Presumably only the clergy or members of a religious order touched the reliquaries after their creation. The three-dimensional detail encouraged viewers to think about touch, the maneuverability of buttons, and their functional role, contributing to the overall liveliness of the reliquary body.[89] The Goldene Kammer Virgin Martyr bust also visualized identity through details of dress. Traces of the original painted family crests, likely of patrons who donated the object, flank her praying hands. The lustrous surface of her buttoned sleeves simulates a roundel-patterned textile, with the motifs in the roundels alternating between a rampant lion and an eagle.[90] Similar heraldic devices appear on other Virgin Martyr reliquary busts, including the *kruseler*-veiled Virgin Martyr bust in figure 3.2. According to Joan Holladay, these shields probably refer to the Kusin and von Palast families, both prominent Cologne patricians.[91]

Comparing the specific details of dress in the Virgin Martyr bust reliquaries with other depictions of desirable dress from the fourteenth century reveals the widespread influence of fashion. The tightly buttoned sleeves that appear on the half-length reliquary busts with praying hands can be compared with a surviving medieval textile, the mid-fourteenth-century quilted pourpoint associated with Charles of Blois (fig. 3.8, center).[92] Although the secular pourpoint is derived from a functional garment, with the padded quilting providing a defensive element, Charles of Blois's version is

---

87 Margaret Scott, *Medieval Dress and Fashion* (London: British Museum, 2007), 108. Additions such as buttons were often officially prohibited by sumptuary laws and could lead to fines and public denouncements of the wearer. Scott notes that in 1351, a Venetian man received a fine because his sixty silver-gilt buttons violated sumptuary laws. Within the context of late medieval Cologne and German-speaking regions more broadly, see Ulinka Rublack, "The Right to Dress: Sartorial Politics in Germany, c. 1300–1750," in *The Right to Dress: Sumptuary Laws in a Global Perspective, c. 1200–1800*, ed. Giorgio Riello and Ulinka Rublack (Cambridge: Cambridge University Press, 2019), 44–53; Maria Giuseppina Muzzarelli, "Reconciling the Privilege of a Few with the Common Good: Sumptuary Laws in Medieval and Early Modern Europe," *Journal of Medieval and Early Modern Studies* 39 (2009): 597–618.

88 For more on the Goldene Kammer bust, see Karpa, *Kölnische Reliquenbüsten*, 59.

89 On touch and the imagination, see Jacqueline E. Jung, "The Tactile and the Visionary: Notes on the Place of Sculpture in the Medieval Religious Imagination," in *Looking Beyond: Visions, Dreams, and Insights in Medieval Art and History*, ed. Colum Hourihane (University Park: Pennsylvania State University Press, 2010), 202–40.

90 Ulrike Bergmann, "Kölner Bildschnitzerwerkstätten vom 11. Bis zum ausgehenden 14. Jahrhundert: Zum Forschungsstand," in Bergmann, *Schnütgen-Museum: Die Holzskulpturen*, 46–8; the Goldene Kammer half-length bust is reproduced as figure 52. See also Karpa, *Kölnische Reliquienbüsten*, 58–59.

91 Holladay, "Relics, Reliquaries, and Religious Women," 68, 111 n. 71.

92 The pourpoint was preserved alongside Charles' hair shirt, kept as a relic in a church treasury in Angers following Charles' death in the 1364 Battle of Auray against Edward III.

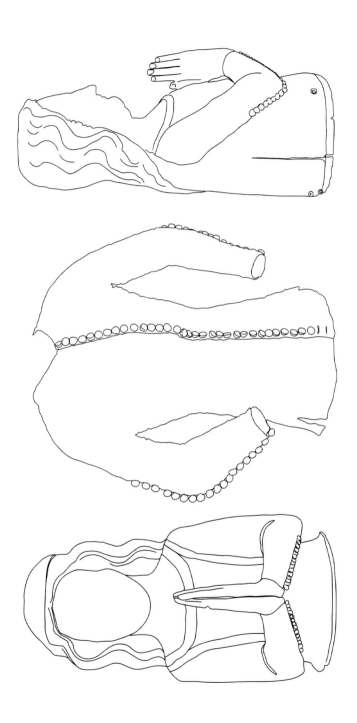

Fig. 3.8: Comparison of sleeve buttons on an extant garment and two Virgin Martyr busts from Cologne. Center: Pourpoint of Charles of Blois, ca. 1370 (Lyon, France, Musée des Tissus, MT 30307). Left: Half-figure bust from the Goldene Kammer (Golden Chamber) of St. Ursula's Church, Cologne. Right, the bust shown in fig. 3.1. Drawing: Claire Kilgore.

the epitome of a luxury garment. It was constructed of lampas silk woven with gold threads and patterned with heraldic lions and winged eagles in geometric medallions. Silk-covered round-headed wooden buttons stretch from above the elbow to the wrist. This physical, fabric pourpoint helps visually place the sculpted, painted buttons used in the dress of the Cologne reliquary busts as intentional reproductions of popular fourteenth-century fashions.[93] The Virgin Martyr reliquary busts that include arms and sleeves make up only a small subgroup of the entire corpus of Virgin Martyr bust reliquaries. However, the incorporation of sculpted buttons on busts within that subcategory reveals the importance of that detail of adornment as a meaningful and recognizable attribute of dress to viewers.

Similar depictions of these fashionable buttons as well as patterned silks can be found in a wide variety of painted images throughout fourteenth- and fifteenth-century Europe, ranging from manuscript illuminations to large-scale wall paintings. For example, intricately patterned silks cut and sewn into dresses featuring tightly buttoned sleeves appear in representations of women in Pisa's *Last Judgment* fresco in the Camposanto, also from the mid-fourteenth century.[94] Close examination of the female elect rising from their graves on the lower left side of the fresco reveals them to be dressed in boldly vegetal-patterned silk dresses with multiple visible buttons extending from the wrist toward the elbow. Similar buttons can be seen on figures portrayed in pilgrim badges from the late fourteenth and early fifteenth centuries.[95] An early-fifteenth-century egg tempera and gold panel painting by Venetian painter Niccolò di Pietro (fig. 3.9) displays St. Ursula and her fellow martyrs in elaborately patterned silks, such as those imported to Venice from the Middle East and Asia or

93 See Coatsworth and Owen-Crocker, *Clothing the Past*, 260. One notable point of difference between the pourpoint and the dresses worn by the Virgin Martyr busts is texture. The pourpoint is quilted and padded, reflecting the design's inspiration from padded armor. Coatsworth and Owen-Crocker note that the pourpoint itself was not likely intended to be used in battle, instead functioning as a showpiece. A non-luxury pourpoint example can be viewed in Ambrogio Lorenzetti's *The Allegory of Good and Bad Government* (ca. 1338), in the Sala dei Nove in the Palazzo Pubblico in Siena. The fresco scene depicting the *Allegory of Good Government* portrays several prisoners being presented to the enthroned male personification of the city of Siena, with the second prisoner in the foreground wearing a white pourpoint visually similar to that of Charles of Blois. In this depiction there are no buttons visible on the man's sleeves due to his arms being tied behind his back, but buttons the same color as his white pourpoint are visible down the front of his garment.

94 The *Last Judgment* fresco is attributed to the painter Buonamico Buffalmacco and was completed in the mid-fourteenth century. It is located in Pisa's Camposanto (Holy Field) cemetery, which contains dirt brought back by ship from Golgotha during the Third Crusade (1189–92). On the Camposanto, see Flavio Boggi, "Pisa Cathedral," in *Encyclopedia of Medieval Pilgrimage*, ed. Larissa J. Taylor et al. (Leiden, Netherlands: Brill, 2010), 568–70.

95 For example, a badge (Museum of London, no. 93.215/1) perhaps associated with the shrine of St. Sithe (Zita), and a milkmaid badge (Museum of London, no. 88.446) from the last quarter of the fourteenth century, excavated in London.

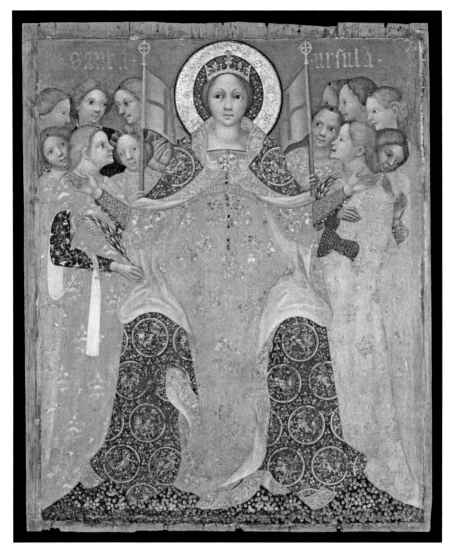

Fig. 3.9: Niccolò di Pietro, *St. Ursula and Her Maidens*, ca. 1410 (New York, Metropolitan Museum of Art, Rogers Fund, acc. no. 23.64). Tempera and gold on wood, 94 by 78.7 centimeters. Photo: Open access, courtesy of the Metropolitan Museum of Art.

produced by Venice's local workshops, which were enhanced through the relocation of Lucchese silk weavers to the city in the previous century.[96] In addition to the Venetian influences that inform the painting's textile motifs, Niccolò's work also indicates familiarity with northern, potentially Bohemian influences, especially his use of nails

96 Del Punta and Rosati, *Lucca una città di seta*, 5–7.

to create the three-dimensional buttons. These tactile details were used in a variety of places throughout the panel painting, including on the sleeves of the frontmost maidens standing to the left and right of St. Ursula as well as on the foreheads of the surrounding martyrs. The raised nails featured prominently in the adornment of St. Ursula, appearing on her red-and-gold patterned sleeves, as well as running vertically down the center of her pink-and-gold foliate-motif dress. Finally, the nails are used to add weight and three-dimensionality to the surface of the large golden brooch used to clasp St. Ursula's elaborate blue cloak, which features phoenixes in large gold roundels. This technique is similar to the use of metal in polychrome wooden sculpture in Northern Europe.[97] In contrast to the previously examined *Ursulaschutzmantelheilige* iconography, here St. Ursula's cloak does not envelop the surrounding martyrs, although the gesture of the martyr on the left with sleeves of black and gold, shown holding a palm, perhaps hints at the sheltering warmth to be found under St. Ursula's sumptuous silk mantle. St. Ursula appears calm and wise, offering strength and comfort to the elaborately dressed women surrounding her, encouraging them and modeling piety and devotion as well as fashionable materiality.

The three-dimensional buttons used in the half-length Virgin Martyr busts communicate a purposeful, textural aspect of clothing, intentionally constructed as part of the dressed identity of the wooden-bust form. As Jacqueline Jung has observed, the tactility of medieval sculpture provided another means of access to the sacred for medieval individuals.[98] The tactile details of clothing present on the reliquary busts offered their beholders the opportunity to imagine dressing themselves in similar garments: fastening buttons, smoothing folds of silk, feeling the weight of bejeweled and embroidered necklines, or adjusting the frilled edge of a *kruseler* veil (fig. 3.2). These tactile gestures, whether enacted in reality or through the mind's eye, allowed beholders to join in with the multitude of Virgin Martyrs as they interceded before God in heaven, wearing garments worthy of the Heavenly Jerusalem.

Recognizably expensive and valuable textiles also appear in reliquary busts that reveal only the upper torso and shoulders of the saints. A Virgin Martyr reliquary bust from the church of St. Kunibert in Cologne, dated to the mid-fourteenth century, incorporates a winged lion or griffin-type figure surrounded by swirling leaves (fig. 3.10, right).[99] This type of animal and its placement draw on motifs associated with

97 Amy Griffin and Antonio Mazzotta, "The Discovery and Conservation of a Nicolò di Pietro in the Cuming Museum, London," *The Burlington Magazine* 156 (2014): 153–58. Bohemian influences should also be viewed as part of the larger artistic and court culture promulgated in the later fourteenth century under the reign of Holy Roman Emperor Charles IV (1316–78), a major artistic patron not only in Prague but also in Aachen and throughout the Holy Roman Empire more broadly. On the artistic influence of Charles IV, see Boehm and Fajt, *Prague, the Crown of Bohemia.*
98 Jung, "The Tactile and the Visionary," 208, 224.
99 The two busts in figure 3.10, like many other Virgin Martyr busts, feature bejeweled necklines. While the bejeweled necklines visually distinguish these trims from typical Cologne *borten*, some reliquary busts, such as Schnütgen A 974, do incorporate trims that might reference locally produced adornments. The jeweled necklines likely recall the

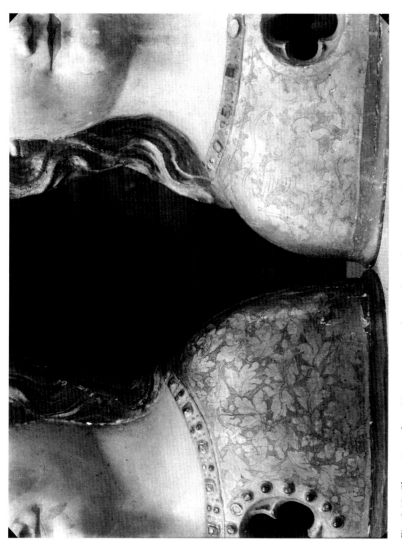

Fig. 3.10: Close view of two Virgin Martyr reliquary busts showing punchwork (*punzierungen*) and (on the bust at the right) a griffin motif (Cologne, Basilica of St. Kunibert, ca. 1400–1500). Photo: Copyright © Rheinisches Bildarchiv Köln, by permission.

the *nasij* or cloths of gold (also known as *panni tartarici*) produced in the Middle East, then under the control of the Ilkhanids, a branch of the Mongols who converted to Islam in the late thirteenth century and ruled territory in Iraq and Persia.[100] The main aesthetic and valuable contribution of *nasij* was through its surface-woven gilded silk thread that was used for both weft and warp.[101] The golden-surfaced reliquary busts from St. Kunibert materially replicate the *nasij* effect, their shimmering surfaces communicating the luxurious materiality of cloth of gold and the material wealth required for its production. Cloth of gold was constructed using gold-wrapped threads, a raw material known to local craftspeople who produced it for local use and export and also saw it incorporated into finished figured silks imported into Cologne.[102]

The Virgin Martyr wearing the griffin-patterned textile includes dual references to the value of her garments through both surface materiality and constructed design. Materially, the garments clothing the fourteenth-century Virgin Martyr busts reflect the heavenly glory witnessed by the saints as they interceded on behalf of their earthly devotees. Their golden-thread woven garments also offered a tactile connection to a female-dominated local gold-spinning industry that provided significant economic contributions and local civic prestige to late medieval Cologne.[103] A Cologne gold spinner or silk weaver could potentially see her craft reflected in the material substances clothing the city's prestigious relics, visible through their display in the city's churches and through the reliquaries that were publicly processed through the city streets on feast days. As Jane Schulenburg suggests in her study of early medieval embroiderers,

---

royal and noble makeup of the group of martyrs, reflecting Ursula's identity as a British princess, or the heavenly splendor befitting the martyrs after death.

100 Maria Ludovica Rosati, "*Panni tartarici*: Fortune, Use, and the Cultural Reception of Oriental Silks in the Thirteenth and Fourteenth-Century European Mindset," in *Seri-Technics: Historical Silk Technologies*, ed. Dagmar Schäfer, Giorgio Riello, and Luca Molà (Berlin: Max-Planck-Gesellschaft zur Förderung der Wissenchaften, 2020), 73–88. A comparable fragment from the collection of the Cleveland Museum of Art (no. 1989.50) features paired hybrid winged animals contained in vertically stacked roundels, although it uses gold thread made with a paper substrate, not the metal-wrapped silk found in Cologne-style spun gold. This is a noticeable material contrast, although the shimmering materiality and heft of the gold thread incorporated into a silk would remain comparable. Produced in central Asia in the middle of the thirteenth century, the Cleveland textile showcases Mongol influence through the use of gold woven into fabric as a sign of power and authority while also drawing on the Mongols' Asian heritage through the incorporation of Chinese cloud motifs visible in the patterning of the hybrid lion's wings. Online at http://www.clevelandart.org/art/1989.50 (accessed Oct. 9, 2024).

101 James C. Y. Watt, *The World of Khubilai Khan: Chinese Art in the Yuan Dynasty* (New York: The Metropolitan Museum of Art, 2010), 6–7. Mackie, *Symbols of Power*, 210–22.

102 Cloth of gold became a desired material and was copied by figured-silk weavers in cities such as Lucca and Venice as well as imported from the Middle East and Asia. Lisa Monnas, "The Cloth of Gold of the Pourpoint of the Blessed Charles de Blois: A Pannus Tartaricus?" *Bulletin du CIETA* 70 (1992): 122.

103 Although women often worked in tandem, including through marital partnership with the male guild of gold beaters. Wensky, "Women's Guilds," 635–38.

female craft practices enabled women to enter into sacred spaces forbidden to them based on their gender through their created objects that were used in the liturgy.[104] For Cologne women involved in textile production, their material familiarity with woven silk and spun gold could enhance their personal devotional visualization of the real and simulated textiles that touched the body of the sacred. This intimate knowledge enhanced their perception of the Virgin Martyr busts and the sacred relics they contained which specifically interceded for Cologne, allowing them to virtually join the ranks of the Virgin Martyrs witnessing the splendor of the Heavenly Jerusalem.

CONCLUSION

The clothing of relics and reliquaries in splendid textiles extends beyond the representative body of the sculpted reliquary to the bodily fragment of the relic itself. Due to the immense quantity of Virgin Martyr relics owned by churches in Cologne, not all were contained within sculpted busts. Windowed reliquary cabinets in the churches of medieval Cologne stored relics, whether contained in reliquary busts such as those discussed throughout this article, wrapped in fabric, or merely stacked neatly. The bones dressed in textiles as well as those contained within wooden bodies existed as paradoxically holy earthly fragments, sacred remnants of the saint in heaven. The relics of St. Ursula and the Eleven Thousand Virgins of Cologne created a collective sensory experience for devotees, reminding viewers of the multitude of saints currently performing as intercessors before God in paradise. Reliquary busts replicating physical bodies enhanced this message. The extraordinary materiality of the textiles adorning their earthly reliquaries further linked the Virgin Martyrs with heaven. The reliquary bodies were clothed in glorious splendor recognizable in substance and in material value to their earthly audience. This message took on additional meaning for devotees intimately involved in the production of similar textiles for the wrapping of relics or adorning of vestments utilized in Cologne's religious institutions.

Polychromed and gilded surfaces simulating elaborately woven silk and cloth-of-gold textiles were not exclusive to Virgin Martyr reliquary busts in medieval Cologne. Busts of male saints and bishops also appeared to wear valuable and desirable textiles. However, the specific inclusion of luxury textiles on the surface of Virgin Martyr reliquary busts and the local connections to female-dominated silk-making and gold-spinning industries merits examination. Gender also plays an important role for the discussion of craft and devotion, with weaving, spinning, and embroidery

---

104 Jane Tibbetts Schulenburg, "Holy Women and the Needle Arts: Piety, Devotion, and Stitching the Sacred, ca. 500–1150," in *Negotiating Community and Difference in Medieval Europe: Gender, Power, Patronage, and the Authority of Religion in Latin Christendom*, ed. Katherine Allen Smith and Scott Wells (Leiden, Netherlands: Brill, 2009), 108–9. While Schulenburg's study ends in the twelfth century, her larger arguments also apply to later medieval contexts.

even functioning as prayers.[105] The recognizable luxury textiles that garb the reliquary busts contribute to their visible identity as Virgin Martyrs, in the same way that their youthfully flushed cheeks and gentle smiles do.[106] Not only do they wear clothing worthy of the heavenly elect, but they also wear clothing familiar in both substance and construction to Cologne's inhabitants. The sensory materiality of textiles juxtaposed with relics, whether through the physical wrapping of bones or simulated in polychrome and gilding upon the reliquary bust surface, helped to visualize the dual residency of the saints on heaven and on earth.[107] Weaving and spinning could be performed by women in a variety of roles, including those pursuing religious life in a convent or beguinage or those working as secular, skilled guild members contributing to the vibrant economy of medieval Cologne. Whether completed inside or outside of a convent, this weaving and spinning recalled the labor of the Virgin Mary as she toiled to craft the temple veil.[108] The Virgin Martyr busts also functioned as models of industriousness, piety, and virtue.

As Michael Camille observed, understanding medieval visuality is more than the study of optics and the physiology of the eye; it instead involves the details of medieval perception and cognition of the whole body.[109] These interactions of perception between object and subject relied on both the significance of vision and impressions of materiality and sensation within the medieval mind.[110] Textiles enhanced the sanctity of the relics, not only through their visual, shimmering beauty and relative material value but also their sumptuous tactility. The relics of the Virgin Martyrs displayed the stark physicality and materiality of bone. This was counteracted by the reliquary containers, which utilized representations of luxury textiles to visualize the material splendor witnessed by the saints in heaven. In addition to their religious message of efficacious intercession and heavenly splendor, the luxury textiles clothing the relics, whether through physical relic wrappings or simulated polychrome, also spoke to the economic power of late medieval Cologne. They symbolized both the raw materials and finished products that circulated through the city's markets and beyond as trad-

---

105 As June Mecham observed in her study of medieval convents in Lower Saxony, nuns used embroidery and counting stitches as prayers in devotional practice. Mecham, *Sacred Communities*, 84–85.

106 Recognizable patterns functioned as markers of identity in medieval devotional iconography, for example the coarsely textured camel-hair garment identifying John the Baptist. Note the mid-fourteenth-century metalwork reliquary bust for the arm of John the Baptist at the parish church of St. John the Baptist (formerly an abbey church) in Aachen, Germany; see discussion and image in Boehm and Fajt, *Prague: The Crown of Bohemia*, 152–53. This phenomenon can also be observed in panel painting and other media.

107 My thanks to Scott Montgomery for this observation.

108 Hock, *The Infancy Gospels*, 5–6, 50–53. See also Vuong, *The Protevangelium*, 74–81.

109 Michael Camille, "Before the Gaze: The Internal Senses and Late Medieval Practices of Seeing," in *Visuality Before and Beyond the Renaissance*, ed. Robert S. Nelson (Cambridge: Cambridge University Press, 2000), 202.

110 Camille, "Before the Gaze," 206.

ed goods. Local connections to the silk-weaving and gold-spinning industries also contributed to the visual importance of the Virgin Martyrs' garments. The elaborately fashionable garments worn by the reliquary busts communicated multivalent messages: the splendor and extravagance of luxury clothing worthy of the Heavenly Jerusalem, the prominence of Cologne as a pilgrimage destination, and the prestigious local industries associated with gendered guilds whose members might have materially contributed to clothing similar to that worn by the reliquary busts, the relics within, or the clerical bodies processing them through the city streets.

The Detailed Lexicon of Ladies' Apparel in Montauban's Sumptuary Laws of 1275 and 1291

Sarah-Grace Heller[1]

In 1275, a set of regulations and fines on women's apparel was passed in the city of Montauban. Included was a clause requiring that the edicts be revisited fifteen years later. Accordingly, they were reviewed and updated in 1291. Comparison of these two documents offers fascinating information on apparel styles, modes of conspicuous consumption, and approaches to moral attitudes over two decades. There are enumerations of terms which clearly denoted sufficiently distinct styles to compel the authorities to distinguish between them, a signal that a fashion culture was at work in the town. A study of the sumptuary laws' vernacular Occitan terminology can serve as an important contribution to the little-studied history of dress and consumption in the medieval Midi, the south of France. Enacted early in the timeline of medieval European sumptuary laws, these edicts also represent a possible model for later ones. Laws in vernacular Occitan (and adjacent Catalan, as well) share certain traits with those emerging in France, Spain, England, and Italy in this period and later, but other characteristics demonstrate that they deserve a place in the comparative work that has justly been called for by Laurel Wilson.[2] Montauban's social and legal context was unique. The dress prohibitions need to be understood within the economic and political framework of this town in the last quarter of the thirteenth century as well as within the broader trend for issuing edicts intended to regulate consumption that was beginning to sweep European municipalities. The first part of this study will place the laws in the context of the town and their codicological transmission. Then it will look at the vocabulary used to denote women and their status, including the women entertainers (*jotglaressas*) and prostitutes or courtesans (*putas*) who were denigrated in the 1291 edict by being allowed to wear clothing prohibited to ladies

---

1 This article expands upon a paper presented in May 2022 at a DISTAFF session at the International Congress on Medieval Studies at Kalamazoo, Michigan.

2 Laurel Wilson, "Common Threads: A Reappraisal of Medieval European Sumptuary Law," in *Legal Encounters on the Medieval Globe*, ed. Carol Symes and Elizabeth Lambourn (Kalamazoo, MI: Arc Humanities Press, 2017), 141–65.

and other women. The third section is a close examination of the lexicon used. To enhance the material philology and offer insights into different contemporary attitudes, I compare representations of women's consumption in Occitan vernacular in such texts as Matfre Ermengaud's *Breviari d'amor* and *Ab greu cossire*, a song in a woman's voice deploring the loss of prized clothing. Comparisons of vernacular clothing terminology in French, Iberian, and Italian literary and legislative sources also serve to help understand the trends in question, and the degree to which Montauban's statutes were unique.

Versions of the 1275 statutes appear in two cartularies. The *Livre des Sermens* (Book of Oaths) contains only those of 1275.[3] The better-known *Livre Rouge* (Red Book) contains a copy of the statutes of 1275 as well as the only extant copy of those of 1291.[4] These edicts have not been widely accessible. An uncertain and abbreviated transcription was published in 1841.[5] This was used by the printer and archivist Edouard Forestié in his analysis of the fabrics and items sold by a fourteenth-century merchant of Montauban, Barthélemy Bonis.[6] In the 1960s, the city's municipal archivist Mathieu Méras paraphrased them into modern French.[7] Close lexical study and comparison of the two decrees has required a new examination of the manuscripts. To make it more available, this study offers a new edition of the 1291 decree accompanied by an English translation (Appendix 4.1).

3 Sarah-Grace Heller, "The 1275 Sumptuary Law in the *Livre des Sermens* of Montauban: An Interpretive Edition and Translation," *Tenso: Bulletin of the Société Guilhem IX* 40 (2025): 17–48.

4 Archives Départementales de Tarn-et-Garonne, MS AA 1, digital version, E(03) 121-AA 1, online at https://bvmm.irht.cnrs.fr/consult/consult.php?reproductionId=2285 (accessed Sept. 11, 2024). The 1275 declaration can be found on fols. 36v–37r, and the 1291 on fols. 74v–75v. All references to the text of the statutes in this article are to the manuscript. Parenthetical citations indicate item numbers. The author thanks Laure Craig for her assistance.

5 L'abbé [Joseph] Marcellin and Gabriel Ruck, eds., *Histoire de Montauban, Par H. LeBret, Prévôt de l'église cathédrale de cette ville, en 1668; nouvelle édition revue et annotée d'après les documens originaux par l'abbé Marcellin et Gabriel Ruck*, 2 vols. (Montauban, France: Rethoré, 1841), 1:411–15. This is a heavily annotated re-edition of Henri LeBret's history, which was written in 1668. Marcellin and Ruck thoroughly combed the municipal archives and added many transcriptions and analyses in annex to LeBret's narrative history. See "Introduction," xxi–xxix.

6 Edouard Forestié, "Le vêtement civil et ecclésiastique dans le sud-ouest de la France," *Société archéologique de Tarn-et-Garonne. Bulletin archéologique* 15 (1887): 161–92, at 168–71; Forestié, *Les Livres de comptes des frères Bonis, marchands montalbanais du XIVe siècle*, 2 vols. (Paris: H. Champion, 1890–94), 1:lviii–lix.

7 Mathieu Méras, "Les Lois somptuaires de Montauban dans la deuxième moitié du XIIIe siècle," in *Bulletin Philologique et historique (jusqu'à 1610) du Comité des travaux historiques et scientifiques: Actes du 89e Congrès national des Sociétés savants tenu à Lyon, 1964* (Paris: Bibliothèque Nationale, 1967), 516–23.

MONTAUBAN'S MUNICIPAL GOVERNANCE: THE EDICTS' FRAMERS

Montauban was founded in 1144 by Alfonse-Jourdain, Count of Toulouse (r. 1109–48). For both military and economic reasons, he wanted a fortified town at the strategic position where the commercial thoroughfare of the Tarn River intersected with the road between his capital at Toulouse and the prosperous city of Cahors to the north.[8] Count Raymond V of Toulouse granted Montauban a charter of unlimited municipal self-governance in 1195, conferring rights and privileges other towns fought for years to receive.[9] The governing body was called the *Capitol*. According to article 45 of the charter, ten respected men were to be chosen to serve as consuls, termed *capitols* or *cossuls* in the original documents.[10] They served for one year and then elected their successors.

The preamble composed by the *capitols* of 1275 indicates the motivations for the declaration. The regulations (*establimenz*) were intended "for the honor of God, our lady Saint Mary, our lord Saint Jacques, and all the saints of paradise, and to guide the honest conduct (*honestat*) of the ladies and for the communal profit (*comunial profieg*) of the city." The end of the document declares that infractions would be fined in units of a thousand *teules*, tiles or bricks. It intimates they were intended for the completion of the church of Saint-Jacques and the bridge over the Tarn, whose construction was a condition of the 1195 charter. Moral and monetary improvement were intertwined.

The opening line indicates the participants. In the name of the king and the *Capitol*, the king's regional representative (*viguier*)[11] Per Ramon Folcaut sanctioned the statutes. His name is followed by those of the *capitols* in that year. After the above invocation to the saints, it goes on to state that he "called a communal *parlement* with trumpets and assembled the townsmen, merchants, and artisans of the commune

---

8 Annie Laforgue, "Naissance d'une ville (12e–13e siècle)," in *Histoire de Montauban*, ed. Daniel Ligou et al. (Toulouse: Privat, 1984), 25–35; Maurice Langevin, "Alphonse Jourdain, fondateur de Montauban, sa vie, son oeuvre," *Bulletin de la Société archéologique et historique de Tarn-et-Garonne* 100 (1975): 65–76; Devals Aîné, *Histoire de Montauban* (Montauban, France: Forestié Neveu et Compagnie, 1855), 1:213–43; Marcellin and Ruck, *Histoire de Montauban*, 1:55–70.

9 Laforgue, "Naissance d'une ville," 32–33.

10 I retain the Occitan terms used in the *Livre des Sermens* in italics rather than translate them with inexact borrowings. To avoid confusion, I capitalize the council (*Capitol*) and indicate the members in lower case (*capitols*). In the 1291 document in the *Livre Rouge*, which was copied later, they are often also referred to as *cossuls*. In Toulouse, the analogous council members were sometimes termed *capitouls* in Occitan, *capitulares* or *consules* in Latin. There were six *capitols* in Montauban in 1176; from 1180 onwards, there were twenty-four. Philippe Wolff and M. Durliat, "Le Premier essor urbain (XIe–XIIe siècle)," in *Histoire de Toulouse*, ed. Philippe Wolff et al. (Toulouse: Privat, 1974), 98–103.

11 The term *viguier* (derived from Latin *vicarious*, cf. English "vicar") signified an executive representative of the counts of the Midi and later the French kings, who held administrative, judicial, financial, and sometimes military functions. They were salaried, rather than farmers of revenues. Joseph Strayer, "Viscounts and Viguiers Under Philip the Fair," *Speculum* 38, no. 2 (1963): 242–55.

in the hall of our lord the king, for a meeting of diligent deliberations with the most respected men of the town" (item 2). Describing the details of the assembly—noting the trumpets, the involvement of all the businessmen of the town, and calling the communal hall "the king's"—shows the importance of recording the intentionally public staging of the declaration. It is worth noting that Montauban had just recently come under French dominion when King Philip III of France (r. 1270–85) inherited both the French throne and the county of Toulouse in 1271, with the deaths of his father Louis IX, his uncle Alphonse of Poitiers, and his aunt Jeanne of Toulouse in Tunis.[12] There is some possibility that Philip's council would have known of Montauban's 1275 law, passed as it was by his *viguier* "in the name of the king" (as well as the *Capitol*).[13] There is no record suggesting that Philip had visited Montauban, however. Via the king's representative, the town was sending a message of homage and commitment to the charter as much as reproof to the husbands of the townswomen. They called it an *establiment p[er] totz temps valedor*, a regulation helpful (*valedor*) for all times and situations. These formulae are essentially repeated in 1291, although the "hall of the king" was replaced by the less obsequious *maizo communal* (lit. communal hall). French sovereignty was no longer new at that point.

REGARDING WOMEN: FEMININE TARGETS

Montauban's regulations focused on women, like those of many other Languedocian, Catalan, and Italian towns. Part of the wording expressing the edicts' purpose in both issuances, *ad honestat de las donas*, signified that they were intended to guide women towards assuming an upright lifestyle. *Dona* (lady) is used twice more to denote the women of the town in 1275 (items 4, 13), as well as being used to invoke Our Lady in the preamble. The term *femna* (woman) appears once as a synonym (item 17). It can be inferred that the term *molher* referred to married women rather than simply women, given that it was used in the singular: no man (*negus hom*) should "put up with" (*sofria*) his wife wearing prohibited trims. Although the list targets only women's clothing, it says that any man or woman (*totz homs e tota femna*) who violated the order would be fined. By 1291, no such mention of men's responsibility for women's clothing infractions is found. Husbands were only required to pay for their wives' infractions concerning lying-in and wedding celebrations (items 7–10). In contrast, the 1279 edict of French king Philip III included a clause saying that both bourgeois

---

12 Philip III formally took possession of the county of Toulouse in October of 1271, through his seneschal Guillaume de Cohardon. Wolff et al., *Histoire de Toulouse*, 171.

13 The *Livre des Sermens* version begins, "Senhor lo rei e·l Capitols, per nom maestre Per Ramon Folcaut" (Per Ramon Folcaut, in the name of his lordship the king and the *Capitol* […]). Note: "Per" is the Occitan equivalent of Peter.

and noble women were required to pay their own fines if they had no husband or lord, whose responsibility it would be otherwise.[14]

In addition to *donas* (ladies), in 1291 the *capitols* included *e autras femnas* (and other women). The addition of this second status category draws a line between noble and common women, emphasizing at least a semantic degree of social awareness of this distinction. However, the rules applied uniformly to both groups. Although the edicts formulaically repeat both status designations, ladies and "other women" were treated as a collective entity when it came to dress and entertaining guests.[15] The effort to distinguish between the knightly and bourgeois classes is quite weak compared to what is seen in certain other sumptuary laws, for instance the French royal laws of 1279 and 1294, which separate different ranks of nobles by income and include a few items on the bourgeoisie, or the English law of 1363 and the 1439 law of Brescia, which expressed complaints that artisans and various types of workers were wearing apparel that was finer than their station merited.[16]

In another contrast with the French royal law of 1279, daughters were not mentioned in Montauban's regulations.[17] No distinction was made between the age and station implied by the terms *dames* in French and *donas* in Occitan, and that of young or unmarried women. Although *damoiselles* are targets in the French law, the corresponding Occitan *donzelas* is absent. Whereas the 1279 law passed by Philip III and his *parlement* had a provision stating that no bourgeois women (*nus bourgeoise*) could have more than one set of clothing lined with vair, the equivalent term *borgesa* does not appear in Montauban's regulations. The French royal laws were more concerned with regulating the number of new outfits per year permitted to many different status

---

14 Henri Duplés-Augier, "Ordonnance somptuaire inédite de Philippe le Hardi," *Bibliothèque de l'école des chartes* 15 (1854): 176–81.

15 Marcellin and Ruck, *Histoire de Montauban*, 1:412–15; Méras, "Les Lois somptuaires," 519.

16 Wilson, "Common Threads," 156; Sarah-Grace Heller, "Anxiety, Hierarchy, and Appearance in Thirteenth-Century Sumptuary Laws and the *Roman de la Rose*," *French Historical Studies* 27, no. 2 (2004): 311–48; Catherine Kovesi Killerby, *Sumptuary Law in Italy, 1200–1500* (Oxford: Oxford University Press, 2002), 81.

17 The 1279 royal law states: "Et que nule dame ne damoisele, en quel estât que ele soit, ou conbien que ele soit grant dame, nc puisse avoir ensemble que iiij paires, si ele n'est fame ou fille de home qui ait plus de .v. .m. livrées de terres à tournois, ou se ele meimes ne les a ; et cele ne pourra avoir au plus que v pères de robes, ne de plus grant pris que de xxx s. de tournois Taune à l'aune de Paris. Et s'aucune foisoit encontre, ses sires paieroit xi libr. de tournois, toutes les foiz que ele feroit encontre, et s'ele n'avoit signeur, ele meimes les paieroit ; et si seroient ces amendes départies si comme il est dit desus." ("No lady or noble maiden of any station, no matter how high, may have more than 4 sets of robes altogether unless she is the wife or daughter of a man worth more than 5000 pounds tournois in lands, or if she owns them herself; and those women may not have more than 5 sets of robes worth no more than 30 sous tournois per yard of Paris. Any lady who violates this shall pay 11 pounds tournois every time she violates it, and if she has no lord she will pay it herself; and the fine shall be distributed as indicated above.") Duplés-Augier, "Ordonnance somptuaire," 180. This translation and all others in this article are my own, unless noted otherwise.

groups.[18] Evidence suggests that Montauban's 1275 law was intended to minimize the visual impression of the town's wealth by prohibiting decorations made of what were essentially monetary materials—gold and silver, principally—on women's apparel, in addition to the moral objective of humility in consumption.[19] The 1291 revision demonstrates some shifts. After fifteen years of *capitols* swearing to uphold the 1275 edicts in the annual initiation ceremony, the directive's force would have been blunted by repetition. The novelty of raising funds for church and bridge construction with fines on gold, silver, and silk on women's clothing would have passed. Like most sumptuary laws, it was probably less than effective. The *capitols* did a thorough job of revising the law fifteen years later, as the first edict dictated that they should. Instead of just fining finery and asking husbands to be responsible for wives' consumption, they attempted to assert a new level of social pressure through shaming ostentatious consumers.

JOTGLARESSAS AND *PUTAS*: CONSIGNING OSTENTATIOUS APPAREL TO FEMALE ENTERTAINERS

In 1291, the "honesty" presented as the ideal for "ladies and other women" was placed on a moral axis whose opposite pole was *jotglaressas* and *putas*, performers and prostitutes. One of the most striking differences in the two laws is the repeated provision in 1291 that ostentatious apparel would continue to be permitted to these categories of women. The formulaic wording indicates that these women of implicitly "dis-honest" professions already possessed such apparel and that it would not be regulated for them, as an exception to regulations imposed on other women.[20] The edicts may have been as much a rhetorical gesture as any kind of active civic management of entertainment and sex workers, asserting that well-dressed women should curb their spending to avoid being confused with those who made their money through singing or sex work. In other words, ill fame would come from being mistaken for a prostitute or a singer, not necessarily from being one. The sartorial permission granted to prostitutes here

---

18 Heller, "Anxiety, Hierarchy, and Appearance," 318–20.

19 Heller, "The 1275 Sumptuary Law."

20 The grammar of these clauses, repeated in items 1–6 and 8, presents ambiguities. For example, item 1, "E que la rauba sia tota redonda, so es assaber que sia tant longua devan coma derriere, a bona fe, exceptadas jotglaressas e putas, *o non / era estada*" (my emphasis), which I translate as "The garment must be round all around, which is to say it must be as long in the front as in the back, in good faith—except for those of performers and prostitutes, *on whom it (the garment) was not (round)*" (see Appendix 4.1). The referents in the phrase *o non ero estada*[-s, it is plural in some items] would be rendered literally as "where (they) were not"; the subject of the plural imperfect verb *eron* must be supplied, and the referent of the past participle of *estar* (meaning to be, to be found, or to be appropriate) must also be supplied. The statutes indicate that entertainers and courtesans could keep apparel they already possessed, and that the styles were appropriate for them but not for "honest women." I am grateful to William D. Paden for his assistance with these clauses.

contrasts with fourteenth- and fifteenth-century regulations of many cities in Mediterranean Europe which forbade them rich attire.[21]

To what extent there was historically a population of professional female entertainers in the region of Montauban is not documented. Efforts to manage prostitution were beginning to occur in the Toulouse region in the thirteenth century, as Agathe Roby has shown. Records have survived of the establishment and management of bordellos within or outside the walls of nearby cities such as Toulouse, Albi, and Foix, as well as Italian towns.[22] Evidence from the port town of Montpellier shows a complex system was in place.[23] Not much has come to light in Montauban's case aside from these edicts. The edicts imply that both *putas* and *jotglaressas* could afford to wear luxury apparel and entertain on a grand scale. There may have been an effort to indirectly regulate men's "honesty" as well, by labeling the dress and consumption of the women with whom they associated as either acceptable or promiscuous. Figure 4.1 contrasts Chasteté (Chastity or Innocence) and Luxure (Lust, cf. Latin *Luxuria*) in the popular moralizing French work known as *La Somme le roi* or *Vices and Virtues*. Finished around 1280 by French king Philip III's Dominican confessor and extant in over 80 copies, this popular allegorical treatise similarly cast women into two moral categories via these figures. This beautiful illumination from a copy made ca. 1294 vividly distinguishes the two groups by dress as well as the flames of perdition extending from Lust's mouth.

The edict is interesting because entertainers had not always been consigned to the same immoral status as prostitutes. The edict shows an intermediate stage in the defamation of performers. It used and repeated the separate terms for the two professions, calling attention to the fact that *putas* and *jotglaressas* were recognized as distinct from one another. At the same time, the effect of the eight provisions explicitly permitting to both types of women the ostentatious apparel which it prohibited to honest ones was to declare they should be treated as morally alike. A *jotglar* or *joglar* (cf. *jongleur* in French) was a performer of the songs of the troubadours. It was not an inherently pejorative term. Some scholars have observed that through the thirteenth century there was growing concern on the part of poets to distinguish between *troubadors* as composers and *joglars* as mere performers. The period from 1245 to 1285 saw a professionalization of poetic activity, which had earlier been practiced primarily by

21 James Brundage, "Sumptuary Laws and Prostitution in Late Medieval Italy," *Journal of Medieval History* 13 (1987): 343–55, at 346.
22 Agathe Roby, *La Prostitution au Moyen Âge: Le commerce charnel en Midi toulousain du xiiie au xvie siècles* (Villemur-sur-Tarn, France: Éditions Loubatières, 2021). There was significant prostitution in Orvieto in Italy; see Carol Lansing, *Passion and Order: Restraint of Grief in the Medieval Italian Communes* (Ithaca, NY: Cornell University Press, 2018), 41–42. See also Leah Lydia Otis-Cour, *Prostitution in Medieval Society: The History of an Urban Institution in Languedoc* (Chicago: University of Chicago Press, 1985), Appendix B, 133. Her corpus of records includes only one sex worker from Montauban, but that example was from the year 1528.
23 Kathryn L. Reyerson, "Prostitution in Medieval Montpellier: The Ladies of Campus Polverel," *Medieval Prosopography* 18 (1997): 209–28.

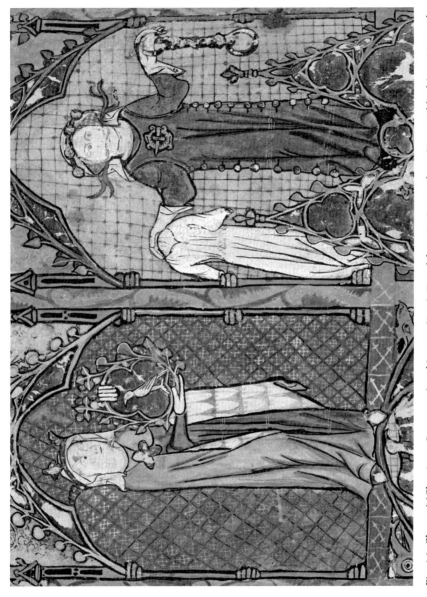

Fig. 4.1: Chasteté (Chastity or Innocence) and Luxure (Lust). Detail from *La Somme le roi* (Paris, Bibliothèque Nationale de France, MS Fr. 938), fol. 120v, 1294. Photo: Courtesy of Bibliothèque Nationale de France.

minor nobles. Some of those new, professional *joglars* were errant performers who sang wherever they could find an audience, in urban streets and taverns as well as courts. However, some professional poets such as Boniface de Castellane and Peire Cardenal were authors of scathing political satires (*sirventes*) whose critiques aroused both supporters and opponents.[24] Either type might have upset the *capitols* of Montauban.

In this period, around 1288–92, Matfre Ermengaud of Béziers (d. 1322) was composing a vast vernacular encyclopedia called the *Breviari d'amor*. Matfre was a lawyer, trained in the two branches of the law, secular (Roman) and ecclesiastical (canon).[25] According to some sources, he may have become a friar late in his life. The prologue sets out his project as an explanation of *fin'amors*, the troubadour love themes of former times (lines 48–78).[26] These often involved free expression of erotic and also adulterous desires. In this later era when the preaching of Inquisitorial and penitential friars held much popular sway, Matfre's apologies for troubadour ethics set their notions of love within the broader context of natural love, protecting them from accusations of frivolity and preserving the dignity of the culture that engendered them.[27] Matfre also worked within the theological tradition. Some sections of the work are social satire, mocking the proclivities of different status groups. A descriptive catalogue of the deadly sins segues into the sins typical of different estates, including kings, simple knights, lawyers and physicians, merchants, shopkeepers, and laborers. At the end, the sins of *joglars* immediately precede those of women, linked at the end of this schematically hierarchical social chain. Comparison of this section with the 1291 sumptuary law can shed light on some of the mentalities surrounding the regulations. Both texts also contain related apparel terms, placing those listed in the edicts in a satirical context.

Whereas Matfre venerated the troubadours of old, when it came to *joglars* he criticized their "lag parlan e putanier" ("ugly, whoring talk," line 18483). Their songs were "the art of the Devil," arousing men to follow their carnal desires (lines 18488–94). Beyond the statutes permitting certain finery only to *jotglaressas* and *putas*, Montauban's consuls sought to vigorously repress performers of both genders in 1291. Item 14 prohibits giving either *jotglars* or *jotglaressas* robes at a wedding feast. Concordantly, the *Breviari* suggests *joglars* were still using satire and mockery in the *sirventes* genre to provoke hosts to be generous, spend lavishly, and indeed to pay them in robes (lines 18464–71, 18459). Item 15 of the 1291 law prohibits *jotglars* or *jotglaressas* from "entering" a home for a wedding, a banquet for a new mother, Christmas, or a Christmas feast. This implies that they were employed to entertain on these

24 Martin Aurell, *La Vielle et l'épée: Troubadours et politique en Provence au XIIIe siècle* (Paris: Aubier, 1989), 119–29, 238–39; Ramón Menéndez Pidal, *Poesia juglaresca y juglares: Aspectos de la historia literaria y cultural de España* (Madrid: Espasa-Calpe, 1962), 81–101.

25 Cyril P. Hershon and Dominique Billy, *Le Breviari d'amor de Matfre Ermenhaud*, vol. 1, *Introduction* (Turnhout, Belgium: Brepols, 2023), 91–101.

26 All references to the text of *Le Breviari* in this article are to the following edition: Peter T. Ricketts, ed., *Le Breviari d'amor de Matfre Ermengaud*, vols. 2–5 (Turnhout, Belgium: Brepols, 1976–2023). Parenthetical citations indicate line numbers.

27 Hershon and Billy, *Le Breviari d'amor*, 145.

occasions. As leverage, the consuls threatened that any who invited them in would be "thrown out of this town and territory for all time." Punishment by permanent exile for welcoming singers seems harsh indeed. It begs the question of what happened to put these performers in such ill repute. Something had caused them to be ardently despised. Montauban's prohibitions do align with a later-thirteenth-century trend towards anti-troubadour sentiment.[28]

The mendicant orders had begun to denounce both feminine excess and jongleurs in the mid-thirteenth century. Diane Owen Hughes has argued that Italian sumptuary laws of the fourteenth and fifteenth centuries encoded messages from their charismatic sermons.[29] Comparison of Montauban's thirteenth-century laws and the *Breviari d'amor* demonstrates the synergy that was already building under the friars' influence a century earlier. Matfre hailed from Béziers, on the Mediterranean side of Languedoc. Béziers was the first town brutally repressed in the Albigensian crusade in a wholesale massacre in 1209. The crusaders later besieged Montauban, another bastion of these so-called heretics ("Cathars") who resisted papal efforts to unify Christendom.[30] Although Montauban finally fell to Simon of Montfort in 1217, there remained a certain number of citizens inclined towards simpler and humbler forms of spirituality that permitted lay interaction. Inquisition records from 1241 contain sentences handed to 99 Cathars and 157 Waldensian "heretics." Emmanuel Moureau proposed that the rapid establishment of the Franciscan order in Montauban may be explained by the strength of these sentiments in the community.[31]

Jotglaressa is not a common term, in contrast with *joglar*. That there were women who composed songs and poetry in Occitan has been much celebrated since the mid-1970s. These women have been termed *trobairitz*, based on the use of the term once in the thirteenth-century romance *Flamenca*. Most works attributed to *trobairitz* are love songs (*cansos*), some of whose erotic sentiments might have seemed steamy to

---

28 Montpellier had passed a similar edict against employing jongleurs for wooing or weddings in 1273; Jeffrey S. Widmeyer, "The Sumptuary Laws of Manuscript Montpellier H119," *Romance Notes* 46, no. 2 (2006), 131–41, at 135.

29 Diane Owen Hughes, "Regulating Women's Fashion," in *A History of Women in the West: Silences of the Middle Ages*, ed. Christiane Klapisch-Zuber (Cambridge, MA: Harvard University Press, 1992), 136–58, at 147.

30 The term "Cathar" is anachronistic in many ways, championed by regionalist historians of the nineteenth century but questioned by many in the twentieth and twenty-first centuries. Institut National de Recherches Archéologiques Préventives (INRAP), "Les Cathares, archéologie d'une hérésie" [audio broadcast with summary], June 18, 2024, https://www.inrap.fr/les-cathares-archeologie-d-une-heresie-18094 (accessed Sept. 11, 2024); Laure Berthet and Laurent Macé, *"Cathares": Toulouse dans la croisade*, exhibition catalogue, Toulouse, Musée Saint-Raymond and Couvent des Jacobins (Toulouse: In Fine, 2024).

31 Emmanuel Moureau, *Vivre en ville au temps des papes d'Avignon: Montauban (1317–1378)* (Cahors, France: La Louve, 2009), 122. Montauban was also a major battleground during the later Wars of Religion. Richelieu made it a target due to its recalcitrant population of Protestants, whose leanings some historians of the city trace back centuries to these earlier movements.

pious ears. Angelica Rieger identified three political satire poems (*sirventes*) as well. That women troubadours could employ this genre might have made them feared as a political threat.[32] But as noted above for their male counterparts, *trobairitz* and *jotglaressas* were different. In Iberia, at least in Castile, Léon, and Galicia, there were women singer-dancers called *soldade(i)ras*,[33] a term that connotes being paid, just as *soldadier* signified a paid soldier. Illustrations of a thirteenth-century collection of Galician-Portuguese *cantigas* influenced by the Occitan tradition, the *Cancioneiro da Ajuda*, depict twelve out of sixteen musical performers as women, as Ana Paula Ferreira observed.[34] *Soldade(i)ras* elicited a variety of reactions in the *cantigas*: they were commonly addressed in the second person in tones varying from admiration to irony to aggression. It is not clear whether *soldadera* was synonymous with *jotglaressa*. However, it is worth noting that at times the vocabulary of this edict of Montauban has more in common with Iberian sources than French, as will be seen below.

The business of gender in sumptuary laws may appear straightforwardly misogynist to modern readers, but it is worth probing. In the *Livre des Sermens* copy, a rubric added centuries later labels the edict *De las donas*. The most obvious translation would be "Concerning women," expressing that archivist's assumption that women were objects of the law rather than an issuing voice. Similar annotations appear in the 1291 copy in the *Livre Rouge*, specifying further that the decrees concerned "what women should wear" (see Appendix 4.1). Although those later rubrics label the edicts' focus as women's clothing, the majority of the regulations of 1291 (items 5 and 7–15, on hosting and special occasions) were addressed to both men and women. Interestingly, in the margin of *Livre des Sermens* a different later hand summarized the 1275 regulations as "that no man or woman shall wear any gold or silver in any style whatsoever on their clothing" ("que home ny femme ne portara sur ses habitz or ny argent de quelle facon que ce soit"), despite the absence of any items directly concerning men's dress. Carol Lansing argues that when male regulators in Italian towns such as Orvieto and Perugia focused on women, it was really an attempt to regulate their own excessive passions.[35] Matfre devoted over 1,200 lines to the sins of men before devoting only around 370 to women. Like many Italian friars as well as Gratian and legal commentators in fourteenth-century Italy, Matfre framed women's sin through the lens of their conspicuous apparel. They condemned women's arrogant belief that they had more intelligence than they did. Perversely, women used what weak judgment they possessed to refuse to

---

32 Angelica Rieger, *Trobairitz: Der Beitrag der Frau in der altokzitanischen höfischen Lyrik: Edition des Gesamtkorpus* (Tübingen, Germany: M. Niemeyer, 1991), poems 44–46; Catherine Léglu, "Did Women Perform Satirical Poetry? *Trobairitz* and *Soldadeiras* in Medieval Occitan Poetry," *Forum for Modern Language Studies* 37, no. 1 (2001): 15–25; Katharina Städtler, "The Sirventes by Gormonda de Monpeslier," in *The Voice of the Trobairitz: Perspectives on the Women Troubadours*, ed. William D. Paden (Philadelphia: University of Pennsylvania Press, 1989), 131–55.

33 Pidal, *Poesia juglaresca y juglares*, 32–35.

34 Ana Paula Ferreira, "Telling Woman What She Wants: The *Cantigas d'Amigo* as Strategies of Containment," *Portuguese Studies* 9 (1993): 23–38.

35 Lansing, *Passion and Order*, 14–15, 47.

follow men's good counsel.[36] Susan Mosher Stuard has remarked that sumptuary laws served as a highly effective tool for perpetuating negative assumptions about woman's nature.[37] A group of male *capitols* framed the two laws. The statements reflect their vision of the appearance the city ought to present. In their view, what women wore impacted men financially, morally, and politically as individuals but perhaps more importantly as a collectivity.

APPAREL REGULATED

The list of items to be fined in 1275 begins:

> Que deguna dona de Montalba en sas raubas ni en sis vestimentas de lana ni en capairo no porto aur fres ni argent fres, ni nulha paradura d'aor ni d'argent, ni de ceda ni d'ermina ni de loira ni de gris ni de perlas ni d'autras peiras, ni nulha *autra* paradura cozuda ni pauzada sobre lo drap.

> [No woman of Montauban shall wear gold or silver orphrey or any gold or silver decoration on her gowns, her woolen garments, or hood; nor any decoration of silk, or ermine or otter or squirrel fur, nor pearls or other gemstones, nor any other ornamentation sewn or attached to the cloth.] (items 4–5)

The guiding principle for all the 1275 proscriptions is in the final clause: ornaments sewn on to clothing. This reveals that a system of fashion was in operation: Montauban's women could change styles regularly by attaching and removing different details.[38]

Multiple forms of gold and silver ornamentation were enumerated. Non-monetary uses of precious metals stand out as the area of greatest concern. The phrase *aur fres ni argent fres* puzzled some of Montauban's archivists, who translated it too literally as "cold silver" (*argent froid*).[39] *Aur fres* signified orphrey, the rich woven or embroidered trim patterned in gold and silver threads mixed with colored silk and even pearls and precious stones, whose use has survived in ecclesiastical vestments and hangings. The umbrella term *paradura* (cf. French *parure*) was used to denote any other type of ornament.

Pearls and precious stones figure in item 5 as embellishments that might be sewn on exterior clothing. Item 9 demonstrates that they might be used for undergarments as well: "on their chemises they shall not wear any ornament of gold or pearls or anything other than linen or silk" ("Item que en camisas no porto aur ni perlas ni re

---

36 "Per ergureilh pecco malamen / quar pesson haver trop de sen, / e, de lur pauper sen uzan, / re qu'om lur cosselhe no fan." ("Through arrogant pride they sin badly because they think they have much intelligence and, using their poor intelligence, they do not do what one [lit. a man] advises them to do.") *Le Breviari*, lines 18507–11.

37 Susan Mosher Stuard, *Gilding the Market: Luxury and Fashion in Fourteenth-Century Italy* (Philadelphia: University of Pennsylvania Press, 2006), 91.

38 Sarah-Grace Heller, *Fashion in Medieval France* (Cambridge: D. S. Brewer, 2007), 30–32, 61–94; Jean Baudrillard, *La Société de la consommation* (Paris: Denoël, 1970), 128, 181.

39 Méras, "Les Lois somptuaires," 518 n. 2; Forestié, "Le vêtement civil," 169 n. 4.

si drap e seda no"). Additionally, they were prohibited on silk cords for mantles and outer garments (item 13). Freshwater seed pearls and small gemstones drilled for use as beads were applied in embroidery techniques in traditions across Europe, from *opus anglicanum* to Russian work. Ceremonial examples have been preserved, notably ecclesiastical garments, altar hangings, and reliquary bags.[40] They are mentioned in a large number of municipal sumptuary laws. Across Italy, edicts of the fourteenth and fifteenth centuries restricted decorative pearls and precious stones on clothing year after year. As Ettore Verga put it, "all the sumptuary laws in Italy declared war on pearls."[41] Prohibitions were not always just for women. For instance, a Venetian ordinance from 1299 forbade borders of pearls for both men and women, except for brides on their wedding dresses.[42] In Barcelona in 1313, both men and women were prohibited from making or commissioning decoration in pearls, precious stones, and gold or silver foil or thread on their clothing, as well as on saddles, harnesses, and other equestrian equipment.[43] Montauban's law additionally forbade that goldsmiths put pearls or gemstones on women's clothing, offering insight into the merchants who sourced these materials. It also shows that some goldsmiths engaged in decorative work on textiles. The link between pearls and goldsmiths suggests the degree of proximity pearls had to the precious metals of coinage. Pearls were associated with the materials of currency and had important exchange value. If gold and silver ornaments were not permissible on public-facing clothing in Montauban because they were akin to wearing money, use of pearls also followed that logic. Diane Owen Hughes observed a mentality of economic protectionism in some later Italian laws in Genoa and Venice, which expressed explicitly how the state was weakened when money that should be

---

40 Maria Giuseppina Muzzarelli, Luca Molà, and Giorgio Riello, *Tutte le perle del mondo: Storie di viaggi, scambi e magnifici ornamenti* (Bologna: Il Mulino, 2023).

41 Ettore Verga, "Le leggi suntuarie milanesi: Gli statuti del 1396 e del 1498," *Archivio storico lombardo* 25 (1898): 5–79, at 9. See also Muzzarelli, Molà, and Riello, *Tutte le perle del mondo*, 52–70; Ronald Rainey, "Dressing Down the Dressed-Up: Reproving Feminine Attire in Renaissance Florence," in *Renaissance Society and Culture: Essays in Honor of Eugene F. Rice, Jr.*, ed. John Monfasini and Ronald G. Musto (New York: Italica Press, 1991), 217–37, at 222.

42 "Item quod aliquis homo, nec mulier aliqua, nec domina, possit de cetero uti frixaturis perlarum, salvo quod sponse possint habere si volunt frixaturas de perlis ad robam sponsalem solummodo, el zoiam unam de perlis tantum, sub pena soldorum XX grossorum." ("Item, that henceforth no man or woman or lady may wear borders of pearls, under penalty of 20 *solidi di grossi*, except that brides, if they wish, may have borders of pearls on their wedding dress a single time.") Cesare Foucard, ed., *Lo Statuto inedito delle nozze veneziane emanato nell'anno 1299* (Venice: Tipografia del Commercio, 1858), 10; translation by Emilie Amt in her *Women's Lives in Medieval Europe: A Sourcebook* (New York: Routledge, 1993), 74–75.

43 Joseph M. Roca, "Lley sumtuaria que aprobada y confirmada per lo princep Anfòs en 10 de febrer del any 1313, publicaren los consellers y prohoms de Barcelona," *Catalana, Revista setmanal* 9.218 (1926): 196–99, at 196. Other Catalan laws followed suit; for instance, see Rafael Conde y Delgado de Molina, "Vestit i societat: Les ordinacions sumptuàries de Cervera (1344)," *Miscel·lània Cerverina* 2 (1984): 25–42, at 37–38, items 1, 2, 4, 5, 11.

in circulation was tied up in clothing. That logic may have existed in Montauban, in the mix with spiritual ideals of austerity and political desires to avoid appearing too wealthy to the French king amid his financial crisis. As Hughes also observed, economic motives can be hard to discern. Although there was a bullion crisis in Europe in these centuries and pearls had exchange value comparable to gold and silver, the laws generally did not address that crisis directly.[44] The "communal profit" cited as a motive in the preambles to Montauban's laws may have been doubly moral and financial.

PEARLS ON CHEMISES AND THE QUESTION OF DÉCOLLETÉ

Prohibiting pearls on undergarments begs questions about how much chemises showed under and around superimposed layers. If illustration practices are to be believed, chemises were minimally visible, if at all, in public in the thirteenth century in France. Chasteté in figure 4.1 may serve as an example. Sleeves on the *cotte* were long. If stylish and tailored to the wearer, a close fit through the arms was achieved by stitching sleeves tight down the arms in the earlier part of the century, or by buttons in later decades.[45] Necklines sat above the clavicle. Gowns passed over the head. The slit permitting this was closed at the neckline with a brooch at the center, or in some cases tied on the side with laces.[46] Under such styles, a chemise embroidered with pearls would have been an invisible luxury, not to mention not terribly practical. The fabric of the gown covering it would rub against the embroidery. The raised texture of the pearls might make awkward indentations. Another possibility is that visual representations do not tell us everything about neckline styles and that embroidered chemises might have been visible to some degree.[47] Or embroidered *camisas* in Montauban may have been influenced by Iberian fashion, not French. In Iberia there emerged a trend around the 1280s of sleeveless overdresses called *brials*, under which women were wearing visible *camisas margomadas* embroidered with colored silk.[48] In what sounds like a similar style, in *Ab greu cossire* the narrator laments not daring to wear her white chemise richly embroidered in yellow, vermillion, black, white, and blue silk with gold and silver thread (lines 76–84).[49] This political satire poem (*sirventes*) has been considered

44 Diane Owen Hughes, "Sumptuary Law and Social Relations in Renaissance Italy," in *Disputes and Settlements: Law and Human Relations in the West*, ed. John Bossy (Cambridge: Cambridge University Press, 1983), 69–99, at 76–79.

45 Camille Enlart, *Manuel d'archéologie française depuis les temps mérovingiens jusqu'à la Renaissance*, vol. 3, *Le costume* (Paris: Picard, 1916), 62.

46 Tina Anderlini, *Le costume médiéval au XIIIe siècle (1180–1320)* (Bayeux, France: Heimdal, 2014), 142.

47 Anderlini (*Le costume médiéval*, 106) has argued that relying too heavily on visual or textual sources to generalize about fashions such as décolleté is problematic.

48 Carmen Bernis Madrazo, *Indumentaria medieval Española* (Madrid: Instituto Diego Velasquez, 1956), 29, plates 59 and 65.

49 All references to the text of *Ab greu cossire* in this article are to the following edition: Carl Appel, *Provenzalische Inedita aus pariser Handschriften* (Leipzig: Fues's Verlag, 1890), online at Corpus des Troubadours, https://trobadors.iec.cat/veure_d.asp?id_obra=515

an invective against the humiliations imposed by the French crusaders during the Albigensian crusade, suggesting a date of 1229–30. However, it only survives in a manuscript transcribed ca. 1300, so the fashion it describes may not necessarily date to the first quarter of the thirteenth century.

Two outer gown styles are mentioned in the law, *gannachas* and *corsetz* (1275, item 12), the cords of which could be of silk but not silver or gold. These styles might have been cut away enough to reveal underlayers. Lighter layers might have been more wearable in Montauban's climate, which was, as in Iberia, warmer than that of northern France.

It is possible that the target was chemises intended only for bed. In literature, wearing only a chemise was synonymous with amorous nudity. In the Occitan romance *Flamenca*, for instance, when the heroine and her lover Guillem succeed in meeting at the baths to make love she declares, "Here I am, just as you would have me, all naked, in my chemise" ("[…] ve·us m'aici bena vostra guisa / tota nudeta en camisa," lines 6130–31).[50] The white chemise Luxure ostentatiously waves in figure 4.1 supports this. The image shows some decoration around the neckline as well as gathering at the waist. In Narbonne, a sumptuary edict of 1297 prohibited any woman from wearing a *camisa* embroidered with silver, gold, pearls, or precious stones except for brides, who were only allowed to wear them in their first year of marriage.[51] A 1350 edict of Montpellier forbade bridegrooms from giving their brides a chemise stitched with gold, silver, or pearls.[52] These suggest that there might have been an established tradition of giving pearl-embroidered chemises as bridal lingerie in the Midi.

In the 1291 revision, prohibitions on pearls disappeared, in an interesting contrast with the obsession for regulating pearls that continued elsewhere for centuries. This

---

(accessed Sept. 11, 2024). Parenthetical citations indicate line numbers. For the translation I draw on Matilda Tomaryn Bruckner, Laurie Shepard, and Sarah Melhado White, *Songs of the Women Troubadours* (New York: Garland, 1995), poem 29. The poem has been dated to 1229–30, when the treaty of Paris ended the crusade and demanded harsh penitence from the towns held to have harbored Cathars. Commentators generally link it with sumptuary laws. However, no extant sumptuary laws date to that early in the thirteenth century except that of James I of Aragon in 1234, which prohibited both men and women from wearing gilt fabrics and jewelry, which some have inferred to be luxury items of Arab origin.

50 François Zufferey and Valérie Fasseur, eds., *Flamenca, édité d'après le manuscrit unique de Carcassonne* (Paris: Librairie Générale française, 2014). The dating of *Flamenca* has been debated. Jean-Pierre Chambon proposed ca. 1208–43, revising earlier hypotheses of 1272–1300 or after 1287; Chambon, "Sur la date de composition du roman de *Flamenca*," *Estudis Romànics* 40 (2018): 349–55, at 350–51.

51 "[…] item que neguna no ause portar camisa en que aia aur ni argent ni perlas ni peiras preciosas, sol novia, quen puesca aver una nuptial tan solament e a quela no ause portar la davant dicha novia mais lo primier an que aura pres marit; estiers, non." Célestin Port, *Essai sur l'histoire du commerce de Narbonne* (Paris: Durand, 1855), 51–52.

52 "[…] camisa cosida ab aur ni ab argen ni ab perlas." Jeffrey S. Widmayer, "Coutumes anciennes de Montpellier (MS. Montpellier, Bibliothèque de Médecine del Univ. de Montpellier, H119)" [critical edition] (Ph.D. diss., University of North Carolina–Chapel Hill,

new clause was introduced, however: no lady or woman "shall dare to wear on any of her garments a neckline that is cut too low" (*cabessalha trop escolatada*, item 6). The consuls specified—ambiguously, for our purposes—that it must be only in the "good manner" (*en bona maniera*). This supports a call for reconsideration of the history of medieval décolleté, commonly thought to appear around the 1320s–30s. Textual sources attest lower necklines in the 1270s, albeit hyperbolically so it is difficult to ascertain the actual style. Around 1270, Jean de Meun's meretricious Old Woman in the *Roman de la Rose* advised women hoping to be seductive to have their gowns cut "open a half foot in the front and back" to show off their pretty necks and white bosoms, if these were some of their best features.[53] The verb is the same as in the 1291 law: *escolete* in French, literally "to separate from the neck." Contemporary with the Montauban edict in the early 1290s, Matfre Ermengaud preached against women wearing their clothing too *escolat*, a behavior contributing to the sin of *luxuria*:

> E porton, per gran malvestat,
> lur vestimen fort escolat,
> e van fort espeitrinadas,
> e mostro lurs caraunhadas
> per los peccadors aloirar
> e decebre e far peccar.

> [And out of great wickedness they wear their clothing so low-cut, and they go around so bare-breasted, and they show their flesh to allure sinners and deceive them and make them sin.] (lines 18742–47)

Matfre's enumerative text brings to life the profusion of ways women could have designed outfits for high visual impact. This passage dramatizes women "parading" themselves to one another as well as leading men towards a path of financial and sexual wrongdoing. The parallels between this encyclopedia and the consuls' declarations are striking, for all that the *Breviari* is far more morally ambiguous. In their shaming and misogynist stances, both texts demonstrate that necklines were a reality that was both fascinating and troubling their audiences. However, note that figure 4.1 does not show any marked difference in neckline style between virtuous Chasteté and lascivious Luxure.

2004), fol. 113, line 5; also fol. 116, line 16, online at Trésor Manuscrit de l'Ancien Occitan (TMAO), http://tmao.aieo.org/CoutMontpW_show2 (accessed Sept. 23, 2024).

53 "S'ele a biau col et gorge blanche, / Gart cil qui sa robe trenche / Si tres bien la li escolete / que sa char paire blanche et nete / Demi pié darriere et devant: / S'en iert assez plus decevant." Armand Strubel, ed., *Le Roman de la rose* (Paris: Librairie Générale française, 1992), lines 13318–22.

FURS AND SILKS

Furs interrupted the initial section on gold and silver *paraduras* on wool garments and hoods in the 1275 law (item 5, see above) and figured similarly in 1291 with one significant change (item 2). As furs are positioned in the same phrase as silk (*ceda*), it makes sense that what the consuls had in mind was linings, although that specific word (*folradura*) is absent. Pre-assembled fur linings (*penas*) would have been sewn in or pulled out according to the seasons. They could be removed for repair or replacement. Like ribbons and fasteners, they were not permanent parts of garments. A *pena* could easily be worth more than the outer cloth it lined.[54]

The fur linings prohibited in 1275 were ermine (*ermina*), otter (*loira*), and grey squirrel backs (*gris*). Regulation of imported ermine and *gris* is not surprising. Valued for their lightweight luxuriance and luminescence, and expensive due to the distances they traveled as well as the high number of the diminutive pelts needed to line a garment, these furs were ubiquitously synonymous with prestige. They are visible in many illuminations lining or edging mantles, for instance the vair *pena* inside Chasteté's in figure 4.1. Note that depicting this fur on the figure was intended to mark her allegorical nobility.

The 1275 mention of otter (*loira*) is less common. It is not a fur that appears often in thirteenth-century prohibitions or literature. While certainly warm and luxurious to the touch, its brown tones were less prized than the luminous white or silvery-variegated ones in this period. Note, however, that it was signaled in the sumptuary declaration of King James I of Aragon in 1234 as a fur that was acceptable for his courtiers only if used as a whole, single pelt along the long edges of capes and sleeve openings.[55]

The section regulating fur was expanded in 1291. No lady or other woman was to be permitted any fur linings of vair, *popra*, or *gris* (item 2). Otter disappeared and was replaced by the enigmatic term *popra*, which does not appear in the principal Occitan or Catalan dictionaries. Forestié translated it as "pourpre," purple cloth, following Marcellin and Ruck's misreading of *porpra* in their edition.[56] While *popra* could be a variant spelling of the close terms *polpra* or *porpra*, connoting rich fabric or garments,[57] *polpra* appears in a later section on rich cloth (item 8). These terms may

54 Robert Delort, *Le commerce des fourrures en Occident à la fin du Moyen Age (vers 1300-vers 1450)*, 2 vols. (Rome: Ecole française de Rome, 1978), 2:299, 465.
55 "Item statuimus quod nos nec aliquis subditus noster non portet vestes [...] nec sedam sudam, nec sembellinum, nec erminium, nec lutriam, nec aliam pellem fractam, vel recoctam [...] vel lutriam integram simplicem, solummodo in longitudine incisam circa capuciaum capae et operaturas manicarum [...]." Juan Sempere y Gauriños, *Historia del Luxo, y de las leyes suntuarias de España*, vol. 1 (Madrid, 1788), 73 n. 1.
56 Forestié, "Le vêtement civil," 170; after Marcellin and Ruck, *Histoire de Montauban*, 1:413.
57 *Dictionnaire de l'Occitan Médiévale*, online ed. (Munich: Bayerische Akademie der Wissenschaften, 2017–; henceforth abbreviated as *DOM*), https://dom-en-ligne.de, s.v. *polpra, porpra*; François Raynouard, *Lexique roman ou Dictionnaire de la langue des troubadours, comparée avec les autres langues de l'Europe latine* (Paris: Silvestre, 1844), s.v. *porpra, polpra*. R. Anthony Lodge glosses *polpra* uncertainly as a "vêtemement d'apparat

have been distinct in the Occitan of Montauban. While it is possible that *popra* was inserted between the two types of squirrel fur to denote a rich type of fabric lining that was equal in monetary value and prestige to vair and *gris*, it is more logical that it would denote a type of fur. Méras hazarded the guess that this was a vermillion fur, probably following Camille Enlart's questionable proposition that there was a four-teenth-century fashion for vermillion-dyed fur.[58] A more plausible explanation is what the fur historian Robert Delort catalogued as *poppe* (also spelled *poples, popel, porpres, pouppes*, among other variants; Lat. *poppii*), lower-value grey squirrels hunted in European forests in spring or early summer when their pelts were turning red-brown.[59] This makes sense as a mid-value fur for Montauban's mixed clientele of bourgeois and local minor nobility who mingled together with far less social stratification than those at the courts of great barons or kings.

In 1275, the *capitols* wanted to confine women's apparel ornamentation to simple linings ("[...] mas tant solament drap e folradura[60] de pels e de sendat," that is "[...] only wear wool garments lined with furs or sendal silk"). They proposed sendal, the least expensive type of silk.[61] A more discreet type of luxury, partially visible at times but not a blatant announcement of wealth, linings did increase a garment's comfort as well as its value. Linings of *pels* (pelts) were also permitted, distinguished from the *penas* discussed above. As opposed to a pre-sewn lining patterned by the piecing of many small pelts, more luxurious partly due to the larger number of animals required, a more modest *pel* might signify a single pelt from a local mammal larger than weasel or squirrel species (e.g. wolves, lambs, rabbits, or cats).

Silks were implicitly prohibited for the construction of outer garments in 1275:

[...] ni fasso deguna rauba ni porto de sendat ni de polpra ni de samit ni de lunh drap d'aor ni de seda, sino era sendat en folradura.

[They may not have made or wear any kind of clothing of sendal, purple, samite, any gold cloth, or silk, unless it is sendal as a lining.] (item 8)

In contrast, there was no listing of these silk types in 1291. This suggests a shift over fifteen years. In 1275, the *capitols* did not want the women of the town to wear

---

[?]" (ceremonial garment); Lodge, *Les comptes des consuls de Montferrand 1273–1319*, online ed. (Paris: Éditions en ligne de l'École des chartes [ELEC], 2006), http://elec.enc. sorbonne.fr/montferrand (accessed Sept. 11, 2024). The Catalan dictionary by Antoni Maria Alcover and Francesc de Borja Moll, *Diccionari català-valencià-balear*, online ed. (Barcelona: Institut d'Estudis Catalans), https://dcvb.iec.cat (accessed Sept. 11, 2024), similarly defines *porpra* as a colorant, the mollusks from which it was derived, a fabric dyed in such a color; but also some kind of tunic or chasuble, i.e. it gives some examples of "blanca porpra" (white purple).

58 Méras, "Les lois somptuaires," 518; Enlart, *Manuel d'archéologie française*, 231.

59 Delort, *Le commerce des fourrures*, 1:45–47.

60 Marcellin and Ruck (*Histoire de Montauban*, 1:411) erroneously interpreted *folradura* as a hem or edging.

61 The Lexis of Cloth and Clothing Project database, http://lexissearch.arts.manchester. ac.uk (accessed May 15, 2024), s.v. *sendal*.

anything that looked rich on their outer layers. Arguably, this was motivated by a desire to prevent any impression that there were precious metals available for coinage that were being kept out of circulation.[62] The law was a fundraiser for church and bridge construction, as noted above, calling for fines paid in building materials (*teules*, tiles or bricks). It was also a public performance of the town's dedication to finishing those projects, whose construction schedules were stretching into multiple decades.[63] There was a significant change by 1291, where only one fine was set in *teules* (item 3, for hair garlands). The other fines are monetary. In addition, each item bore a clause saying that the garments in violation should be "given" (*seria/-o donat/-ada/-adas*) to whomever (*a qui*) the consuls decided, when (*o/on*) they knew about it or according to their judgment (*a lor conoguda*). Specific intents and procedures are not explained. Surrendering garments implicitly constituted a fine since they had substantial resale value. Demanding relinquishment of the apparel would serve the moral purpose of demonstrating upright behavior, the political purpose of repressing the image that the town had extra funds to waste, and the fiscal purpose of raising funds. However, the indication that items would be sold or donated suggests that the garments would have remained in circulation in the area, ineffective for cleansing the town of feminine sartorial excess, unless they were reused for other purposes such as church vestments or burials.[64] That is possible. In any case, the Montauban edicts do not call for "bonfires of the vanities" in the manner Bernardino of Siena, as were enacted in multiple Italian cities in the 1400s.[65]

BROOCHES AND FASTENERS

The impulse to enumerate speaks to the presence of fashion in Montauban's culture in the later thirteenth century. A reader perceiving the efforts to cover every possible variation of a garment or accessory might get the impression that the *capitols* were struggling to keep up with the vocabulary and different styles. This vocabulary makes this law stand out. The 1275 edict lists four different kinds of prohibited garment fasteners and prohibits two materials, gold and silver.

---

62 The availability of gold and silver fluctuated over the medieval period, and they were often in short supply relative to demand. Several Italian laws discuss this explicitly. Kovesi Killerby, *Sumptuary Law in Italy*, 45–46; Hughes, "Sumptuary Law and Social Relations," 76–78.

63 Heller, "The 1275 Sumptuary Law," 31–34; Méras, "Les Lois somptuaires," 522–23.

64 For instance, Julie Glodt, "Fripes ou vêtements de luxe? La dernière vêture des prêtres et des prélats à la fin du Moyen Âge (1250–1550)," paper presented at Les Sources Macabres [study day], University of Lausanne, Switzerland, Nov. 19, 2019, online at https://hal.science/hal-03931716 (accessed Sept. 23, 2024), 1–17.

65 Kovesi Killerby, *Sumptuary Law in Italy*, 109.

[…] ni porto cadenas d'argent ni afubialhs ni mealhas ni fermalhs, ni aor ni argent en deguna maniera, en rauba ni sob[re]-rauba de lana.

[(…) nor may they wear silver chains, mantle clasps (*afubialhs*), medallions (*mealhas*), or brooches (*fermalhs*) of gold or silver in any manner on garments or woolen outer garments.] (item 7)

In distinguishing between two layers of outer garments, the text makes it clear that all these accessories were normally seen on the exterior. While small annular brooches were often used as fasteners for underlayers such as chemises and the long-sleeved gowns (*cotas*) worn over them, the items listed in this paragraph were all more ostentatious (if also functional) objects. Linking archeological or visual sources with lexical ones is always conjectural, but comparison can give insight into what was available. Earrings, bracelets, and necklaces do not figure, for instance.[66] They would have conflicted with the styles of the time. The edges of tight, long sleeves and high necklines were already sites of decoration, and headwear such as veils and *bendas* obscured the ears.

A silver chain (*cadena d'argent*) would serve to connect the two top corners of a mantle. Such an accessory is seen with some frequency in visual representations. Although some might imagine "chains" as necklaces, the archeological record does not support that for this period.[67] *Cadenas d'argen* figure on Matfre Ermengaud's list of ornaments with potential to lead women towards the mortal sins of envy and vanity (to be discussed below).

Somewhat more challenging to visualize and translate is an *afubialh*.[68] As the word is semantically related to the verb *afublar* meaning to put on a mantle or garment, it is logical that it was an ornament in that service.[69] It may have been a two-part clasp sewn on to the two top corners of a heavier outer garment, of which there are examples. Compare a 1313 sumptuary law of Barcelona which permitted women *aflibays* of silver and two mantles.[70] In thirteenth-century Castilian, *aflibados* referred to men's semicircular mantles attached with fibulae. The word for the pin may have been used

---

66 Marian Campbell, *Medieval Jewellery in Europe 1100–1500* (London: V&A Publications, 2009), 40; Anderlini, *Le costume médiéval*, 94–95; Guido Gregorietti, *Jewelry Through the Ages*, trans. Helen Lawrence (New York: Crescent, 1969), 167.

67 Geoff Egan and Frances Pritchard, *Dress Accessories 1150–1450* (London: Boydell, 1991), 318–20.

68 This word is difficult to read in the manuscripts. It is not a common Occitan term in this period. Forestié ("Le vêtement civil," 169) read *afuxals*, which he translated as "affiquet"; Marcellin and Ruck (*Histoire de Montauban*, 1:411) saw *afulvalhs*, which makes less sense; Méras ("Les Lois somptuaires," 518 n. 3) read *afulualhs*, which he interpreted as a jewel pinned on to a garment or most often to the hair. DOM glosses *afiblalh* as a brooch to attach a mantle, derived from Latin *fibula*.

69 Sempere y Guariños, *Historia de luxo*, 73 n. 1, item 7 of the law. In thirteenth-century Castilian, the term *aflibados* referred to a man's semicircular mantle attached with a fibula. Bernis Madrazo, *Indumentaria medieval en Española*, 22.

70 Roca, "Lley sumtuaria," 196.

synecdochically for the cloak.[71] The contexts are similar. Note that the evidence suggests these decorative closures were used by men as well as women. The large piece clasping Chasteté's mantle at the neck in figure 4.1 might correspond to this type.

A *fermalh* denotes a pin designed to close (*fermar*) a slit permitting a chemise or robe to go over the head, worn by both sexes. Clergy used large ones for chasubles. Images often represent annular brooches used for this purpose, and artifacts suggest that this was the predominant brooch form as well.[72] There are many examples of rich *fermails* described in medieval French literature in texts from the 1170s onward, often made of gold set with precious stones.[73] Luxure's huge brooch in figure 4.1 gives an example of how they could draw prominent attention to the neck and bosom. To give an idea of how an accessory like this might have been monetized, in March 1345 Barthélemy Bonis gave a man named Sir (*senhen*) Bertran 15 sols and 10 deniers for a silver one he was pawning to pay for medications. Bonis returned the *fermalh* when Bertran repaid the debt in 1346.[74]

Mealhs is more of a puzzle when it comes to apparel. The word appears derived from "medallion," the round pieces of bronze or occasionally gold or silver embossed with portraits produced in ancient Greece, Rome, and Byzantium. While such medallions reappeared in the sixteenth century, they were not produced in this period. Occitan *mealha*, a feminine noun, denoted a tiny coin, a half denier.[75] This was probably a borrowing from *medaglia*, a half penny in circulation in northern Italy in the

---

71 This might correspond to a two-part type of clasp pierced with holes for sewing each half to the edges of a garment. One classified as being for a secular garment, made of gilded copper, champlevé enamel, and gemstones, from thirteenth-century France, is now in the Walters Art Museum, Baltimore (acc. no. 44.16), online at https://art.thewalters.org/detail/23964 (accessed Sept. 11, 2024); a "mors de chape" of silver and gold filigree with precious stones is held in the Musée des Beaux-Arts, Dijon (inv. no. CA T 1339), online at https://www.pop.culture.gouv.fr/notice/joconde/01370021972 (accessed Sept. 11, 2024).

72 Compare the sculptural images and museum objects collected by Anderlini, *Le costume médiéval*, 84–86.

73 Eunice Rathbone Goddard, *Women's Costume in French Texts of the Eleventh and Twelfth Centuries* (Baltimore: Johns Hopkins University Press, 1927), 115–16.

74 Edouard Forestié, *Les Livres de comptes*, 1:lxxvii, 5. Forestié says a merchant's wife also bought one set with pearls. Bonis dealt primarily in cloth, candles, and mercery but handled many other things occasionally. He also was a sort of banker as seen here, making loans on collateral which was often gold or silver jewelry like this. As Emmanuel Moreau notes, it is difficult to know exactly how jewelry was obtained. It may have been largely resale. Emmanuel Moreau, *Un marchand au Moyen Age: Regards sur la vie quotidienne au XIVe siècle: Les comptes de Barthélemy Bonis (1345–1365)* (Cahors, France: La Louve, 2012), 13.

75 *DOM*, s.v. *mealha, mezalha*. It appears in toll records; for instance, in the cartulary of Albi in an edict dated 1245, if someone wanted to cross the bridge over the Tarn with a quantity of copper weighing more than a pound, they paid one *mealha*; Auguste Vidal, "Costumas del Pont de Tarn d'Albi," *Revue des langues romanes* 44 (1901): 481–513, at 491, online at https://gallica.bnf.fr/ark:/12148/bpt6k198685/f493.item (accessed Sept. 23, 2024).

thirteenth century.[76] In French, *maille*, sometimes spelled *mealle* or *mehaille*, had the same sense.[77] Were *mealhs* coins reused as something like buttons or beads, with holes punched in them so that they could be sewn on? Perhaps, but whereas the noun connoting a small coin (*mealha*) was feminine, *mealhs* is masculine and would normally denote something different. Pilgrimage badges or "medals" came into vogue and were produced in large numbers to the fourteenth and fifteenth centuries. However, this instance appears decades earlier, and banning an object of piety seems contradictory to the mission. The term does not appear in Bonis' records, nor in contemporary Iberian edicts. It might correspond to some kind of brooch with an integral pin, in the style of early medieval disc brooches.[78] Compare a line in *Ab greu cossire*:

> can me remire ab pane lo cor no.m fen,
> ni mos huelhs vire que gart mos vestimens
> que son rics e onratz
> e ab aur fi frezatz
> e d'argen *mealhatz*

> [(…) when I gaze at myself my heart almost cracks, and my eyes fail me when I look at my clothes, rich and noble, trimmed with gold orphrey and *mealhatz* with silver] (lines 4–11; my emphasis)

Here, *mealhatz* is a past participle rather than an apparel item per se. Literally, it describes rich garments "metaled" with silver. Could it be translated as "medallioned," or "laminated"? It may refer to some type of fabric printing. In their edition, Matilda Tomaryn Bruckner, Laurie Shepard, and Sarah Melhado White settled for the ambiguous "worked." Note the reference to gold orphrey trim here, as well—another item on the 1275 list.

The 1275 edict returns to closures for outer layers several items later:

> Item que no porto espinlas, ni fermalhs en gannachas ni en garda-cors ni en gannags, ni re mas tant solament tro a .x. botos en cada raoba de valor de .iij. tornes cascu daqui en aval.

76 Etymology for *médaille* from *Trésor de la langue française informatisé* (Paris: Centre National de la Recherche Scientifique, 1994), via Ortolang online portal, Centre National de Ressources Textuelles et Lexicales, https://www.cnrtl.fr/etymologie/medaille (accessed Sept. 11, 2024).

77 Frédéric Godefroy, *Dictionnaire de l'ancienne langue française*, 10 vols. (Paris: F. Vieweg and E. Bouillon, 1888), 5:72, s.v. *maille*, 2.

78 Archeological finds in London attest that this type of brooch reappeared in large numbers only in the later fourteenth and fifteenth centuries, but there may be a few examples from the late thirteenth; Egan and Pritchard, *Dress Accessories*, 260–6+2. Compare the jeweled brooch of the Colmar treasure, Musée National du Moyen Âge (Musée de Cluny), Paris, no. Cl. 20672, early fourteenth century, online at https://www.musee-moyenage.fr/collection/oeuvre/fermail-du-tresor-de-colmar.html (accessed Sept. 11, 2024).

[They shall not wear pins or brooches on their over-garments or surcoats, or anything except up to ten buttons per garment worth 3 [deniers] tournois[79] apiece, and only up to that price.] (item 12)

Espinlas signified "pins," but the type and how they would be used is not clear here. Like *mealhs*, the term does not appear in the Bonis records, nor in other sumptuary laws in romance vernaculars from adjacent regions. Straight pins in brass and copper alloys were produced and sold by the thousands in these centuries.[80] They were used primarily for constructing headdresses and attaching veils, at times for securing clothing as well. In excavated burials of women, archeologists sometimes find a dozen or more located around the thorax.[81] It is unlikely that such common and utilitarian objects would be the subject of the ban, however. There are occasional archeological finds of straight pins with decorative heads from the thirteenth century, far fewer in number than simple wire pins. In London, a few embellished with coral heads have been found in twelfth-century deposits and a few with colored glass heads from the first half of the fourteenth.[82] In one copy of the Parisian *Livre des Métiers* (1268), a note adjacent to the regulations of the button makers mentions *espingles* "pierced with glass," saying no glass was acceptable except that of Montpellier.[83] The *espinlas* restricted here must have been decorative in some manner, perhaps with a decorative head.

A spinner painted in the margin of a Bible from Toulouse dated to the early fourteenth century sports several fashionable accoutrements (fig. 4.2).[84] The style of the image is distinct from those by scriptoria in the north. Her neckline is striking. A wide facing in dark blue stands out in sharp contrast with the red of her gown and the pink of the blue-lined mantle draped over her lower half and her staff. While not showing any cleavage, it is set further down from her throat than what is seen in many

79 The cost per buttons varies between the two extant manuscripts: the *Livre des Sermens* says the maximum should be 3 tournois (*.iij. tornes*) each, whereas the *Livre Rouge* copy says 5 (*.v.*). I quote here from what I believe to be the earlier copy. Moreover, 3 is in conformity with the 1291 maximum price, so I conclude that this is the more consistent reading for both edicts.

80 Olivier Thuaudet, "La fabrication des épingles à tête enroulée: Réflexion à partir des épingles retrouvées au château d'Apcher (Lozère)," in *Artisanat et métiers en Méditerranée médiévale et modern*, ed. Sylvain Burri and Mohamed Ouerfelli (Aix-en-Provence, France: Presses Universitaire de Provence, 2013), 57–59, online at https://shs.hal.science/halshs-01926174 (accessed Sept. 23, 2024).

81 Olivier Thuaudet, "Linceul ou inhumation habillée? Les épingles, lacets, boutons et autres attaches dans les sépultures du XIIIe siècle au début du XIXe siècle en Provence," in *Rencontre autour de nouvelles approches de l'archéologie funéraire*, ed. Solenn De Larminat et al. (Paris: Publication du Gaaf, 2017), 127–36.

82 Egan and Pritchard, *Dress Accessories*, 297–304.

83 This note in manuscript B was in a different hand than the statute and was very likely added later than the original 1268 compilation. Georges-Bernard Depping, ed. *Règlemens sur les arts et métiers de Paris, rédigés au XIIIe siècle et connus sous le nom du Livre des métiers d'Etienne Boileau* (Paris: Crapelet, 1837), 187 n. 2.

84 Toulouse, France, Bibliothèque d'Étude et du Patrimoine, MS 15, 145r, online at https://arca.irht.cnrs.fr/iiif/6247/canvas/canvas-1234373/view (accessed Sept. 11, 2024).

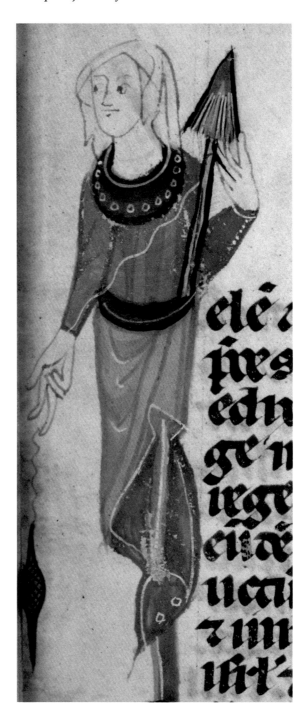

Fig. 4.2: Woman spinning. Marginal image from Bible (Toulouse, France, Bibliothèque d'Étude et du Patrimoine, MS 15), fol. 145r, early fourteenth century. Photo: Courtesy of Bibliothèque d'Étude et du Patrimoine.

images where the gown is pinned tight at the throat. Indeed, there is no visible neck slit at all, nor a brooch. A thin band of white—silver?—runs around the blue facing, perhaps set a thumb-width away from the edge. A dozen small round circles are spaced regularly on the wider part of the blue. Do these represent a type of metallic trim such as *mealhs*, or silver buttons? Could they be pearls? I think they represent a style akin to some of those targeted by the edicts and listed by Matfre. She appears in the book of Haggai (Aggaeus in Latin), one of the twelve minor prophets. While biblical illustrations tend to show anachronistic styles in certain artists' attempts to evoke ancient times, in some cases hints of contemporary styles traced a moral bridge to the present. For instance, on feminine figures such as Mary Magdalene, the Whore of Babylon, and the Wise and Foolish Virgins, touches of exaggerated fashionable details are shorthand for the story. The short book of Haggai preaches the need to rebuild the temple. The Lord spoke to Haggai asking if the people were dwelling in paneled houses when the house of the Lord was in ruins (Haggai 1:3–4). Haggai poses rhetorical questions about the ironies of living a life of vain consumption: you have sowed much but reap little, you have eaten but not enough to be satisfied. This is spot-on for an illustration representing fashion. In another verse Haggai apostrophizes, saying: "You have clothed yourself but don't have enough to keep warm" (Haggai 1:6).[85] A neckline pulled away from the neck would have been an effective way to express the futility of mortal vanity intended by that line. A collar into which time and wealth had been invested to ornament it with silver or pearls could have been an effective way to depict the final irony, that the one who has worked to earn a living puts his salary in a purse full of holes (Haggai 1:6). A decorative neckline is quite literally a hole. The concern over neckline ornamentation in Montauban in these years makes it clear that a symbolic link would have been powerful.

BUTTONS

Buttons (*botos*), unlike the above-listed fasteners, were discussed at length in both sets of edicts, showing that this trend in decorative clothing fastening was evolving. In 1275, the button maximum was set at ten per garment. This begs the question of how many buttons people were attempting to sew on their outfits. Luxure in figure 4.1 is depicted with nine fastening one side of her surcoat and eleven fastening the other. The "Prince of the World" adjacent to the Foolish Virgins at Strasbourg Cathedral (ca. 1300) was sculpted with sixteen buttons on his right and twenty-three on his left of the two open slits in his surcoat, for a button total of thirty-nine. Even more may be counted on the late-thirteenth-century effigy of the Count of Alençon, which is conserved at the Musée National du Moyen Âge in Paris. It depicts him soberly dressed, with the exception of a closely sewn row of over five dozen buttons running from ankle to thigh on each

---

85 International Standard Version, online at https://biblehub.com/haggai/1-6.htm (accessed Sept. 23, 2024).

side of his robe, discreetly layered between pleats.[86] Perhaps more representative of women, six buttons are shown on the left sleeve of the woman in figure 4.2. According to Montauban's laws she goes just a little bit too far, unlike the above men.

Button ostentation and expense continued to vex the town's conscientious leaders into the 1290s, part of a broader anti-button movement that would sweep Europe in the fourteenth century. The maximum number of ten was repeated in 1291 (item 4), but with greater concern for specific materials. Gold, silver, and silk buttons were limited, as was any decoration: the buttons had to be "plain, round, and flat." Clearly, the available choices were multiplying. Raised buttons stamped with patterns or other forms were in circulation.[87]

How would customers have obtained buttons? In Montauban some decades later, Barthélemy Bonis noted that he gave a goldsmith (*daulelier*) 4 sous for twelve silver buttons for the edges of a chainmail hood, which itself cost 20 sous.[88] Bonis often sold the requirements for making and trimming a garment (*guarnitura* or *guarnizo*) along with the cloth, and he acted as a middleman between clients and tailors, mercers, and other artisans as in this case. While he had many female clients, there are no entries for women purchasing buttons. Indeed, this is the only specific example of a button transaction in the registers, which suggests they might not have been sold along with fabric as "notions" as they are now. If women bought them, they may have gone directly to the goldsmith. To wear buttons was to wear ornamental bullion, not just fasteners. In *Ab greu cossire*, buttons are mentioned: "que.ls verstirs an naffratz / e desencadenzatz / e desenbotenatz" (lit. "because through clothing they have wounded us, and un-chained us, and un-buttoned us"), meaning they have taken away our fine silver chains (cf. *cadenas*, above) and buttons. The narrator later exhorts goldsmiths, as well as ladies who are their customers ("Senhors dauraires e los dauriveliers / donas e donzelas / que es de lur mestier," lines 46–49) to beseech the pope to excommunicate town consuls for their harsh regulations as well as the friars who demanded loathsomely penitential dress in their preaching.

Button regulation would become a regular feature of later sumptuary regulation. The target of regulators was often superfluous buttons rather than those used as functional fasteners. Barcelona permitted solid silver or gold-plated buttons on the sleeves of women's gowns in 1313, where they would have functioned to draw the sleeves tight on the arms.[89] Another Catalan law, that of Cervera in 1344, permitted plain silver or gold buttons used only on sleeves and at the neck (*cabeç*).[90] Montauban's emphasis on sleeve placement implies that uses elsewhere might not be acceptable, but the statute

---

86 Musée National du Moyen Âge (Musée de Cluny), Paris, no. Cl. 23408, online at https://www.musee-moyenage.fr/collection/oeuvre/pierre-d-alencon.html (accessed Sept. 11, 2024).

87 Anderlini, *Le costume médiéval*, 86–87, shows some stamped and granulated examples.

88 Forestié, *Les livres de comptes*, 1:236–37.

89 "Puxen encara portar, en màngues de gonelles o de brials, botons dargent plans o daurats." Roca, "Lley Sumtuaria," 196.

90 Conde y Delgado de Molina, "Vestit i societat," 25–42, at 37, item 1.

is not openly prohibitive. In subsequent decades in Tuscany, the evidence is clear that the button fashion shed the bonds of utility. The fourteenth-century Florentine chronicle of Giovanni Villani describes measures in 1330 taken to curb women's excessive apparel, including "gilded silver buttons paired together and often in four to six rows."[91] Florence banned nonfunctional buttons in the 1350s.[92] From 1360 there survive Florentine court records of charging fathers for superfluous buttons on their children's clothing. One boy had eighteen silver buttons on a cloak, with gold ribbon running down either side of them; an infant son had a particolored hat trimmed with gold ribbons and tiny silver buttons; a toddler daughter's gown was adorned with twenty-six enameled silver buttons at the breast and eighteen on the sleeves, running up past her elbows.[93] The Montauban edicts predate these by several decades and represent an earlier stage of button history. Stella Mary Newton observed that buttons did not figure in the English royal inventories before around 1337–38, which prompted her to speculate on the timeline for the arrival of button fashions in England.[94] The Montauban laws document that buttons of significant value were being used on clothing in Occitania at least fifty years before they appear in extant accounts for the English court and show that changes in button usage and styles were occurring well before the fourteenth century.

In 1275 it was simply buttons that were targeted, whereas the 1291 statute specifically targets buttons of gold, silver, and silk that feature in the above-mentioned fourteenth-century regulations.[95] Archeological digs in the Thames unearthed numerous buttons in copper and lead/tin alloys dating to the thirteenth and fourteenth centuries. Many were solid and plain. Some were hollow, of tin. A number were of brass sheeting stamped with patterns or beaded edges. Some would have had a decorative piece of stone or glass embedded in the center.[96] These materials correspond to those described in the statutes of the button and thimble makers of Paris recorded in the *Livre des Métiers*, which specify brass, copper, and copper-zinc alloy (*archal*).[97] Silver and gold buttons are not mentioned there. They may have been manufactured by goldsmiths, as well as sold by them as discussed above.

In 1275, the maximum button price was set at "3 tournois," which implies that many buttons cost more. In 1291, that was still the admissible price maximum, but the money was now expressed as *tornes negres*, lit. "black tournois." Neither text specifies

---

91 Giovanni Villani, *The Eleventh and Twelfth Books of Giovanni Villani's New Chronicle*, trans. Rala Diakité and Matthew T. Sneider (Kalamazoo, MI: Medieval Institute Publications, 2022), chapter CLI, 180. I am grateful to Gloria Allaire for this reference.

92 Stuard, *Gilding the Market*, 85; Ronald E. Rainey, "Sumptuary Legislation in Renaissance Florence" (Ph.D. diss., Columbia University, 1985), 669.

93 Kovesi Killerby, *Sumptuary Law in Italy*, 154–55.

94 Stella Mary Newton, *Fashion in the Age of the Black Prince: A Study of the Years 1340–1365* (1980; repr., Woodbridge, UK: Boydell, 1999), 15–18.

95 The mention of silver buttons as well as a number of other items makes me wonder if *Ab greu cossire* could be later than the date of ca. 1230 that has previously been theorized.

96 Egan and Pritchard, *Dress Accessories*, 272–80.

97 Depping, *Règlemens sur les arts et métiers*, 184–87.

the units for these button prices, in contrast with the *sous tournois* units specified for silk braid closures (1275, item 13). Silver coins tarnished more as the base metals in the alloy increased, particularly when more copper was used. This slight difference in the two texts may be an indicator of the devaluation occurring in the later thirteenth century. Devaluation was much worse for the money of Cahors, a city north of Montauban, but was happening with the French coinage as well.[98] Note that the price was expressed in tournois coinage rather than that of Cahors, which was in more common use in the region. Cahors' deniers were worth barely more than half those of Tours.[99] In 1291, fines in other sections were assessed in *caorces*, the ordinary coins of daily transactions. It is interesting that button prices were set in French royal coinage rather than the local currency. It may suggest that they came from Paris or other northern French sites of production.

Buttons were fairly costly in the French currency of the time. If *tornes negres* refers to the penny coinage, the maximum permitted cost of ten buttons would have come to 30 deniers, or 2½ sous. The *Livre des Métiers* records that craftsmen would be fined 5 sous if their shanks were badly soldered such that the buttons came off,[100] a penalty equivalent to two sets of buttons for an honest citizen of Montauban. In contrast, the silver- and gold-plated buttons that figure in the 1291 edict and later laws of other cities would have been worth as much as coins themselves, in terms of their content of precious metals. Comparative prices for goods are notoriously difficult to find, as are accurate records of wages and salaries at given points in time. These documents can contribute towards understanding of the costs of medieval clothing, which still deserves greater study, but they do present ambiguities.

If metal closures were forbidden, what did the *capitols* think women ought to use to attach their mantles and affix their layered garments? Item 13 of the 1275 edict presented the concessions:

> Empero volo e autreiaro que las donas posco portar e·ls mantels una tressa de seda pura ses als, de pretz de .v. sols de tornes, e d'aqui en aval; e cordos en lors gannachas e en lors corsetz de ceda ses aur e ses argent e ses peira e ses als.

> [However, they grant that ladies may wear a simple silk braid on their mantles, but only one at a price of 5 sous tournois, and no more than that; and on their laced over-gowns (*gannachas* and *corsets*), cords of silk without gold or silver or gems or anything else.]

In this ideal vision of the honest city, men could wear hard metallic fasteners, but women were to have soft ones. A silk braid was permitted to cost twice as much as the maximum number of buttons, so price was not the only consideration.

---

98 Jacques Le Goff, "Du XIIIe au XIVe siècle, l'argent en crise," in his *Le Moyen Âge et l'argent* (Paris: Perrin, 2019), 133–50.

99 Mireille Castaing-Sicard, *Monnaies féodales et circulation monétaire en Languedoc (Xe–XIIIe siècles)* (Toulouse: Association Marc Bloch, 1961), 47–49.

100 Depping, *Règlemens sur les arts et métiers*, 185.

Matfre Ermengaud listed both metal and textile accessories in his rhetorical *enumeratio* of the ways women could sin by their desire for apparel:

> Ni ja no hauran pro *botos*
> Ni vels ni bendas[101] ni *cordos,*
> Ni hauran pro *fermalhamen*
> Ni guarlandas d'aur e d'argen
> O de *perlas* ni senturas
> Ni borzas ni frezaduras,[102]
> *Cadenas d'argen* ni tessells[103] […]

> [They will never have enough buttons, or veils or *bendas* or cords, nor will they ever have enough brooches, or garlands of gold or silver, or pearls or belts or purses or orphrey trims, or silver chains or braids […]] (lines 18514–20, my emphasis on terms appearing in the edicts)

Montauban's *capitols* and Matfre Ermengaud were clearly thinking about many of the same objects. It almost seems they were both following a familiar script. If the *Breviari* was designed on the model of a book of prayers and hymns, this was a litany to be sung of the perils of apparel. If modeled on Gratian's law codes, it was a text for jurists to memorize and repeat when cases arose. The sumptuary documents state that they were to be read aloud and the consuls and men of the town were to swear to uphold them every year (1275 items 18–20, 1291 items 17–18). These lists of ornaments were performed, in both cases. Like passages from the liturgy, the time for reading them would come regularly once a year. They both expressed their concerns in the vernacular rather than Latin, whose vocabulary was too limited. Regulations in Latin referring to clothing and other contemporary things simply latinized vernacular terms, often clumsily. Both were castigating a popular audience.

---

101 The term *benda* is difficult to translate. It signified a strip of linen in some contexts, e.g. a bandage in the Occitan translation of Albucasis' text on surgery. In *Flamenca* the heroine wore one over her face in church so she would not be seen ("davan sa cara ges de benda," Zufferey and Fasseur, *Flamenca*, line 2416, also 3135); Guilhem, frustrated in coming all the way there to meet her only to not see her face, declares he will teach her how to deceive her jealous husband and avenge her for having to wear it ("de la benda·t venjarai," lines 2463–66); it was pulled tightly over her ears ("Li benda sai que m'a trait / que·l tenc las aurellas serradas," lines 4002–3). For Montauban and Matfre, however, it was a fashionable item. Figure 4.1 shows several veils. A *benda* might be one of those layers. In the mid-to-late thirteenth century there was a fashion for bands of linen running under the chin, over the ears, and pinned at the top of the head to which veils, hair nets (French *crespinetes*), and other headpieces could be pinned. Cf. Anderlini, *Le costume médiéval*, 116–20.
102 *Frezaduras,* cf. *aur fres ni argent fres,* 1275, item 4. Variants in the manuscripts include "fuselduras," seemingly related to "fusel" signifying a bobbin; also "frauseduras."
103 Variants include "tressels," suggesting a braid; also "tercels," "tezels," "tacells," "texels," which might suggest a woven band. The variety of variant terms is impressive.

RICH FABRICS

The 1275 edict prohibits another group of showy items that could be sewn on to women's visible garments, these characterized by particularities of fiber and textile finish. There are some singular terms in this group, as well. However, attention to textile ornamentation was completely abandoned in 1291.

In 1275, item 8 says that women also may not have made or wear any kind of clothing of sendal, "purple," samite, any gold cloth, or silk, unless it is sendal as a lining ("fasso deguna rauba ni porto de sendat ni de polpra ni de samit ni de lunh drap d'aor ni de seda, sino era sendat en folradura"). Similarly permitting only discreetly hidden uses of silk, item 9 allows silk embellishment on chemises in addition to the fabric they are made of, but not gold or pearls or anything else ("en camisas no porto aur ni perlas ni re si drap e seda no"). Simple silk marked the limit between honesty and worldly vanity, and it was better to hide it than flaunt it.

Imports of sendal and samite appear together in the *leudas* (tariff list) of Montpellier ca. 1350 and were taxed at the same rate. Merchants were to pay 2 deniers for either of them, in contrast with 4 deniers for a "worked silk" patterned either by weave or embroidery.[104] Sendal was a plain weave. It was the most common and least expensive medieval silk, usually of a lighter weight suited to linings, such as the 1275 statute permits (item 4). Samite was a heavier, lustrous silk in a twill weave, imported from Byzantium and later Italy.[105] Both were ubiquitous in literary texts. Several of these prohibited silks were used in the allegorical portraits of Guillaume de Lorris' *Roman de la Rose* (ca. 1225), where the figure of Deduit (Pleasure) wore samite figured with birds of beaten gold (lines 819–20); Richesse (Wealth) wore purple (*pourpre*) covered in gold figured embroidery and orphrey (lines 1055–57); Largesse (Generosity) wore "Saracen" purple (line 1161).[106] Sendal was omitted, however, as it was apparently too common for representing qualities with such power over lovers. Ramon Llull's narrator placed layers of samite on the lover who died of love in his "Tree of the Philosophy of Love" (*Arbre de filosofia d'amor*, ca. 1293): a white samite showing the stains of his sins, then a red samite representing his martyrdom by love, and finally a gold one proving he had been loyal.[107] In this mystical text, samite had connotations both of pomp and perhaps of a textile befitting a holy context.

---

104 "Cendat e samit e cirici .ii. d.; Trastot drap de ceda obrat .iiii. d.," Widmayer, "Coutumes anciennes de Montpellier," fol. 172, lines 21–22; fol. 227, lines 6–7.

105 Tina Anderlini, "Dressing the Sacred: Medallion Silks and Their Use in Western Medieval Europe," *Medieval Clothing and Textiles* 15 (2019): 101–36; Anna Muthesius, "Silk in the Medieval World," in *The Cambridge History of Western Textiles*, ed. David Jenkins (Cambridge, UK: Cambridge University Press, 2003), 1:332–37, 343.

106 Strubel, *Le Roman de la rose.*

107 "E cobriren-lo ab un bell sàmit blanc, a significansa que l'amic era mundat de sos peccats. Sobre aquel sàmit blanc posaren un altre sàmit vermel, a significansa que l'amic era màrtir per amor; e sobre aquel sàmit vermell posaren un altre sàmit d'aur, a significansa

Based on the Bonis registers, sendal was the principal silk sold in Montauban.[108] Of the many colors he sold, red and green were the most popular. In contrast, the practical reality of purchasing "purple" (*polpra*) in Montauban is hard to discern. Appearing in this section enumerating fabrics, it is not to be confused with the fur *popra* mentioned above (1291, item 2), for all the closeness of the spellings. It was famous as the ancient symbol of fabulous wealth and power in scripture and romances, but it hardly appears in practical sources of this time. There were many dozens of different fabrics sold in the Bonis shop two generations later, many of which he bought wholesale each year at the fair of Lendit in Saint-Denis. He did not sell a *polpra*, either as a color or a weave. Later, records from the dyers of Tuscany show a wide range of hues and dyestuffs. *Porpora*, a "purple" from murex or other shellfish, did appear occasionally, according to Maria Giuseppina Muzzarelli.[109] Dominique Cardon identified a medieval Mediterranean "pourpre" as produced by overdyeing a woad blue base with a red bath.[110] A Catalan tariff document records a *porpra* cloth whose provenance was Spain or the Holy Land (*Oltramar*); another mentions a *porpra vermella*, indicating that it was made with vermillion dye, perhaps tinged red. But Catalan literary sources called *porpra* "precious" and associated it with emperors.[111] In short, a "purple" textile product did seem to have existed, at least in the fourteenth and fifteenth centuries. However, it does seem to have been more mythically associated than commercially available, making it easy to prohibit. It is possible that prohibiting *polpra* may have had more elements of moral performance than a response to a real spending problem in thirteenth-century Montauban, but the opposite may be true as well. It is worthwhile to note that "purple" had been prohibited in multiple laws from antiquity, such the *Lex Julia* of 46 BCE. Pearls were prohibited there, as well. Roman laws may have served as models of civic virtue in Italy, Occitania, and Iberia, where Roman law was practiced in the Middle Ages.[112]

Item 11 prohibited several styles that are somewhat lexically challenging. One was a *rauba vetada de ceda*, literally a garment "striped" with silk.[113] What did this

que l'amic era provat e estat leyal a son amat e amor […]." Ramon Llull, *Arbre de filosofia d'amor*, ed. Gret Schib (Barcelona: Barcino, 1980), chap. 83, 129.

108 Moureau, *Un marchand au Moyen Age*, 37.

109 Maria Giuseppina Muzzarelli, *Guardaroba medievale: Vesti e societa dal XIII al XVI secolo* (Bologna: Il Mulino, 1999), 155.

110 Dominique Cardon, "Violets des pourpres, bleus de pastel ou d'indigo: Le monde des indigoïdes," in her *Teintures précieuses de la Méditerranée: Pourpre, kermès, pastel* (Carcassonne, France: Musée des Beaux-arts, 1999), 22–29.

111 Isidra Maranges i Prat, *La Indumentària Civil Catalana, segles XIII–XV*, 2nd ed. (Barcelona: Rafael Dalmau, 2018), 153–54. See also Germán Navarro Espinach, "Textiles in the Crown of Aragon," in *Textiles of Medieval Iberia: Cloth and Clothing in a Multi-Cultural Context*, ed. Gale R. Owen-Crocker, María Barrigón, Nahum Ben-Yehuda, and Joana Sequeira (Woodbridge, UK: Boydell, 2022), 93–122, at 110–11.

112 Kovesi Killerby, *Sumptuary Law in Italy*, 9–14.

113 *DOM*, s.v. *vetat*, gives "rayé," striped; s.v. *vetadat* which references Emil Levy, *Provenzalisches Supplement-Wörterbuch* (Leipzig: Reisland, 1894–1915), who translates *vetadat* as

signify in practice? Extant images from Northern Europe do not show contemporary women wearing noticeable stripes. The passage continues to further prohibit *drap cozut ab autre*, literally "fabric sewn with something else." One possibility is to translate *vetada* here as "appliquéd," to emphasize the idea of stitched-on trims that might be removed in accordance with the rest of the line, *ni de drap cozut ab autre*, nor cloth stitched with anything. A *veta* could signify a ribbon, cord, or band. Narrow lines of color do appear around the edges of sleeves, mantles, and necklines as in figure 4.1, so perhaps this is the most likely interpretation. Bonis had an entry for a sale to a wealthy bourgeois of some green silk to sew (on?) a hood for his own use, where similarly a past participle form of the verb *vetar* was used as a qualifier to indicate how the hood would be decorated (".i. ochau seda vert per cozer .i. capairo a son ops vetat").[114] A Barcelona edict of 1313 in Catalan prohibited any man or woman of the city, no matter what their estate, from adding sewn-on embellishment (*sobreposades o cosides*) to clothing, using the verb *vetar* along with several others. It prohibited these acts of trimming as well as having garments made with images on them unless they were woven into the fabric.[115]

Another prohibition is *rauba picada ni aor pelada*. The first term is clear enough, as *picada* means "stitched" with gold. This is in keeping with earlier references to embroidered embellishment. The second verb, *pelar*, has several connotations: to plume, to peel, to skin, i.e. to remove the feathers or fur from an animal. That is the use for the word in French sources, but not associated with fabric. Looking south instead, there is an analogue in Catalan. *Peladas* were an item sold by the piece in a tariff document.[116] That suggests something that might be applied to a garment decoratively rather than used as the main support. Does this signify fabric somehow gilded, and if so by what process? A "pelé" has not been documented in French sources. Tonia Brown-Kinzel has identified a few extant fabrics from this period that were gilded by stamping or block printing, whose places of origination have been identified as ranging from Egypt to Yemen to Iran. It is possible that such imports traveled as far as Montauban.[117]

"gestreift," striped (8:714a). Walther von Wartburg et al., eds., *Französisches Etymologisches Wörterbuch*, 25 vol. (Bonn: F. Klopp, 1928–2002), 14:570a glosses the example of a striped fabric in a Montalbanese document of 1370, but that was eighty years later; online at https://lecteur-few.atilf.fr/lire/140/570 (accessed Sept. 11, 2024).

114 Forestié, *Les Livres de comptes*, 1:144. Forestié suggested it was a ribbon used as border trim ("ruban pour bordure").

115 Item 3. "Item: que null hom ne neguna dona de Barchinona o qui estia en Barchinona, de qualque condiciò que sia, no gos daqui avant listar *ne vetar* per forsa, ne batcegar, negunes vestadures, ne fer fer en aquelles ymages dauçells o daltres qui sobreposades o cosides hi sien, si donchs tixent no si fahien." Roca, "Lley sumtuaria," 196.

116 Marages i Prat, *La Indumentària Civil Catalana*, 144–45.

117 Tonia Brown-Kinzel, The Printed Textiles Project, pers. comm. Cleveland Museum of Art nos. 1950.353 and 1950.524 are ikats (woven with yarn pre-dyed to create patterns) printed with gold from Yemen; no. 1950.558 is a mulham from Iraq or Iran, a checkerboard pattern figured with printed gold lions. No. 1933.96 is also attributed to that region, but it is a very small sample, making it difficult to analyze.

THE LEXICON OF LAYERED GARMENTS

In 1275, the *capitols* used a concise vocabulary for different types of outer garments in what appears to be an attempt to cover every possible exemption that consumers might claim. In 1291, this attention to terminology was abandoned, reduced to "any garment for going outside" (*en neguna salhadura*, the verb *salhar* signifying to exit or go out) in the item regarding buttons (item 4). In 1275, the blanket phrase for anything where metallic accessories might be used is *en rauba ni sobre-rauba de lana*, literally "garments or over-garments of wool" (item 7). When they returned to specify further metallic accessories, they also listed three types of over-garments: pins and brooches were not to be worn *en gannachas ni en garda-cors ni en gannags* (item 12). Next, they did permit unadorned cords of silk on their *gannachas* and *corsets* (item 13). There have been attempts by lexicographers and costume historians to gloss analogous terms in other languages, but many of those authors admit that conclusively pinning down and explaining the nuances between styles is an elusive goal. There is a strong sense that they were evolving quickly, relatively speaking.[118] Luxure wears a garment of one of these types in figure 4.1. Chasteté is shown in only a *cote*, in contrast.

NEW DIRECTIONS IN 1291: TRAINS AND GARLANDS

In 1291 the *capitols* added items regarding trains. The first leapt to the top of the list, displacing all discussion of trims, brooches, and rich fabrics. No proper lady or other woman of Montauban might dare to wear:

> negu rosset en deguna dessas raubas, mas quant tan solament / de .i. palm de drap outra terra, e no plus. E que la rauba sia tota redonda, so es assaber que sia tant longua devan coma derriere, a bona fe

> [any kind of train on any of her garments, unless it is one with only a palm[119] of fabric on the ground, and no more. The garment must be round all around, which is to say it must be as long in the front as in the back, in good faith] (item 1)

Trains appear in literary texts and frequently in sumptuary laws,[120] but often they are described paraphrastically in terms of how much extra fabric dragged on the

---

118 Anderlini, *Le costume médiéval*, 154; Maranges i Prat, *La Indumentaria civil catalana*, 35. Stella Mary Newton (*Fashion in the Age of the Black Prince*, 15) calls the corset of fourteenth-century English records "enigmatic," for instance.
119 A palm or *pan* was a length unit corresponding to the width of the fingers when splayed. The exact measure could vary between towns. In the nineteenth century in Montauban it was recorded as equivalent to 23 centimeters; M. Duc de La Chapelle, *Métrologie Française ou traité du système métrique décimal à l'usage du département du Lot* (Montauban, France: Fontanel, 1807), 8. Forestié ("Le vêtement civil," 15) assumed this length held for medieval Montauban, but it is difficult to be certain.
120 There were bans in Siena in 1249, San Gimignano in 1251, and Parma in 1258–66. See Kovesi Killerby, *Sumptuary Law in Italy*, 26.

floor. For instance, in the *Lai de l'ombre*, the exquisite lady is described as wearing a delicate white summer gown (*chainse*) that trailed more than two yards (*qui trainoit plus d'une toise*) behind her on the rushes on her floor.[121] The French verb *trainer* is the source of the English noun "train." Italian laws were usually in Latin, but forms of this French verb appear. In Sienese statutes from 1277–82, an edict prohibited fabric "training" on the ground in back (*pannos trainantes sui dorsi per terram*) for young ladies (*fancella*).[122] The royal law of Sicily in 1290 used words harking back to ancient Roman hem decoration (*ystitam seu fimbriam*) when it prohibited all women from wearing robes with such edging longer than four palms on the ground (*longiorem palmis quatuor supra terram*).[123]

In contrast, the Occitan word *rosset* is striking as a nominal form that labeled the style, rather than described the act of dragging on the floor or a length to be measured. It is not to be found in any Occitan dictionary in that form. The verb *rosegar* does signify "to pull or drag" in Occitan, like *rossegar* in Catalan.[124] The term seems to have been limited to Languedoc and Catalonia. It is unlike many other words used to indicate trains such as Latin *coda* or French *queue*, whose Occitan equivalent would be *cauda*; in Italian there is *stracisco*, which expresses the notion of "extra" fabric. The term is uncommon in sumptuary laws. The only comparable instance I have found is in a Perpignan edict of 1313. It mandated that "no lady or maiden shall dare to wear on their robes a train longer than two palms of Montpellier, on pain of (a fine of) 100 sols which shall be paid from her dowry ("neguna dona ni donzela no gaus portar en lurs robes *rossegues* oltre .ii. palms de Montpeller, sots pena de .c. qui seran pagat de lur dot," item 4, my emphasis).[125] In a further parallel, both municipalities extended the prohibitions to hold tailors accountable for creating gowns with trains. In Perpignan in 1313, tailors and any person who might make garments would be penalized with the same fines as consumers. Montauban was significantly more draconian: the penalty for tailors was a fine of 20 sous and being prohibited from tailoring any clothing again in the town or territory. Note that these provisions came several items after the ban on trains (Montauban 1291, item 16; Perpignan 1313, item 5[126]). This suggests that the governing body had time to think about potential loopholes in an early model of the law, and this then became a widespread pattern. Montauban was the most conservative of the above examples when it came to length: one palm, versus two in Perpignan and four in war-torn Sicily where king Charles II was urging spending limits to direct

121 Jean Renart, *Le Lai de l'ombre*, ed. Alan Hindley and Brian J. Levy, trans. Adrian P. Tudor (Liverpool, UK: University of Liverpool Press, 2013), 40–41, lines 314–17.

122 Curzio Mazzi, "Alcune leggi suntuarie senesi," *Archivio storico italiano*, ser. 4, vol. 5 (1880): 133–44, at 136, item 2.

123 Heller, "Angevin-Sicilian Sumptuary Statutes of the 1290s: Fashion in the Thirteenth-Century Mediterranean," *Medieval Clothing and Textiles* 11 (2015): 79–97, at 89.

124 *DOM*, s.v. *rosegar*; Alcover and Moll, *Diccionari català-valencià-balear*, s.v. *rossegar*.

125 *Livre des Ordinacions*, Archives municipales de Perpignan (MS AA7), 74r. My transcription and translation.

126 *Livre des Ordinacions*, 74r.

resources to the military effort. Even the latter was less than half that of Jean Renart's lady in the French text. Montauban permitted only a tenth of that length.

Also newly introduced in 1291 were garlands (item 3). These are another near-constant feature of municipal sumptuary laws across Europe from the thirteenth to fifteenth centuries. The head, as the most visible part of the body, was an ideal site for attention-seeking consumption and fashion innovation. Luxure sports an exaggerated garland in figure 4.1. Montauban's prohibitions echo the garlands of gold, silver, and pearls which Matfre signaled among the apparel that paved the path to sin (lines 18517–18). The *capitols* of 1291 seem attentive to the message of the preachers' calls and Matfre's satire. He warned that if husbands gave in to women's demands for garlands and mantles, they would be led into poverty (lines 18594–95, 18618–26) and compelled to multiply their sinful acts, namely lying, stealing, and cheating. In turn, the *capitols* declared that acceptable garlands were to be cheap, priced in penny coinage. Two was the limit. They were expected to be relatively short-lived as well, permitted "as long as they last" (*aitant quant aquelas duraran*). Acceptable garlands were made of greenery, flowers, leaves, or herbs (*de flors, o de fulha, o d'erba*). These would have been disposable, the "fast fashion" of the later thirteenth century. Buying a garland could permissably mark a celebratory moment, but not constitute an investment. Similarly, *Ab greu cossire* includes the complaint that along with orphrey and the work of goldsmiths, women could no longer wear veils and *bendas*. Their garlands could only be of flowers in summer (lines 27–30).

CONCLUSIONS

Montauban's sumptuary edicts of 1275 and 1291 enacted prohibitions on many women's apparel items that were frequent targets of laws in Occitania, Catalonia, Italy, and elsewhere: gold and silver, pearls, silks, furs, trains, and garlands. The more one looks at the sumptuary laws across Europe, the more formulaic they can seem. One curtailment can blur into the next, from year to year and from town to town. It seems there was something contagious about them: they spread, mutating along the way. The originality of the Montauban laws lies partly in the details that emerged from its unique context and population. For instance, Montauban's *capitols* proposed blacklisting tailors cutting fashionably long gowns for women and barring them from ever working there again, while other city councils chose merely the threat of fines. *Jotglars* and *jotglaressas* were threatened with similar banishment for entertaining, even as *jotglaressas* were permitted to keep finery that honest ladies should be ashamed to wear.

Montauban appears to have been a prosperous commercial town, yet also one with a significant sector of its population bearing a penchant for spiritual austerity which manifested as "Cathar," "Waldensian," and Protestant beliefs over the centuries, and a warm welcome to the mendicant orders in the mid-thirteenth century. The sentiments of many of its inhabitants had been branded heretical in the earlier half of the century. In the last quarter, by enacting these laws and rapidly funding and erecting houses for the preaching orders, the consuls and men of the town publicly enacted gestures of humility by imposing restrictions on wives. Comparison of the two edicts and other narrative sources from the region suggests that the preaching of the friars and municipal sumptuary regulation in Languedoc were potently intertwined. *Ab greu cossire* explicitly blames the sartorial misery experienced by those targeted for cruel penitence on the Inquisition (*los prezicadors*) and the preaching friars (*los fraires menors*) (lines 54–60). Contrast this song of lament with sources celebrating the ecstatic joys of sartorial denial. The *Life of Saint Douceline* (ca. 1215–74), a mystic who brought the Beguine order to Marseilles and who professed great devotion to St. Francis, tells how she would wear a pigskin next to her skin and bind her body with a knotted cord but over them wear "beautiful elegant robes, as if she loved colourful fabrics."[127] A contemporary model of Franciscan renunciation, Douceline's life also tells of her vision of two humble ladies in black with heads covered in mantles who told her they were wearing clothing pleasing to God (chapter 2.4). Renunciation of apparel elicited dramatic responses, that much is clear.

In the past, some scholars have taken these Montauban sumptuary edicts as evidence of the profusion of luxury goods available in the town and the frivolity of its female inhabitants. Such a view risks reading the edicts too much at face value. What is targeted in women's behavior masks greater consumption by men, products sold by men, and garments tailored by men. There is more to the story than women running amok with their dress shopping. Women were the overt targets of misogynist preachers and also municipal leaders influenced by them, as well as by the models of sumptuary legislation arising as a trend all over Europe. Less obvious may be the ways that women were used as a screen for men to critique each other's behavior. While the Montauban law fined silk, fur, and metallic trimming on women's clothing, it must be noted that men's clothing was so trimmed as well. It is a modern prejudice that only women cared about fashion. In municipal laws, it is women who were regulated, but they were not the only ones richly arrayed; indeed, their spending ranked second to that of the men in their households and communities. It is worth noting that *Ab greu cossire* presents gender ambiguity with regard to clothing since it seems to present a female narrator but was attributed to a male one, "P. Basc." Men were wearing gold, silver, vair, and silk as much as women, if not more. Many clerics were, too. The wealthy Benedictine monks were often criticized for the splendid cloth and objects in their treasuries. Confiscated women's clothing may very well have been transformed for liturgical use. Complexly mixed with these moral pressures, consuls were also responding to more and more pressing financial needs. They were obliged to fund civic construction projects as well as cope with monetary instability. Women's clothing was an easier target than

---

127 Kathleen Garay and Madeleine Jeay, trans., *The Life of Saint Douceline, Beguine of Provence* (Cambridge: D. S. Brewer, 2001), 27–28 (ch. 1.10–11). The original Occitan is "e desus, illi portava vestirs bels e paratz, jassisisso que draps de lur propria color amava e portava […]." J.-H. Albanés, *La vie de Sainte Douceline, fondatrice des Béguines de Marseille composée au treizième siècle en langue provençale* (Marseille: Camoin, 1879), 10.

the consumption of their powerful male compatriots. Targeting it was made easier by the righteous support of the minor orders and the models of other towns.

Another originality is the vernacular vocabulary of Montauban's edict. It contrasts with the Latin used in Castile, Italian cities, and other areas. It can take the reader further into everyday commerce and sartorial choices in this region than formulae drawn from Roman law. Comparative examinations of specific terms show that the ways people in this part of Languedoc were talking about their apparel were often closer to those of Barcelona or Perpignan than those of Paris or Florence. The people of Montauban were concerned about certain modest luxuries that the inhabitants of more ostentatious places did not bother to regulate. They discussed mediocre *popra* fur, not just vair and *gris*; *espinla* pins, and not just big *fermails*. Using the right vernacular term for the moment mattered there. A train was not just something to be measured and adjusted. It was a named element of style, a *rosset*. Occitan is a rich language at the crossroads of what are now France, Spain, and Italy, now subsumed due to political shifts over the centuries. These sources deserve a place in the glossaries at the disposition of historians of dress, law, and Mediterranean culture. There are more texts in Occitan and Catalan that merit study and that deserve to be considered in comparative sumptuary studies. The relatively early date of these regulations suggests that they may have been influential and not just parroted.

Appendix 4.1

Transcription and Translation of the 1291 Sumptuary Law of Montauban

Following is a transcription of the edict of 1291 from the *Livre Rouge* (Archives Départementales de Tarn-et-Garonne, MS AA 1, digital version, E(03) 121-AA 1, https://bvmm.irht.cnrs.fr/consult/consult.php?reproductionId=2285), fols. 74v–75v, along with a translation of each section.[1] I have added section numbers in brackets for reference purposes. In the transcription, italics are used to signal expansions of abbreviations. Words in ellipsis are supplied in brackets. In the translation, I use italics to retain certain Occitan terms rather than render them with inexact borrowings.

[Fol. 74v]
[Rubric, circled, top left]
en l'an m.cc.lxxxx et primo foro fag los establimens escriutz

[in the year 1291 the edicts written were passed]

[Rubric, circled, top right]
Los establimens fags dels paramens de las donas

[The edicts made regarding the apparel of ladies]

[Rubric in cursive below those two, in later French]
Des habillemenz [que] doivent porter les fames de Montauban

[Concerning what the women of Montauban must wear]

[Preamble]
Conoguda causa sia qu'en Ramon Borrel, viguier de Montalba, per nostre senhor lo rey, / el capitol *per* nom….
Ad honor de Dio e de nostra dona s*an*ta Maria e de mosenhor *san* Jacme e dels s*ans* de paradis, e ad / honestat de las donas et per lo cominal profeg de la vila de Montalba,

---

1   The author is much indebted to William D. Paden for his paleographic and interpretive assistance.

apelat parlament com*un*ial / ab las trompas et e avistat los borzes e·ls mercadiers e·ls menestrairals e·l comunal de la vila en la maizo comunal de Montalba et agut diligent tractament ab los plus sains homes de la vila, *per* comunal / acort fero et establiro et aordenerero totz aquetz establimens sotz escriutz *per* totz temps valedors / so es assaber:

[Let it be known that Sir Raymond Borrel, *viguier* of Montauban for our lord the king, and the *capitols*, by name (…list of names), for the honor of God, our lady Saint Mary, our lord Saint Jacques, and all the saints of paradise, and to guide the honest conduct of the ladies and for the communal profit of the city, called a communal *parlement* with trumpets and assembled the townsmen, merchants, and artisans of the commune in the town hall, for a meeting of diligent deliberations with the most respected men of the town. By communal accord they will make and establish and order these regulations, which shall be valid for all times, which is to say:]

[1] Item q*ue* deguna dona ni autra femna d'esta vila ni de la honor no porte ni auze portar, / ab gen nis ses gen, negu rosset en deguna dessas raubas, mas quant tan sola-ment / de .i. palm de drap outra terra, e no plus. E que la rauba sia tota redonda, so es assaber que sia tant longua devan coma derriere, a bona fe, exceptadas jotglaressas e putas, o non / era estada, en pena de *per*dre la rauba en que lo rosset seria; e que seria donada a qui on / los cossols establirio, e a lor conoguda.

[No lady or other woman of this town or of the territory shall wear, in public or in private, any kind of train on any of her garments, unless it is one with only a palm of fabric on the ground, and no more. The garment must be round all around, which is to say it must be as long in the front as in the back, in good faith—except for those of performers and prostitutes, on whom it (the garment) was not (round)—on pain of losing the garment with the train. The garment shall be given to whomever the consuls decide, and as they know of it.]

[2] Item q*ue* neguna dona ni autra femna d'esta vila ni / de la honor no aja, ni pusca aver ni portar en totas las suas raubas pena de vaires, ni de / popras, ni de gris; mas quant tant solament una pena e non plus en qualque rauba se vulha, / exceptat un capairo folrat d'aitals penas coma dessus, laqual pusca aver e no plus, exceptadas / jotglaressas e putas, o non ero estadas, en pena de *per*dere la folradura de la pena e la rauba en que seria. Que seria tot donat a qui on los cossols establirio, a lor conoguda./

[No lady or other woman of this town or the territory may have on her garments, or be allowed to have, or wear, in all of her clothing, fur linings of vair, pople, or *gris*. She may only have one fur lining, which she may have and no more, on any garment that she may choose, except for a hood lined with such furs as listed above—except for those of performers and prostitutes, on which (the furs) had not been (thus limited)—on pain of losing the fur lining and the clothing on which it is found. It shall all be given as the consuls decide, and as they know of it.]

[3] Item que deguna dona ni autra femna d'esta vila ni de la honor no porta ni auze portar / garlanda de neguna maniera ni de neguna cauza, mas quant tan solament de pretz / de .x. sols de tornes negres o d'aqui en aval entrefatcho, e als. E que non aia / ni pusca aver mas quant doas et no plus daquel aval for, o daqui en aval, aitant quant aquelas dura/-aran si no era de flors, o de fulha, o d'erba, exceptadas jotglaressas e putas, o n'en era estada, en / pena de un milhier de teole pla e de perdre la garlanda. Que seria tot donat a qui on / los cossols establirio, et a lor conoguda.

[No lady or other woman of the territory may wear or dare to wear a garland of any material or of any style, but only (one) offered at a market price of 10 black sols tournois or less, and otherwise.[2] She will not and may not have more than two at that market price, and no more—or from that price down—or for as long as (the garlands) will last, unless it is made of flowers, greenery, or herbs—except for those of performers and prostitutes, in whom it (the garland) had not been (regulated)—on pain of a fine of a full one thousand bricks and losing the garland. It all shall be given as the consuls decide, and as they know of it.]

[4] Item que deguna dona ni autra femna d'esta vila / ni de la honor no porte ni auze portar botos d'aur ni d'argen ni de seda ni de ne-/guna autra cauza, sino o fazio tro a .x. botos en cascuna rauba; e aquels botos que sio redons / e plas, ses tota autra obra; e que cascu boto sia de pretz de .iii. tornes negres, e d'aqui en aval; / entre fatcha e als. Et que non meta n'auze portar en neguna salhadura, exceptadas jot-/glaressas e putas o non era estada, en pena de perdre los botos e la rauba en que seria. Et que seria / tot donat a qui on los cossols establirio, e a lor conoguda.

[No lady or other woman of this town or the territory shall wear or dare to wear buttons of either gold, silver, silk, unless (it is) up to ten buttons per garment. The buttons should be round and flat, not worked in any other fashion, and only offered at a market price of 3 black tournois and no more, and otherwise. No one should put them on or dare wear them on any outdoor garment—except for performers and prostitutes, on whom it had not been (regulated)—on pain of losing the buttons and garment on which they are found. It all shall be given to whomever the consuls decide, and as they know of it.]

[5] Item que deguna dona ni au-/tra femna d'esta vila ni de la honor, quant levara dessas jassilhas, no fassa ni auze far /ditnar, ni manjar, ni negu autre covit de neguna persona, si no era que estes en l'ostal / de la jazent, exceptadas jot-glaressas e putas o non era estada, en pena de .v. sols de caors per cada / persona que manjaria; e que'l maritz de la jazent seria tengutz e destreg de pagar, per cada persona

---

2   "Otherwise" might indicate coinage other than tournois, or perhaps garlands made of other materials. The referent is unclear.

[Fol. 75r]
que manjaria e per cada vegada, aqui on los cossols establirio, e a lor conoguda.

[No lady or other woman of this town or the surrounding territory, when she rises from her lying-in, may invite or dare to invite any guests to dine or eat, or other person, if it is not in the home of the new mother, except entertainers and prostitutes, on whom (this edict) did not bear, on pain of a fine of 5 sous of Cahors for each person who is eating. The husband of the new mother shall be held and obliged to pay for each person who is eating, each time, to whomever the consuls decide, according to their judgment and to their knowledge.]

[6] Item que /neguna dona ni autra femna ni d'esta vila ni de la honor no porte ni auze portar en ne- / guna dessas raubas cabessalha trop escolatada, mas quant en bona maniera, exceptadas / jotglaressas e putas, on non era estada.

[No lady or other woman of this town or the territory shall dare wear on any of her garments a neckline that is cut too low, but only one in the good manner—except for performers and prostitutes, for whom it had not been (regulated).]

[7] Item que neguna dona ni autra femna ni d'esta vila ni / de la honor no cortege ni auze cortejar neguna jazent, si no era cozina segonda d'elas / o de so marit, o cozina germana, o d'aqui en amont, o comaires; e aquelas que o pusco far / tant solamen lo ditmigne, e no a negun autre dia de la setmana, exceptadas jotglaressas e putas / o n'en era estada, en pena de .v. sols de caors per cada persona e per cada vegada; e qu'el maritz seria tengut e destreg / de pagar per la molher, aqui on los cossols establirio, e a lor conoguda.

[No lady or other woman of this town or the territory should visit or dare to visit any new mother if she is not at least her second cousin, or that of her husband, or first cousin, henceforth, or godmothers; and they may only visit on Sundays, and no other day of the week, on pain of a fine of 5 sous of Cahors per person, each time. The husband will obliged and compelled to pay for his wife, as the consuls decide, and as they know of it.]

[8] Item que / neguna dona ni autra femna d'esta vila o de la honor no covide ni auze covidar ni anar / covidar per nossas ni per autres manjars, mas quant tant solament de .iiii. donas, e no plus / exceptadas jotglaressas e putas, o non ero estadas, en pena de .v. sols de caors per cada persona, e per cada / vegada; e que li marit serio tengut e destreg de pagar per las molhers, aqui on los cossols / establirio, e a lor conoguda.

[No lady or other woman of this town or the territory may invite, dare to invite, or go to invite, more than four ladies to weddings or other feasts, and no more—except for performers and prostitutes, for whom it has not been (regulated), on pain of a fine of 5 sous of Cahors per person on each occasion. The husbands will be obliged and compelled to pay for the wives, as the consuls decide, and as they know of it.]

[9] Item que negus hom ni neguna fenna d'esta vila ni de la honor / no sia ni pusca esser a negunas fermalhas de nobia, mas quant tant solament .x. prozomes / e .x. donas de cada partida, exceptat l'escriva, en pena de .v. sols de caors per cada persona e per cada / [vegada] e que los maritz serio tengutz e destregs de pagar per lors molhers, aqui on los cossols establirio, e a lor co-/noguda.

[No man or woman of this town or territory may be present at any wedding engagement, but only ten good men and ten ladies for each side, not including the scribe, on pain of a fine of 5 sous of Cahors per person per (time). The husbands will be held and obliged to pay for their wives, as the consuls decide, and as they know of it.]

[10] Item que negus hom ni neguna femna d'esta vila ni de la honor no fasso ni auzo / far covit ni manjars per razo de fermalhas de nobia, ni quant anara a gleia, en pena / de .v. sols caorces per cada persona e per cada vegada e que li marit serio tengutz e destregs de / pagar per las molhers, a qui on los cossols establirio, e a lor conoguda.

[No man or woman of this town or territory shall hold or dare to hold a feast or meal for a marriage engagement or when they go to church, on pain of a fine of 5 sous of Cahors per person per time. The husbands will be held and obliged to pay for the wives, to whomever the consuls decide, and as they know of it.]

[11] Item que negus hom / d'esta vila ni de la honor no ane ni auze anar ab neguna nobia, per assolassar per / carriera, si no a fazia quant lo maritz la prendria e la cobiaria, tant solament, en pena / de .v. sols de caors per cada persona e per cada vegada. Et seria donat a qui on los cossuls establirio, e a / lor conguda.

[No man of this town or territory shall go or dare to go with any bride to escort her through the streets, if not doing it when the husband will take her and accompany her, and only then, on pain of a fine of 5 sous of Cahors per person on each occasion, and it shall be given as the consuls decree, and according to their judgment.]

[12] Item que negus hom d'esta vila ni de la honor, que pregna molher, no / done ni auze donar, ni home ni fenna per lui ni e nom de lui, ab gen ni ses gen, neguna / maniera de joias, a neguna persona, foras de l'ostal en que seria la nobia, en pena de / .xxx. sols de caors, que.lh costaria per cada persona a cui ne daria. Los quals serio donat a qui / on los cossuls establirio, e a lor conguda.

[No man of this town or territory, when he takes a wife, shall give or dare to give, nor any man or woman (to give) for him or in his name, in private or in public, any kind of jewels to any person, outside of the home where the bride will be, on pain of a fine of 30 sous of Cahors, that it would cost him for each person to whom he would give any; which (sous) would be given to whomever the consuls would decide, and as they know of it.]

[13] Item que negus hom ni neguna fenna d'esta / vila ni de la honor, que fassa filhol o filhola, quel pairis no'lh done ni'lh auze donar, ab / gen ni ses gen, mas quant de .i. dinier d'argent, o daqui en aval, e la mairina autre / denier aital meteihs o daqui en aval. E tot lo romanent d'albolas e d'als, tro en .vi. sols de caorces, en pena de .xx. sols de caors per cada vegada. Que serio donat a qui / on los cossols establirio, e a lor conoguda.

[No man or any woman of this town or territory, when they consecrate a godson or goddaughter, the godfather shall not give nor dare to give him, in public or in private, more than one silver denier, and the godmother another denier just the same, and no more, in public or in private. And all the remainder for the baptismal gown and anything else, up to 6 sous of Cahors, on pain of a fine of 20 sous of Cahors each time, which shall be given to whomever the consuls would decide, and as they know of it.]

[14] Item que negus hom ni neguna femna / d'esta vila o de la honor, a negunas cortz de nobia, no done ni auze donar, ni home / ni femna per lui ni e nom de lui, ab gen ni ses gen, raubas a jotglars ni a jotglaressas/
[Fol. 75v]
d'esta vila ni de foras, en pena de .xx. sols de caors per cada rauba et per cada vegada. E serio / tot donat a qui on los cossols establirio, e a lor conoguda.

[No man or woman of this town or territory, at any wedding feast, shall give or dare to give—or any man or woman in their name, in public or private—clothing to jongleurs or jongleuresses, either from this town or from elsewhere, on pain of 20 sous of Cahors per garment per time. And they (the sous) would all be given to whomever the consuls decide, and as they know of it.]

[15] Item que negus jotglars / ni jotlaressas, privatz ni estranhs, no intre ni auze intrar en ostal d'esta vila ni / de la honor, a nossas ni a covitz, ni a jazens, ni a nadal, ni en las festas de nadal, si ape-/latz o no i era, per aquela persona que mas de poder y auria; que aquel o aquela que o / faria / seria for jetatz d'esta vila e de la honor, per totz tems.

[No jongleurs or jongleuresses, from here or elsewhere, may enter or dare enter a home in this town or this territory, for a wedding, a lying-in, Christmas, or a Christmas feast, whether (he was) invited or not by the person who had the most power to do so. The man or woman who did it will be thrown out of this town and territory for all time.]

[16] Item que negus sartre d'esta vila / ni de la honor no talhe ni auze talhar neguna rauba, a neguna dona de esta vila ni de / la honor, mas quant tan solament que aia .i. palm de drap outra terra, e no plus, e que la rauba / sia tota redonda, so es assaber

que sia tan longua denant coma darreire a bone fe, en pena / de .xx. sols d*e caor*s, e q*ue* no talharia may rauba en esta vila ni en la honor.

[No tailor of this town or territory shall cut or dare to cut any garment, for any lady of this town or the territory, that has any more than a palm width of fabric on the ground, and no more, and the garment must be the same length all around, which is to say the same length in the front and the back, in good faith, on pain of a fine of 20 sous of Cahors and being prohibited from tailoring any clothing again in this town and territory.]

[**17**] Item establiro / q*ue* cascu capitol, quant sera mes en creat, cascu an noelament juro a gardar e a manten/-ner los establimens sobrescriutz.

[They decreed that every consul, when put in place and created, each year, swear to uphold and maintain the abovesaid decrees.]

[**18**] Item q*ue* tug li home d'esta vila et de la honor, de .xv. ans / en amont, juro a tener e a gardar e a mantener e a conservar los establimens sobredigs / quant p*er* lo capitol ne serio requeregut. Tots aquestz establimens sobredigs fero / lo viguier el capitol sobredigs. Salva e retenguda la volontat de nostre senhor lo rei / defransa e dessa cort. Lo capitols sobredigs e tug li autre prodome sotz escriutz jurero / los .iiij. sanz avangelitz a tener e a gardar e a mantener totz los establimens sobrescriutz/p*er* totz temps; et aisso a jurar en la forma sobredicha.

[The men of this town and territory, from the age of fifteen up, swear to keep and uphold and maintain and preserve the abovesaid decrees, when they will be required (to do so) by the *Capitol*. All these abovesaid decrees were made by the *viguier* and the *Capitol* as said above. With all respect for the will of our lord the King of France and his court, the abovesaid consuls and all the other good men, undersigned, swore to keep and uphold and maintain all the abovesaid decrees for all time and to swear this in the abovesaid form.]

Semper Ubi Sub Ubi: Representations of Male Underwear in Northern European Art, 1140–1450

Carla Tilghman[1]

Semper ubi sub ubi is an old joke among Latin students that translates as "always where under where," but is, of course, heard as "always wear underwear." It is a cute joke and recalls the motherly adage that one should always wear clean underwear in case of an accident. Embedded in such sayings are powerful cultural ideas about protection, modesty, and cleanliness—all of which can be afforded to an individual through the wearing of undergarments.

Undergarments, despite being an often humble and usually hidden piece of apparel, are foundational, both physically and ideologically. Underwear worn by male-presenting figures (referred to as *braies* or *braga* in French, Italian, English, and Spanish medieval literature) appears in both secular and sacred images.[2] By focusing on a selection of Northern European illuminations and panel paintings created between 1140 and 1450, I examine the metonymic nature of visual representations of *braies*: underwear as a stand-in for the body and ideas about the body.

The verism predominant in Northern European images also allows for a close examination of stylistic as well as ideological evolutions of *braies* as they appear on depictions of male figures. The garment reveals and reinforces ideas of constructed masculinity, male prowess, cleanliness, sanctity, shame, and lack of shame. *Braies* also serve to emphasize the voyeuristic nature of looking at images: the viewer, gazing at scantily clad men, can encounter didactic lessons on humility, admire the outline of shapely buttocks, or both.[3]

While little has been written about underwear in general and even less about *braies* in particular, three authors have discussed some specific examples of medieval

---

1 A version of this paper was presented at a session organized by DISTAFF at the 2023 International Congress on Medieval Studies in Kalamazoo, Michigan.
2 From French *braies*, from Old French *braies*, plural of *braie*, from Latin *braca*. For a detailed discussion of the etymology, see E. Jane Burns, "Ladies Don't Wear *Braies*: Underwear and Outerwear in the French *Prose Lancelot*," in *The Lancelot-Grail Cycle: Text and Transformations*, ed. William W. Kibler (Austin: University of Texas Press, 1994), 152–53.
3 For other references that discuss garments and the construction of meaning, see Désirée Koslin and Janet Snyder, eds., *Encountering Medieval Textiles and Dress: Objects, Texts,*

literature where *braies* are mentioned and used as a metaphor. E. J. Burns, in analyzing the French *Prose Lancelot*, sought to understand uses of male underwear but discovered that "… as I read more and more, I learned less and less. Indeed, the very characteristic that defines underwear—its being worn beneath another garment—makes it literally invisible and historically elusive."[4] Through literary references, Burns notes that *braies*—whether loose or tight-fitting—are an exclusively male garment.[5] Stephanie Hathaway discusses *braies* specifically as they relate to the tale of Guillaume d'Orange in the *chanson de geste Le Moniage Guillaume* (covered in more detail below).[6] Hathaway analyses how Guillaume's *braies* work as a literary stand-in for ideas of trickery, prowess, and spirituality, and that *Le Moniage Guillaume* is not the only medieval tale where *braies* were used to represent these notions. Guillaume's adventures happen outside of the monastery to which he has retired. Leah Shopkow's article "Mooning the Abbot" focuses on the wearing (or not) of undergarments inside Benedictine orders and the shunning of such fanciness among the Cistercians.[7]

While these pieces, published between 1994 and 2017, were written by women, using a variety of analytical lenses, Sarah-Grace Heller has observed that most of the literature from and about the 1140–1450 time frame considered in this paper was written by men, whose descriptions of garments tended to emphasize the male gaze toward the female body, clothed or disrobed.[8] The visual arts in the same period were predominantly commissioned, and almost exclusively made, by men for targeted male consumption. And while there was certainly no lack of female figures (clothed and unclothed) for the male gaze, there were also male figures, presented singly or in groups, displaying sartorial elegance or near nakedness, exhibiting political prowess or abject devotional humility, who were also subject to the male gaze. This paper will consider how the portrayal of *braies* on the male body intertwined religious ecstatic mysticism with heteronormative and homoerotic readings by both covering and revealing the body and cultural meaning.

Images (New York: Palgrave Macmillan, 2002); Louise Sylvester, "Technical Vocabulary and Medieval Text Types," *Neuphilologische Mitteilungen* 16, no. 1 (March 2016): 155–77; E. Jane Burns, *Sea of Silk: A Textile Geography of Women's Work in Medieval French Literature* (Philadelphia: University of Pennsylvania Press, 2009); Roze Hentschell, "Treasonous Textiles: Foreign Cloth and the Construction of Englishness," *Journal of Medieval and Early Modern Studies* 32, no. 3 (2007); Kristen Tibbs, "'Semiotics of the cloth': Reading Medieval Norse Textile Traditions" (M.A. thesis, Marshall University, 2012); Charlotte Newman Goldy and Amy Livingstone, eds., *Writing Medieval Women's Lives* (New York: Palgrave Macmillan, 2012).

4 Burns, "Ladies Don't Wear *Braies*," 153.

5 Burns, "Ladies Don't Wear *Braies*," 159.

6 Stephanie Hathaway, "*Pour ses braies se porra courecier*: The Preservation of Guillaume's Pants in *Moniage*," *Journal of the Australian Early Medieval Association* 5 (2009): 55–64.

7 Leah Shopkow, "Mooning the Abbot: A Tale of Disorder, Vulgarity, Ethnicity, and Underwear in the Monastery," in *Prowess, Piety, and Public Order in Medieval Society*, ed. Craig M. Nakashian and Daniel P. Franke (Leiden, Netherlands: Brill, 2017), 179–98.

8 Sarah-Grace Heller, "Anxiety, Hierarchy, and Appearance in Thirteenth-Century Sumptuary Laws and the *Roman de la Rose*," *French Historical Studies* 27, no. 2 (2004): 311–48.

What are *braies*?[9] The word comes from French and Latin, but there are other ways of describing this garment that was worn under clothes, around the hips (often loosely), tied at the waist, and made from undyed cloth (fig. 5.1). The Carolingians referred to the upper-class version of such a garment as *femoralia* because it touched and covered the thighs, while the lower-class equivalent was called a *subligaculum*, often worn as a loincloth cinched at the waist and passing between the legs more like a cloth diaper.[10] François Boucher wrote that Charlemagne was described as wearing a linen *femoralia* beneath his gaiters (*tibiales*).[11] French thirteenth- and fourteenth-century literature consistently uses the term *braies* when such an undergarment is (rarely) mentioned. Rather than risk confusion with contemporary meanings by trying to translate *braies* into English ("shorts," "drawers," "underwear," "briefs," "panties"?), *braies* will be used here to describe the various iterations that evolved from the knee-length, trouser-like garments of the twelfth century to the short, snug briefs seen in the fifteenth century.[12]

The only apparent extant example of *braies* comes from Lengberg Castle, Nikolsdorf, Austria. It dates from approximately the fifteenth century, and was found not as part of a burial, but rather the infill of building work.[13] Constructed of an hourglass-shaped piece of linen and held together by narrow strips of linen that would tie around the hips, this garment still raises more questions than it answers. Typically identified in current literature as "male underwear," it is still unclear if this was a specifically gendered garment.[14] What argues for a "male" garment is the similarity to mid-to-late-fifteenth-century depictions of a "bikini brief" style.[15]

Mentions of clothing in literature and depictions in art are source material for researchers when such garments no longer survive. In the case of male undergarments, Gale Owen-Crocker has noted that "authors of Old English heroic poetry were only interested in garments which were war-gear [...] of the garments worn underneath the mailcoat [...] we are told nothing."[16]

---

9 For general discussion of undergarments, see Stella Mary Pearce, "The Study of Costume in Painting," *Studies in Conservation* 4, no. 4 (Nov. 1959): 127–39; Chrystel Brandenburgh, *Clothes Make the Man: Early Medieval Textiles from the Netherlands* (Leiden, Netherlands: Leiden University Press, 2016), 25–52; Andrea Denny-Brown, *Fashioning Change: The Trope of Clothing in High- and Late-Medieval England* (Columbus: Ohio State University Press, 2010), 11, 13–26.

10 Doreen Yarwood, *Costume in the Western World: Pictorial Guide and Glossary* (New York: St. Martin's Press, 1980), 5.

11 François Boucher, *20,000 Years of Fashion* (New York: H. H. Abrams, 1987), 157.

12 I am indebted to Burns for her struggles with trying to translate *braies*. Burns, "Ladies Don't Wear Braies," 152–55.

13 Elizabeth Coatsworth and Gale R. Owen-Crocker, *Clothing the Past: Surviving Garments from Early Medieval to Early Modern Western Europe* (Leiden, Netherlands: Brill, 2018), 273–78.

14 Coatsworth and Owen-Crocker, *Clothing the Past*, 273–308.

15 Coatsworth and Owen-Crocker (*Clothing the Past*, 278) cite one example in the *Flagellation of Christ* in Chapelle Saint-Antoine at Bessans, France.

16 Gale R. Owen-Crocker, *Dress in Anglo-Saxon England*, revised and enlarged edition (Woodbridge, UK: Boydell, 2004), 20–21.

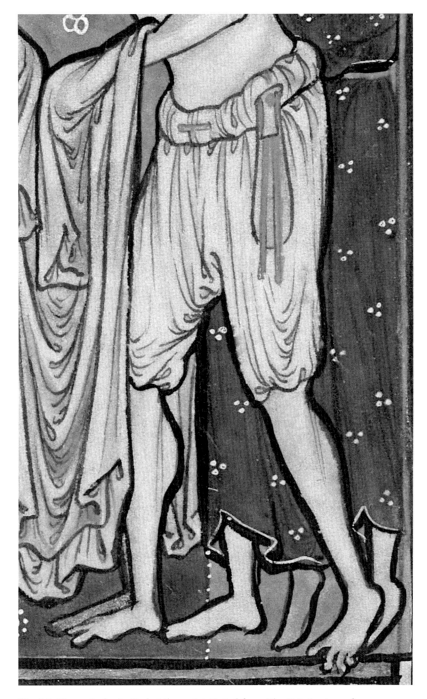

Fig. 5.1: Figure in *braies* tied at the waist. Detail from The Trinity Apocalypse (Cambridge, England, Trinity College, MS R.16.2), fol. 30r, 1250. Photo: The Master and Fellows of Trinity College, Cambridge, by permission.

Little is known about the construction of linen male undergarments, unlike, for instance, woolen garments that have survived in the anaerobic conditions of bog burials largely intact.[17] However, the evolution of male *braies* is evident in depictions of the garment in the visual arts. The *Martyrologe-Obituaire de Saint-Germain-des-Prés* (ca. 1250–90) shows rye threshers wearing loose, knee-length *braies* that are rolled over a belt or cord at the waist (fig. 5.2). Yet the wheat harvester pictured in the Vienna *Tacuinum Sanitatis* (ca. 1380–99) is wearing the much shorter, tighter set of *braies*, often pictured paired with hose and worn under shorter robes (fig. 5.3). *Braies*, it would seem, followed the same evolution as male outerwear, moving from loose, draping garments to tighter and more fitted ones from the twelfth to the fifteenth centuries. *Braies* are consistently pictured as white- or cream-colored, undyed cloth, and it is reasonable, given chronology and geography, to assume that they were made from linen.

At their most basic, *braies* provided a multidirectional protective barrier. The body was protected against friction from outer garments, which were, in turn, shielded from bodily oils, sweat, urine, feces, and other fluids. Braies also functioned like outer clothing in that they insulated the wearer from the weather. But as Sarah-Grace Heller notes, "Clothing is a guarantee of protection and shelter beyond the simple way it covers the body; it grants the wearer 'space' in the community."[18] For upper classes with, at times, fairly rigidly constructed modes of acceptable dress, wearing *braies* incorrectly could result in ridicule and damage one's community "space." For example, by the fourteenth century, there was a distinction between "inner" (unlined) and "outer" (lined) *braies*. An account of Edward III's wardrobe includes six pairs of lined *robarum* and twelve pairs of "old style" (unlined) *robarum* for wear underneath a robe.[19] Unlined braies were appropriate to wear under longer garments, while the lined, and presumably thicker, braies were to be worn under fashionable shorter tunics. Improperly fashioned or lack of outer *braies* might lead to youthful wearers being mocked for showing their bottoms to all when bending over to serve their lords, at least according to the anonymous author of the *Grandes Chroniques de France* (1344–50). The author attributed the loss of the French at the battle of Crecy (1346) to God's punishment for the pride and indecency seen in contemporary French fashion.[20] *Braies*, in this example, became the seat of friction between English and French identity, moral and immoral presentation, and (homo)sexual tension among upper-class men. Underwear represented identity, decency (or lack thereof), humor, and desire, all topics that are covered below in more depth.

For peasant laborers, *braies* not only provided protection from sun, dust, and chaff during the summer and fall harvesting seasons but also may have functioned to

17 Naomi Tarrant, *The Development of Costume* (Edinburgh: National Museums of Scotland, 1994), 40.
18 Heller, "Anxiety, Hierarchy, and Appearance," 330.
19 Stella Mary Newton, *Fashion in the Age of the Black Prince: A Study of the Years 1340–1365* (Woodbridge, UK: Boydell, 1980), 17.
20 Newton, *Fashion in the Age of the Black Prince*, 10.

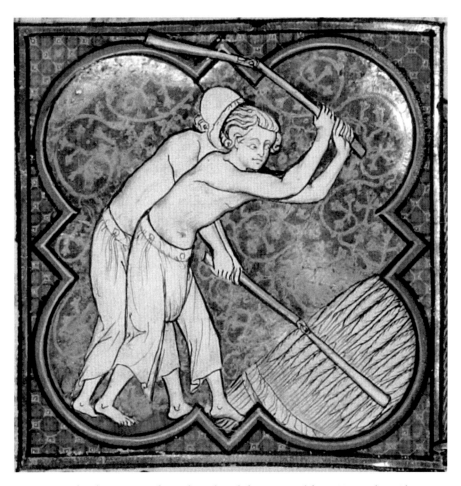

Fig. 5.2: Rye threshers wearing loose, knee-length *braies*. Detail from *Martyrologe-Obituaire de Saint-Germain-des-Prés* (Paris, Bibliothèque Nationale de France, MS Lat. 12834), fol. 64v, ca. 1250–90. Photo: Courtesy of Bibliothèque Nationale de France.

mark the wearer as a part of the larger enterprise of harvesting, an activity that both served their overlord and provided food for the community (fig. 5.4). While being partially clothed during communal labor could be positively experienced as inclusive, the removal of outer garments could also be exclusive. The stripping of martyrs was generally done to remove the protection, both physical and psychological, of outer clothes ahead of physical torture and execution. Images of male martyrs shown only in their *braies* suggest that they have been forced into a greater state of vulnerability, allowing easier access to the corporeal body (fig. 5.6).

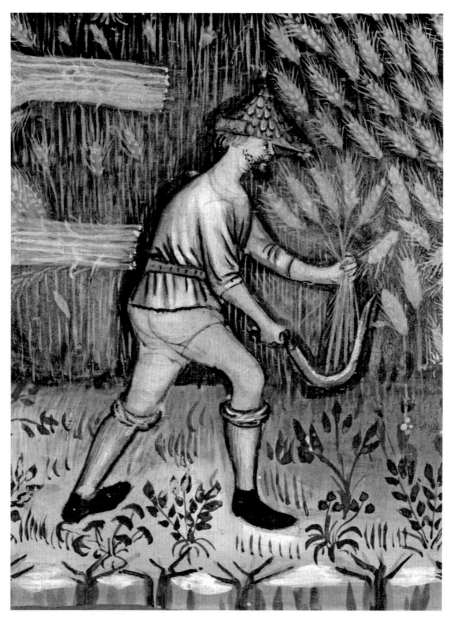

Fig. 5.3: Harvester wearing *braies* and rolled-down hose. Detail from *Tacuinum Sanitatis* (Vienna, Österreichische Nationalbibliothek, Cod. ser. n. 2644), fol. 46v, ca. 1380–99. Photo: Courtesy of Österreichische Nationalbibliothek, by permission.

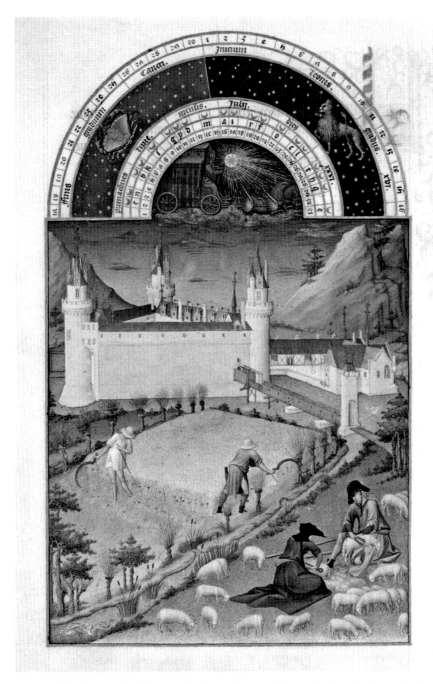

Fig. 5.4: Calendar page for July, showing harvesting and sheep shearing. Limbourg Brothers, *Les Très Riches Heures du Duc de Berry* (Chantilly, France, Bibliothèque du Musée Condé, MS 65), fol. 7v, 1412–16. Photo: Courtesy of Agence Photographique de la Réunion des Musées Nationaux.

MAKING IDENTITY

In terms of social rather than physical function, we know that medieval clothing was used to indicate class difference, to distinguish individuals through heraldry, to identify religious orders, and to "single out pilgrims, Jews, Muslims, heretics, lepers, prostitutes, the insane and individuals condemned to death."[21] Laws from the thirteenth and fourteenth centuries, particularly in France, show that arbiters of fashion were mostly concerned with stabilizing class hierarchy through the limiting of clothing consumption and display.[22] As Heller notes, the "French laws of 1279 and 1294 are intent on regulating the correlation between status, income, and expenditure on materials for clothing. Unlike typical laws from the fourteenth century onward, they do not attempt to regulate the minutiae of particular styles, cuts, or modes of embellishment."[23] Despite their appearance in literature such as the *Chroniques, braies* are not mentioned in the reams of sumptuary laws. In France, such laws became increasingly focused on garment details such as trim, cut, length, and color, and gradually included the lesser nobles and knights in the middle-income brackets, yet *braies* do not make an appearance in sumptuary law. Underwear seemed to have little to do with upward social mobility.[24]

CONSTRUCTED MASCULINITY

Clothes do not necessarily make fixed identities. It is not unusual to find an examination of constructed "masculinity" approached by putting it in opposition to constructed "femininity."[25] Male maturation was often characterized by the separation of young men from "female" environs and sites of womanliness. Secular law and biblical doctrine during the late Middle Ages served to reinforce ideas of sexual inequality that had been inherited from the classical world. Attitudes toward gendered behavior and activity were made and then remade through evolving stereotypes in literature and visual arts.[26] For instance, Christ in the diminutive *Book of Hours of Jeanne D'Evreux* (1324–28) is depicted as a well-muscled, mature man (fig. 5.5). His genitals are covered so that the young queen and her ladies could avoid prurient voyeurism and instead

21 E. Jane Burns, *Courtly Love Undressed: Reading Through Clothes in Medieval French Culture* (Philadelphia: University of Pennsylvania Press, 2004), 2.
22 Heller, "Anxiety, Hierarchy, and Appearance," 317.
23 Heller, "Anxiety, Hierarchy, and Appearance," 318.
24 Heller, "Anxiety, Hierarchy, and Appearance," 318.
25 For scholars who are dealing with the fluidity of gendered clothing and visual presentation, see Joan Cadden, *Meanings of Sexual Difference in the Middle Ages: Medicine, Science, and Culture* (Cambridge: Cambridge University Press, 1993), 70–117; Susan Crane, *Gender and Romance in Chaucer's Canterbury Tales* (Princeton, NJ: Princeton University Press, 1994), 93–131; Roberta L. Krueger, "Constructing Sexual Identities in the High Middle Ages: The Didactic Poetry of Robert de Blois," *Paragraph* 13 (1990): 105–31.
26 Burns, *Courtly Love Undressed*, 17. Such depictions were often "then enshrined in legal, religious, educational, scientific and political doctrines."

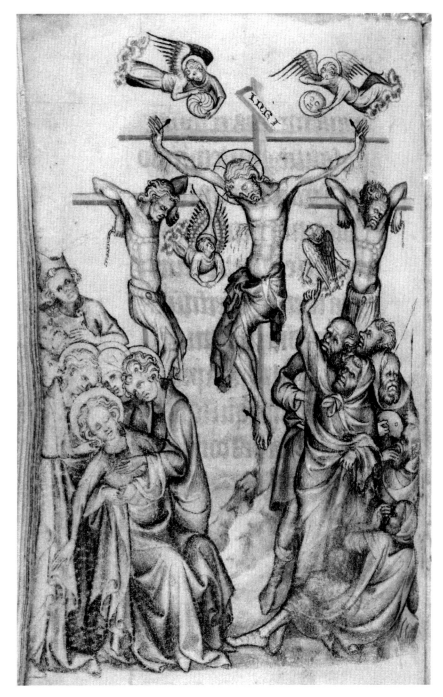

Fig. 5.5: Crucifixion. Jean Pucelle, *Hours of Jeanne D'Evreux* (New York, Metropolitan Museum of Art, Cloisters Collection, MS 54.1.2), fol. 68v, ca. 1324–28. Photo: Courtesy of the Metropolitan Museum of Art.

focus on the mortification of his flesh and ideal sacrifice. Yet even artworks seemingly made for women were ultimately about masculine performance. The *Hours of Jeanne d'Evreux* was commissioned for her by her new husband Charles IV le Bel (d. 1328), and while it functioned as a private prayer book for female use, it still spoke more of masculine desire (in this case for a male heir) than of female piety.[27]

But not all constructions of masculinity pitted "male" against "female." Particularly among the upper and knightly classes, competition between men and domination of other men were even more important than the maintenance of hierarchical power over women.[28] Male-for-male performance took many forms such as real and staged combat, political maneuvering, land ownership, object acquisition, and ensuring the continuation of lineage. Men commissioned works of art in order to display their wealth, education, and generosity. For example, Rogier van der Weyden's altarpiece the *Descent from the Cross* (before 1443) was commissioned by the Leuven Guild of Archers (*Schutterij*) for the Chapel of Our Lady Outside the Walls at Leuven where it would be on display for everyone, but particularly other masculine guild members, to see and admire.[29] Such guild commissions were both politic and pious, a way for guild members (most of whom were men) to display their civic pride (and power), their humble devotion, and their wealth to their community, but especially to members of other guilds.[30]

A more intimate confluence of *braies* and masculinity played itself out in the workaday spaces of monastic communities. During the Middle Ages, the rules for monastic clothing came largely from the Benedictine Rule. Monks did not usually wear undergarments, but a communally owned pair of *braies* kept in the monastery's wardrobe could be "checked out" by a monk embarking on a journey so long as the drawers were washed and put back upon return.[31] *Braies* shared among men in this way represented communal space rather literally and, in this instance, occupied a liminal space between secular and sacred. *Braies* were worn out into the secular world for both practical and spiritual reasons. The garment provided protection from the environment, and presumably added a bit of comfort to anyone riding a donkey while traveling. *Braies* also afforded a monk modesty, covering their genitalia and buttocks from view and offering a practical and psychological barrier to any temptations toward sin.[32]

---

27 Madeline H. Caviness, "Patron or Matron? A Capetian Bride and a Vade Mecum for Her Marriage Bed," *Speculum* 68, no. 2 (April 1993): 333–62.

28 Ruth Mazo Karras, *From Boys to Men: Formations of Masculinity in Late Medieval Europe* (Philadelphia: Pennsylvania University Press, 2003), 67–75.

29 Rogier van der Weyden, *Descent from the Cross*, oil on panel (Madrid, Museo Nacional del Prado, no. P002825), viewable at https://www.museodelprado.es/en/the-collection/art-work/the-descent-from-the-cross/856d822a-dd22-4425-bebd-920a1d416aa7 (accessed July 16, 2024).

30 Lorne Campbell and Jan van der Stock, *Rogier van der Weyden 1400–1464: Master of Passions* (Leuven, Belgium: Davidsfonds, 2009).

31 Karras, *From Boys to Men*, 62.

32 Shopkow, "Mooning the Abbott," 179–98.

In a more spiritual sense, masculinity among sacred communities was expressed not just in terms of communal responsibility, but also through religious courage or resolve. Katherine Lewis writes "hagiography suggests that nothing defined a monk's manly strength better than the struggle for virginity or chastity."[33] As in the secular upper classes, men in sacred communities, especially cloistered ones, inevitably performed their religious masculinity for one another.

However, the saints themselves and religious followers rarely led absolutely chaste lives.[34] Even if the martyrs struggled with their religious resolve, paintings and illuminations of them could act as moral stand-ins: visual representations of perpetually chaste figures designed to be used not only as devotional images for prayer but also as visual reminders to the laity of the ultimate goals of devotional masculinity. However, the secular and sacred versions of performative masculinity often clashed. P. J. P. Goldberg shows that "[a]s part of discussion of the evils of lechery, pastoral texts often noted that men who committed this sin were keen to advertise it. *Dives and Pauper*, a fifteenth-century commentary on the Ten Commandments, possibly authored by a Franciscan friar, laments that the shameful state of affairs is such that men are more embarrassed by chastity than lechery."[35] Medieval and early Renaissance constructions of masculinity were complex, and different communities were served by distinct and sometimes contradictory formations.

SACRED *BRAIES*

Devotional images that were commissioned and produced by men were generally available to both the lay and religious male communities. Martyred male figures clad only in *braies* were routinely on public or semi-public display, such as on altarpieces that showed crucifixion scenes like the *Kaufmann Crucifixion* (ca. 1340).[36] The *braies* on a martyred body functioned in several seemingly contradictory ways. *Braies* as a cover for the male genitalia reminded the viewer of Adam's original sin in disobeying God's commandments—eating from the Tree of Knowledge and becoming aware of shame and his own nakedness. *Braies* as a genital cover also reinforced the sanctity of martyrs even as the carnality of the otherwise naked body was exposed to the elements and to torture. The white cloth of *braies* created a visual contrast with the (sometimes torn and battered) flesh and so emphasized the unclothed body as a site of devotion for the viewer and religious physical ecstasy for the martyr. Late medieval and early Renaissance paintings and illuminations, particularly in Northern Europe,

33 Katherine J. Lewis, "Male Saints and Devotional Masculinity in Late Medieval England," *Gender and History* 24, no. 1 (April 2012), 114.

34 Virginia Burrus, *The Sex Lives of the Saints: An Erotics of Ancient Hagiography* (Philadelphia: University of Pennsylvania Press, 2004), 45–68.

35 P. J. P. Goldberg, "Masters and Men in Later Medieval England," in *Masculinity in Medieval Europe*, ed. Dawn M. Hadley (London: Longman, 1999), 56–70, at 63.

36 Unknown artist (Berlin, Gemäldegalerie, Staatliche Museen, no. 1833), viewable at https://smb.museum-digital.de/object/61522 (accessed Dec. 30, 2024).

incorporated contemporaneous details such as clothing, furniture, and architecture to create humanist images with which the viewer could feel a greater affinity. The outer garments pictured in images such as the *Martyrdom of St. Hippolytus*[37] (ca. 1490–1500; fig. 5.6) and the *Kaufmann Crucifixion* seem to accurately reflect garment styles and fashion evolutions; it is not a stretch to assume that the *braies* are similarly reflective of contemporary fashion.

In the central panel of the *Triptych with Scenes from the Life of Christ and Mary* by the Master of the Collins Hours[38] (ca. 1440), a continuous narrative presentation of Christ and the two thieves being led to their deaths is in the foreground, and in the background the three figures are crucified before a crowd. Dressed in a pink robe with jeweled borders, belted at the waist, Christ carries his cross, while the two thieves are wearing white knee-length tunics. On their respective crosses, they are all naked except for a loin covering. The two thieves appear to be wearing opaque linen *braies*, while Christ is wearing a transparent drape. The groin coverings are used to create visual distinction between the sacred statuses of the figures: Christ's sanctity and ultimately unearthly holiness are suggested through both the nod to opulence in his pink (possibly faded from red) robe and the ephemeral modesty drape.[39] He is visually and spiritually separate from the more mundane thieves who wear contemporary garb. Christ's garments are ageless, fictional coverings that speak to his sanctity, his otherworldliness, and the transient nature of the physical body itself.

Even private devotional books use distinguishing undergarments. The Crucifixion scene in the *Hours of Jeanne d'Evreux*, delicately crafted in grisaille by Jean Pucelle, crowds biblical figures together along with small winged beings who flit among the crosses (fig. 5.5). The bodies below Christ are dressed in generic robes that signal the historicity of the figures. Christ's hips are covered with a thick, improbably draped cloth, while the thieves are each clothed in early-fourteenth-century knee-length *braies*. Just as the unknown artist did in *Scenes from the Life of Christ and Mary*, Pucelle intentionally used recognizable, contemporary undergarments to create visual distinction between the sacred figures and the more mundane thieves and to allow the viewers to see themselves in the thieves. The tiny depiction of *braies* invited young

37 Unknown artist (Boston, Museum of Fine Arts, Walter M. Cabot Fund, acc. no. 63.660.1).
38 Madrid, Museo Nacional del Prado, no. P002538, viewable at https://www.museo-delprado.es/en/the-collection/art-work/triptych-with-scenes-from-the-life-of-christ-and/39740f98-336b-4d80-8120-bd6e0c4bd96f (accessed Oct. 28, 2024).
39 In some instances, red paint has been noted to have faded to pink. It's not clear whether that is the case in this instance, nor has there been a study done on *Scenes from the Life of Christ and Mary* to determine whether the original paint was red or pink. Irina Petroviciu, "Red Dyes from West to East in Medieval Europe: From Portuguese Manuscript Illuminations to Romanian Textiles," in *Textile Crossroads: Exploring European Clothing, Identity, and Culture Across Millennia*, ed. Kerstin Droß-Krüpe, Louise Quillien, and Kalliope Sarri (Lincoln, NE: Zea Books, 2024), online at https://digitalcommons.unl.edu/texroads/6 (accessed Aug. 7, 2024).

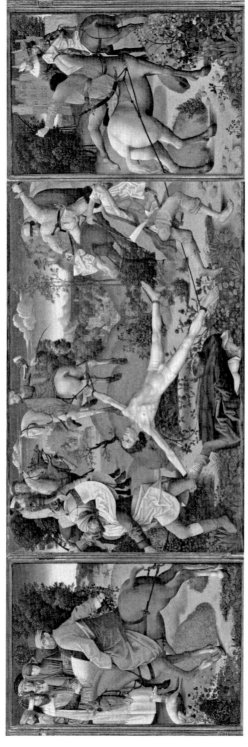

Fig. 5.6: Unidentified artist, *Martyrdom of Saint Hippolytus*, Netherlands, ca. 1490–1500 (Boston, Museum of Fine Arts, Walter M. Cabot Fund, acc. no. 63.660.1). Tempera and oil on panel, 99⅝ by 34½ inches. Photo: Copyright © 2025, Museum of Fine Arts, Boston, by permission.

Queen Jeanne—she was born in 1310 and married in 1324—to meditate on Christ's sacrifice and to think of sin and redemption as contemporary.

These powerful didactic paintings and illuminations focused viewer attention on the more relatable "living" body, especially late medieval and northern Renaissance works chock-full of realistic and contemporary details. Such images stimulated the viewer's physical senses, creating an embodied experience. The use of recognizable, contemporary *braies* brought these images into the viewer's present reality, aiding in reflection on the nature of their contemporary lives, even as the images also served as meditations on mortality (*memento mori*).

The *Martyrdom of St. Hippolytus* fuses contemporary visuals (recognizable *braies*) with *memento mori* reflection on the nature of martyrdom, death, and sacrifice (fig. 5.6). Hippolytus' body is centered in the foreground of the middle panel of the triptych. The pale flesh and white linen *braies* contrast with the green grass and foliage. His taut, static body is juxtaposed with the moving figures and flapping clothes of the torturers. The visual line of Hippolytus's stretched limbs leads the viewer's eye beyond the picture frame and into their physical space. Viewers face a lesson in the art of saintly sacrifice but are also titillated with horrified anticipation as they wait, breathless, for the rending of flesh and tearing of Hippolytus's body by horses that seem about to gallop out of the picture frame, past or over the viewer. The use of implied orthogonal lines makes the viewers part of an audience participating in the torture rather than merely observing a depiction of it.

As previously noted, *braies* serve several different functions in such images: modesty coverings, reminders of man's original sin, and examples of contemporaneous fashions. But there are two more concepts that *braies* pictured in martyrdoms seem to signify: cleanliness and shame. "Cleanliness" is a tricky concept to understand within the medieval and early Renaissance cultural framework, especially as the concept encompasses both physical and spiritual ablutions.

In images of martyrs, where *braies* are visible, they can be seen to represent a kind of physical cleanliness. Even in the midst of torture, the notion of cleanliness attaches to the martyrs through the wearing of white linen tunics and/or *braies*. St. Vincent of Saragossa was grilled, yet in Bernat Martorell's *Altarpiece of Saint Vincent* (1438–40),[40] Vincent is shown wearing perfectly clean, snug white linen *braies* while roasting on the grate. The same is true of St. Vincent as he is pictured in *Saint Vincent at the Stake* (1455–60).[41] Even as he is tortured, his visible body and *braies* remain untouched by the ashes and grime that surround him, the *braies* thus protecting him from not only soil, but also the humiliation of total nakedness. He stays "clean" physically but also spiritually by being revealed not as a carnal body, but as someone already experiencing the divinity associated with martyrs. The saints are in the midst of sloughing off their mortality, their earthliness, and their secular maleness. As Burns points out, the portrayals of nakedness or near-nakedness of those being martyred, while presenting

40 Barcelona, Museu Nacional d'Art de Catalunya, inv. no. 015797-CJT. The scene discussed here is at the upper right of the altarpiece.
41 By Jaume Huguet; Barcelona, Museu Nacional d'Art de Catalunya, inv. no. 024135-000.

primarily a form of torture and humiliation, also show the saints stripped of all earthly wealth and accouterments of the secular male. They are revealed as not just "male" but as men without the false trappings of social status.[42]

The early Christians saw the physical sacrifice and torture of martyrs as the greatest form of devotion to Christ where the "abjection of the flesh went hand-in-hand with the exaltation of divinity."[43] Radical martyrdom, prevalent in the first to third centuries, produced many of the saints pictured in thirteenth- and fourteenth-century images as models for devotion, though not necessarily emulation.[44] Martyrdom—and the particular version of shame experienced by the martyr—was seen as a transcendent experience that held the promise of eternal life as ultimate reward for physical suffering but also allowed the saint to experience torture as a way to be released from the carnality of the flesh. As Julia Kristeva puts it, "the abject is edged with the sublime."[45]

There are several forms of shame at play here: disgrace or dishonor, internalized shame as self-contempt, and the transformative experience of shame. Stripping martyrs down to their *braies* was a way to disgrace them and put them on dishonorable public display. The intent was to humiliate them and create a state of self-contempt. However, Virginia Burrus argues that the shame experienced by martyrs was not humbling, but rather was a transcendent experience that allowed them to truly experience the love of the divine by shedding attachment to their body and the mundanity of the moment. *Braies* here act not only as a stand-in for their spiritual cleanliness, but also for their ability to move beyond physical shame.[46]

Shame is felt, but also witnessed. Audiences consuming images of martyrdoms were ideological witnesses to the shaming of saints. Viewers were not simply passively observing pretty pictures. Instead, they were psychologically present at the martyrdom through prayer and devotion. This need for presence was made all the more real through the artistic techniques employed by the late medieval and early Renaissance artists of Northern Europe. As in the van der Weyden *Descent from the Cross* and the anonymous *Martyrdom of Saint Hippolytus* discussed earlier, the artists strove to create images that broke the visual lines of physical frames and pushed into the viewer's material and psychological space. The realistic and contemporary details routinely included in these paintings and illuminations reinforced the audience's experience of pictured action happening in real time. Because *braies* were painted to mimic current undergarments, they contributed to the overall illusion of the martyrdom happening in a modern setting. But *braies* also functioned as more than just one member of a chorus

42 Burns, *Courtly Love Undressed*, 113.
43 Virgina Burrus, *Saving Shame: Martyrs, Saints, and Other Abject Subjects* (Philadelphia: University of Pittsburgh Press, 2007), 47; Paul Middleton, *Radical Martyrdom and Cosmic Conflict in Early Christianity* (New York: T&T Clark, 2006), 172.
44 The practice of radical martyrdom (volitional death) was eventually decried by Clement of Alexandria (ca. 150–ca. 215). Teresa Berger, *Gender Differences and the Making of Liturgical History: Lifting a Veil on Liturgy's Past* (Farnham, UK: Ashgate, 2011), 26–32.
45 Dino Felluga, "Modules on Kristeva: On the Abject," in *Introductory Guide to Critical Theory* (New York: Routledge, 2015), 12–13.
46 Burrus, *Saving Shame*, 42–79.

of realistic details. The garment that was left after the body was stripped of the outer trappings of wealth, masculinity, dignity, or physical protection still served multiple yet distinct purposes. In one sense, *braies* functioned as an instrument of shaming.

The figures around Hippolytus are dressed in thick, deeply dyed wools with touches of velvet, while his own fur-edged *cote* lies abandoned on the ground. The clad figures are in control of the setting, yet they are in the background and side panels of the triptych. Hippolytus, as noted earlier, is centered before the viewer, making it clear that his martyrdom *is* the performance at hand. His identity as sanctified sacrifice comes from having been stripped down to his *braies*, and it is in that garment alone that he performs the role of martyr—the role of the shamed, for both the painted audience and for viewers of the painting. Through that performance, in that garb, shame becomes transformed into a defiant spectacle of shamelessness; a martyr who is ready to be tortured and sacrificed as a willing warrior of Christ and as a moral spur for, in this case, the congregation of Saint-Hippolyte in Poligny where the triptych may have first hung.[47] In the secular context of the *Grandes Chroniques de France* mentioned above, seeing *braies* leads to the mocking of the wearer and embarrassment and moral risk for the viewer. This same notion comes into play with sacred images of martyrs. We come to know the sanctity of the unclad figures *through* their lack of clothes, through their endurance of mocking and shaming.

For later medieval and early Renaissance audiences, shame was not something to slide by or "get over"; rather, it was supposed to be transformative. Shame and guilt are tightly intertwined here, and both are being used as tools to push the viewer toward embracing Christian humility.[48] Increasingly, many of those commissioning and consuming art throughout the fourteenth and fifteenth centuries were wealthy merchants and aristocrats: purveyors and owners of luxury. One can also reasonably assume that they understood that images of martyrdoms were intended to make them reflect on the potential danger to their faith and afterlife if they did not feel a certain amount of shame and guilt about their good lives while looking at images of suffering.[49]

Another aspect of shame with these works of art connects to the spiritual mortification associated with nudity as expressed in Catholic medieval church doctrine.[50] *Braies* not only served as the uniform of the martyr who was being shamed, but they also functioned to protect the viewer from shameful feelings that could arise from gazing at the martyr's nakedness. In *L'Être et le néant*, Jean-Paul Sartre sees shame as a primary means of comprehending an encounter with the other: shame is what enables the possibility of comprehending the mutual regard between other and self.[51] James Mensch shifts the problem of shame from existential to phenomenological by positing that "I am ashamed before the actual other, that is, before his or her concrete

---

47 Burrus, *Saving Shame*, 9.
48 Shame is a painful experience, unexpected and disorienting, something that is done to us. Guilt is based in our own actions, something that we have done or knowingly left undone.
49 Burrus, *Saving Shame*, 4, 33–42.
50 Burrus, *Saving Shame*, 9.
51 Jean-Paul Sartre, *L'Être et le néant* (Paris: Gallimard, 1943).

presence. I internalize this presence […] and regard myself through their regarding of me. This regard is painful."[52] Viewers of *Hippolytus* become aware not only of his performance and the figures in the painted field but also of other viewers. The *braies* covering Hippolytus's genitals serve as a visual barrier between the viewer and full nudity: a necessary fig leaf, protecting the upright sensibilities and spiritual cleanliness of the viewer. Burrus reminds us that audiences viewing depictions of bodies, especially revealed bodies, have never been monolithic or necessarily heteronormative. Queer, sadomasochistic, seductive, transgressive desires are all in play parallel with shame.[53] *Braies*, fig leaves, and flimsy bits of flowing cloth have been added to paintings often to calm a public outcry of moral turpitude. Yet as a garment of last resistance to nudity, *braies* operate as both visual protection and erotic invitation.

SECULAR *BRAIES*

Sacred figures are not the only ones who strip or are stripped down to their *braies*. The image of secular men stripping down to their *braies* in preparation for battle has been used as a literary device to present contradictory pictures of masculine warriors. Elizabeth Howard argued that in the late-tenth- or early-eleventh-century Old English poem *Beowulf*, the hero's divesting himself of the accouterments of a warrior and stripping down in preparation for his battle with Grendel was a version of un-manning himself. In order to defeat a monster, a creature that is neither man nor beast, Beowulf has to divest himself of his maleness, his warrior prowess as a man, and become a beast himself. Howard wrote that Beowulf strips himself of armor and outer garments to become less than a warrior and to suffer that humiliation to defeat his foe.[54] Conversely, in *Chanson de Guillaume* (ca. 1140), Guillaume d'Orange, a retired knight, strips down to his underwear as part of a clever plan to defeat bandits bent on robbing him. His act of allowing the bandits to rob him of his clothes (and seemingly unman him) permits him to enact a previously hatched plan to both defend himself and also thwart an annoying abbot. In this case, the wearing of only *braies* becomes a demonstration of warrior cunning and braggadocio.[55]

In Chrétien de Troyes' unfinished poem *Perceval ou le Conte du Graal* (ca. 1190), Perceval finds himself in bed with a temptress but takes comfort in the fact that he still has on his *braies*, which apparently act like a chastity belt preserving his virginity/ honor.[56] In the *Roman de Tristan* (twelfth century), Tristan's wearing of *braies* convinces

52 James Richard Mensch, *Hiddenness and Alterity: Philosophical and Literary Sightings of the Unseen* (Pittsburgh: Duquesne University Press, 2005), 103–4.

53 Burrus, *Saving Shame*, 22.

54 Elizabeth Howard, "The Clothes Make the Man: Transgressive Disrobing and Disarming in *Beowulf*," in *Styling Texts: Dress and Fashion in Literature*, ed. Cynthia Kuhn and Cindy Carlson (Youngstown, OH: Cambria Press, 2007), 18–19.

55 Hathaway, "*Pour ses braies se porra courecier*," 59–60.

56 Chrétien de Troyes, *Perceval (Or the Story of the Grail)*, trans. Ruth Harwood Cline (Atlanta: University of Georgia Press, 1985).

King Mark of Cornwall (erroneously) that no adultery with Iseult has taken place. In this case, the presence of *braies* is no protection against fornication and indeed, as with Guillaume, actually represents male prowess through clever trickery.[57] *Braies* represented in both literary and visual sources function not just as a fluid signifier of "masculinity" but also as iconographic symbols to perform contradictory versions of maleness.

What the images and literature discussed thus far have in common is their representation of the upper classes which, in the medieval worldview, would have included the martyrs. Peasants, the lowest class, are depicted as having a somewhat different relationship with displays of *braies*.

Images of peasants engaged in labor developed as a regular part of calendar cycles of occupations of the months sometime in the late Carolingian era but only became widespread during the twelfth century. Peasants are one of the three classes commonly depicted in medieval visual arts such as the tenth-century *Winchester Chronicle*: the noble, the cleric, and the peasant, or "those who fight, those who pray, and those who labor."[58] Such rustic images were commissioned and consumed by royalty and the aristocracy for their own amusement.[59] Images such as the rabbit-hunting scenes in the fifteenth-century tapestry set *Rabbit Hunting with Ferrets* served as a counterpoint to the visual and social complexities of court life.[60] Clean, productive peasants like those in the *Très Riches Heures du Duc de Berry*[61] (ca. 1412–16), which was commissioned by John, Duke of Berry, for private viewing, served as pictorial confirmation of the successful functioning of a hierarchical social system that primarily benefited the aristocracy. The happy peasant was one stereotype, while the dissolute, vulgar peasant was another, demonstrating immoral behavior which was not to be emulated, but was, nevertheless, amusing for the aristocratic viewer. Such images became aphorisms for both the aristocracy and lower classes, showing that good stewardship of lands and villeins on the part of the upper classes would lead to hardworking, content lower classes, producing crops that supported everyone.[62] In the case of the *Très Riches Heures*, the bounty of nature (and by extension God's grace) and the ephemeral qual-

---

57 Burns, *Courtly Love Undressed*, 159–60.
58 Georges Duby, *The Three Orders: Feudal Society Imagined*, trans. A. Goldhammer (Chicago: University of Chicago Press, 1981), 12.
59 Johan Huizinga, *The Waning of the Middle Ages: A Study of the Forms of Life, Thought and Art in France and the Netherlands in the XIVth and XVth Centuries* (Garden City, NY: Doubleday Anchor, 1954), esp. 128–38.
60 Woven of wool and silk by unknown weavers around 1460–70 in the Burgundian Netherlands, the set consists of three monumental tapestries: *Peasants Preparing to Hunt Rabbits with Ferrets* (Glasgow, Burrell Collection, no. 46.56), *Rabbit Hunting with Ferrets* (Fine Arts Museums of San Francisco, acc. no. 39.4.1) and *Halte de chasse ou collation de paysans* [hunting stop or peasants' picnic] (Paris, Musée du Louvre, no. OA 10441). For a more detailed discussion of these tapestries, see Kate Dimitrova's "Class, Sex, and the *Other*: The Representation of Peasants in a Set of Late Medieval Tapestries," *Viator* 38, no. 2 (2007), 85–125.
61 Limbourg Brothers (Chantilly, France, Musée Condé, MS 65).
62 Panofsky, *Early Netherlandish Painting*, esp. 70–72.

ity of life were suggested by the peasants seen moving through the different seasons. While not overtly religious images, their placement in a Book of Hours connects the painted laborers to medieval Christian ideas of a virtuous life and salvation through good works.[63]

Both the *Rutland Psalter*[64] (ca. 1260; fig. 5.7) and the *Martyrologe-Obituaire de Saint-Germain-des-Prés*[65] (ca. 1250–90; fig. 5.2) show rye or wheat threshers in mid-swing. The *Rutland* figure wears *braies* that are secured at both knee and waist with a small purse attached. The two figures from the *Martyrologe* are both wearing loosely fit mid-calf-length *braies*, secured at the waist. Presented in a roundel and a quatrefoil respectively, the figures are isolated with their labor, exemplars of the benefits of hard work. *Braies* here illustrate their class and secure their appropriate modesty.

Laboring peasants like those shown in the *Rutland* and *Martyrologe* texts are fairly typical of images found in a wide array of religious manuscripts. The peasants who appear in secular tomes, such as the different versions of the *Tacuinum Sanitatis*, still have a rather moralizing tone to them but are shown engaged in a greater variety of activities and moods. Medieval *Tacuinum Sanitatis* (tables of health) were Latin translations of an eleventh-century Arab medical treatise, *Taqwīm as-sihha bi al-Ashab al-Sitta*, written by the Christian physician Ibn Butlan of Baghdad (d. 1068). The *Taqwīm* synthesized information from extant Greek-derived medical science and health traditions and discussed 280 items that affect health, such as food, drink, climate, physical activity, and clothing (like linens that can be washed). The first Latin edition, completed by 1266, was commissioned within the ambit of the Court of Naples and Sicily, possibly by Charles I of Anjou or his predecessor Manfred, and inspired several others.[66] The Latin editions were dominated by illustrations useful for literate and non-literate nobles alike. In the images, idealized courtiers were fashionably dressed and shown engaged in "healthy" activities already familiar to the aristocratic viewer, such as horseback riding and dancing.

Male peasant figures in the Paris *Tacuinum Sanitatis*[67] (ca. 1400) are shown wearing different combinations of shoes, hose, *braies*, linen shirts, and wool tunics. Several figures appear in *braies* alone or paired with a short, white linen shirt. In the boar hunting scene, we can plainly see the short, snug *braies* on the figure in the foreground thrusting a phallic spear into the side of a boar being torn at by dogs (fig. 5.8). There is a salacious quality to the portrayal of the man's prominently displayed round rump and muscular legs. The curious lack of outer garments (that *are* worn by the figure in the background hunting rabbits), especially while hunting wild boar, seems to draw even

---

63 J. C. Webster, *The Labors of the Months in Antique and Medieval Art to the End of the Twelfth Century* (Evanston, IL: Northwestern University Press, 1938), 102.

64 London, British Library, MS Add. 62925, 5r.

65 Paris, Bibliothèque Nationale de France, MS Lat. 12834, 64v.

66 Cathleen Hoeniger, "The Illuminated *Tacuinum Sanitatis* Manuscripts from Northern Italy ca. 1380–1400: Sources, Patrons, and the Creation of a New Pictorial Genre," in *Visualizing Medieval Medicine and Natural History, 1200–1550*, ed. Jean A. Giens, Karen M. Reeds, and Alain Touwaide (Aldershot, UK: Ashgate, 2006), 53–55.

67 Paris, Bibliothèque Nationale de France, MS Nouv. Acq. Lat. 1673.

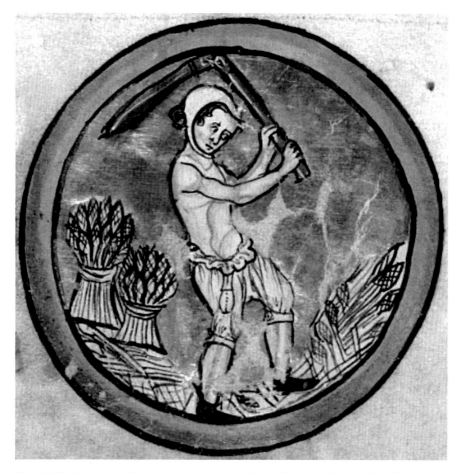

Fig. 5.7: Worker wearing knee-length *braies*. Detail from the *Rutland Psalter* (London, British Library, MS Add. 62925), fol. 5r, ca. 1260. Photo: British Library, by permission.

more attention to his partial nakedness. There is a similar depiction in the painting of truffle hunting: a male figure clad in rolled-down hose, *braies*, and white shirt in the foreground, slightly bent over, with his backside facing the viewer (fig. 5.9). Two figures in the background wear shoes, hose, wool tunics, and even a hat. We are again presented with a conspicuously displayed bottom and naked thighs. In both these images, the figures are going about their business, much like we have seen peasants in Books of Hours do. Yet there is a distinct flavor of jocular humor with homoerotic overtones that here are more overtly displayed.

The painted page shown in figure 5.10 is a more complex scene and one not generally found in Books of Hours: drunks fighting. Four standing figures are shown around a table covered in containers. In the foreground is a man again clad in only *braies* and shirt, and facing him across the table is a second man quite well turned out

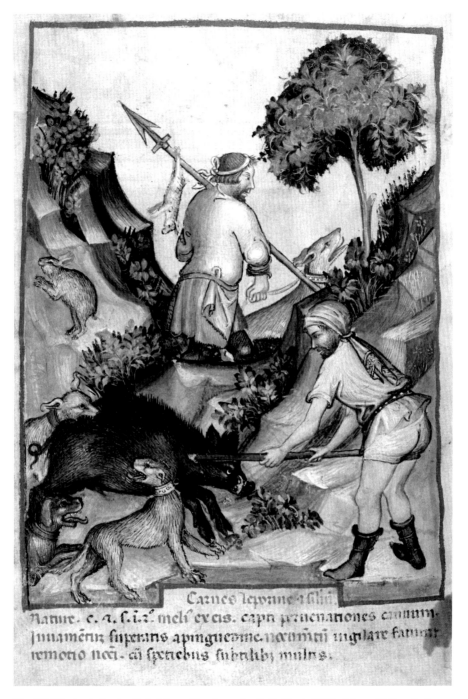

Fig. 5.8: Hunter in *braies*. Detail from *Tacuinum Sanitatis* (Paris, Bibliothèque Nationale de France, MS Lat. nouv. acq. 1673, fol. 91v), ca. 1390–1400. Photo: Courtesy of Bibliothèque Nationale de France.

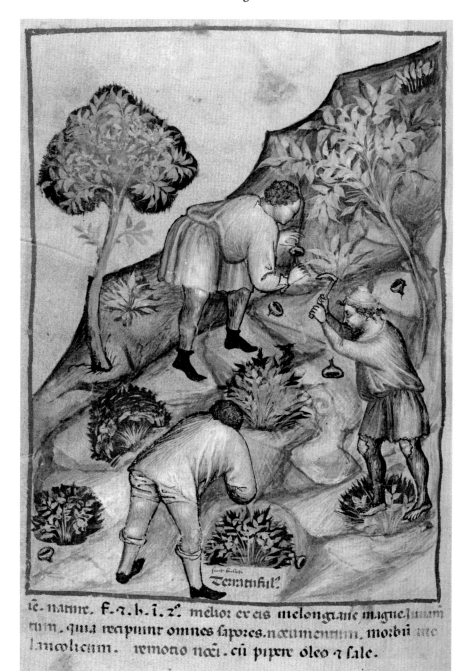

Fig. 5.9: Truffle collector in *braies* and rolled-down hose. Detail from *Tacuinum Sanitatis* (Paris), fol. 39v. Photo: Courtesy of Bibliothèque Nationale de France.

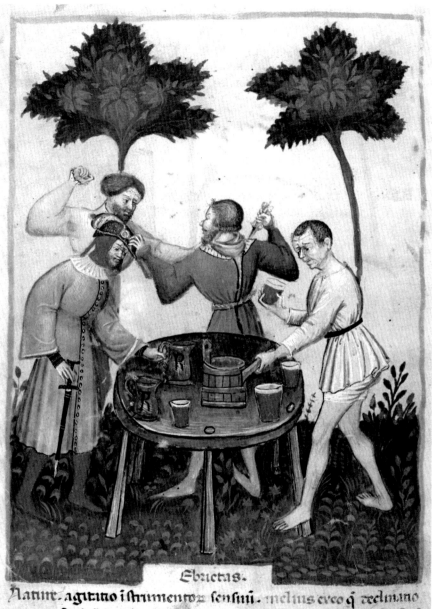

Fig. 5.10: Men drinking, with one in braies. *Tacuinum Sanitatis* (Paris), fol. 88v. Photo: Courtesy of Bibliothèque Nationale de France.

in shoes, hose, a long blue wool *cote*, white collar, hood, and hat, holding a sheathed sword. These gentlemen are both reaching for vessels that presumably hold alcohol. The two fully clad figures in the background, one of whom has a drawn knife at the ready, are engaged in a fist fight. The foreground figures seem unconcerned or unaware of the scuffle as they busily imbibe. The dangers of too much alcohol are clear here: fights and possibly losing one's clothes. It is not at all coincidental that the writing on the page outlines medical uses of wine and what might be a hangover cure. While the *Tacuinum* technically lay outside of the geographic parameters for works considered in this article, they are a useful visual foil to both the style and content of the northern works.

Peasants of the Paris *Tacuinum* are positioned and dressed to be objects of humorous derision and voyeuristic gaze by the noble classes. The same kind of classed voyeurism appears in the *Très Riches Heures du Duc de Berry*, which, as noted above, was commissioned by the Duke for private viewing. The twelve monthly calendar vignettes are the most striking of the book's illuminations, each topped with a zodiac calendar and swimming in lapis lazuli blue. Five of the months show aristocratic pursuits, while seven show peasants working in fields with backdrops of ducal architectural holdings. Calm, orderly scenes convey a sense of ideal social order where aristocrats are elegant and always entertained, and peasants work diligently, content with the simplicity of their rustic lives. It is all, of course, an illusion created for the pleasure of the Duke. In a private devotional book made specifically for him, John could be assured that he would find the images pleasing and specifically to his liking. In the *Très Riches Heures*, sacred devotion and secular carnality are combined.

Michael Camille uses the lens of erotica and queer theory to propose that John did not use the book just to gaze at lands and buildings, but indeed to stare at the male figures, many of whom are only partially clad. While the naked-legged and short-*braies*-wearing figures are not placed as obviously as they are in the Paris *Tacuinum*, they are still present. The July page of the *Très Riches Heures* shows a male figure in the distance, scything a field of grain, barefoot and wearing short white *braies*, a white short-sleeved shirt, and a hat (figs. 5.4 and 5.11).[68] February's page is subtle and simultaneously far more blatant in displays of flesh and the crude realism of peasant life (fig. 5.12). Winter has arrived in a scene where three figures toil in the cold while another three warm themselves by the fire inside a hut. Hay is stacked neatly, beehives are all tucked up, birds feed on grain, and the sheep are snugly crammed into their pen. A figure in the background cuts wood to keep the fire going while another walks across the frozen ground, breath visible in the cold air. All is orderly and well kept. As a viewer, we are closer to the hut, as it takes up a third of the foreground space, almost as if we are invited to come in and enjoy the warmth of the fire. A woman in a blue dress and white chemise holds her skirt up to

---

68 Michael Camille, "'For Our Devotion and Pleasure': The Sexual Objects of Jean, Duc de Berry," *Art History* 24, no. 2 (April 2001): 169–94.

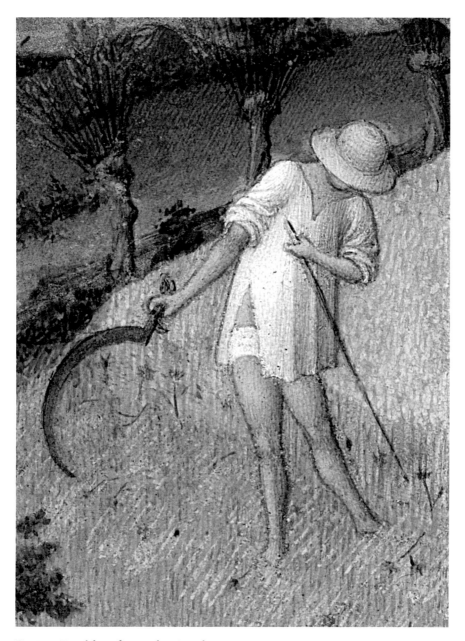

Fig. 5.11: Detail from fig. 5.4, showing a harvester.

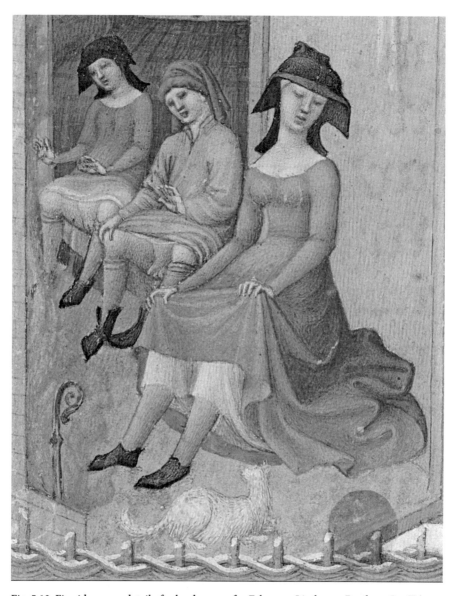

Fig. 5.12: Fireside scene, detail of calendar page for February. Limbourg Brothers, *Les Très Riches Heures du Duc de Berry*, fol. 2v. Photo: Courtesy of Agence Photographique de la Réunion des Musées Nationaux.

her knees so that the fire will warm her legs. Beyond her are two figures (male and female) who are sitting open-legged, warming their nude genitalia.

In the sacred scenes of martyrs and secular Arthurian tales discussed earlier, *braies* acted as a visible barrier against carnal desire, whether real or imagined, actual or trickery. Here, in the February page, that barrier has been removed. The Duke might gaze upon tiny representations of splayed nudity. The figures with their garments raised to show their genitals are tucked into a corner of the page and sit in partial shadow. It is easy to miss their display or to think little of it. But when this image was published in *Life* magazine in the 1950s, the genitals of these peasant figures were airbrushed out so as not to offend viewers with the casual display of body parts that usually remain covered.[69] Camille points to the Duke's admitted sense of "plaisance" in choosing objects for his collection, which sometimes included young men at the same time as the Duke was arranging for his second marriage to keep the lineage secure and strengthen political alliances.[70] The Duke's sexual fluidity "show[s] that he did indeed have an interest in looking at the genitals of the lower classes, both male and female."[71] While the peasants most certainly represented moral performances of industriousness in Books of Hours, it also seems reasonable to note that peasants were essentially owned by their overlord and were objects of carnal physical desire and prurient gaze as well. Unlike all of the other peasant and martyr scenes so far discussed, in the February scene, it is the lack of *braies* rather than their presence that seems meaningful.

Braies are humble garments. They are not difficult to construct. Medieval re-enactors find them comfortable to wear. Artists of the Middle Ages and early Renaissance periods included their contemporary versions of *braies* in scenes of shame and torture, harvesting and drinking, swimming, sleeping, and dying. Figures from the humblest of beggars and laboring peasants to revered martyrs are pictured wearing an incarnation of the white linen undergarment.

By working from the micro to the macro, we can ask why such a humble garment—so often hidden by other more opulent clothes, rarely mentioned in literature, and discounted by some costume historians as lacking significance—shows up so often in late medieval and early northern Renaissance works of art? Depictions of *braies* do not lack meaning, but many of those meanings have been relatively unexplored. When *braies* are depicted in certain artworks, they not only contribute to and support the primary meaning created by other pictured objects but sometimes create meaning in and of themselves. In scenes of Calvary, contemporarily styled, realistically rendered *braies* make the two thieves more specifically tangible for the male viewing audience. *Braies* on martyrs speak to multiple meanings of shame, humiliation, vulnerability, and being revealed to another but also the divine ecstasy experienced by the radical martyr. On a peasant pictured toiling in a field or bending over to pick truffles, *braies* can suggest modesty, poverty, and practicality or be suggestive of the erotic pleasures that lie beneath. Clothing layers meaning, and *braies* all the more so.

69 Camille, "For Our Devotion and Pleasure," 174.
70 Camille, "For Our Devotion and Pleasure," 171.
71 Camille, "For Our Devotion and Pleasure," 174.

The Trade in Knitted Jersey Stockings, and Their Creation by Child Knitters in Norwich and Yarmouth Around 1600

Lesley O'Connell Edwards[1]

In his work *An Account of the State of England in Anno Domini 1600*, which included details of England's economy in 1600, Thomas Wilson wrote that in Norwich, children between the ages of six and ten years earned £12,000 sterling annually towards their keep, chiefly by knitting fine jersey stockings. He also stated that "every child being able at or soone after seven yeares to earne 4 shillings a week att that trade, which the marchants uttered [i.e. put for sale[2]] att London; and some tradeing with France and other parts."[3]

Hand knitting in England was a domestic employment in this period, with no structure or regulatory body, which means no systematic records exist. A wide range of archival records, including household accounts and national and local government documents, shows that knitted jersey stockings were well known in England at this date. Wilson's comments are a very rare thing: information on the work of child textile workers in a specific area of England in 1600, and the markets for their product, complete with numerical data. Although other evidence shows that Wilson's estimate of earnings of four shillings a week for children is far too high, other sources confirm the existence of child knitters in Yarmouth and Norwich and a trade in jersey stockings in the late Tudor period. These include Yarmouth export port books, which detail both the trade in jersey stockings and their traders who can be linked to Norwich, and the 1570 census of the poor in Norwich, which records child knitters.

---

1 I would like to thank Professor Gale Owen-Crocker who heard a version of this paper at the 2023 conference of the Medieval Dress and Textile Society, and encouraged me to develop it. I would also like to thank the anonymous peer reviewers and the editors for their comments and encouragement.
2 *Oxford English Dictionary*, online ed. (New York, Oxford University Press, 2000–; henceforth OED), https//:www.oed.com, s.v. *utter*, v.1.
3 F. J. Fisher, ed., *The State of England Anno Dom. 1600, by Thomas Wilson*, in *Camden Miscellany* 16, Camden Society, 3rd ser., 52 (1936): 20. For details on Wilson's original, see note 84, below.

Norwich was the second city in the land in 1600, with a population of twelve thousand to fifteen thousand in the later sixteenth century.[4] Norwich is in Norfolk, and its nearest port is Yarmouth. The city had close trading links with the Low Countries since at least medieval times, and also received refugees from war and natural disasters there.[5] Figure 6.1 shows the position of Norwich relative to Yarmouth, Ipswich and London, and the near continent.

Little research has been published on the history of hand knitting in England. Some research has been carried out on hand-knitted stockings: Joan Thirsk's classic paper published in 1973 about the stocking knitting industry in general is still a vital source today on production and trade, and often cited; Pauline Croft's study of the export trade in stockings from London in the late sixteenth to the mid-seventeenth centuries provides a general overview of selected port books from different decades; and more recent research has studied the stocking knitting industry of the later sixteenth century in Norwich, concentrating on the production process, the volume of production, and the socioeconomic background of the knitters.[6] A. R. Michell studied trade in general to and from Yarmouth between 1550 and 1714 for his doctorate in the 1970s, but his research seems never to have been published.[7]

This paper is the first to provide a detailed study of one type of stocking, examining the evidence for its production in Norwich and Yarmouth especially around the end of the sixteenth century and the beginning of the seventeenth. The export of stockings from the head port of Yarmouth for a two-year period falling over the years 1600 to 1602 will be analysed, including destinations, volume, and the traders' backgrounds. *The State of England* will be placed in its context, then the existence of child knitters in Norwich and elsewhere will be discussed. Possible wages for children will be examined before consideration is given to how Wilson might have arrived at his numerical data and how far these can be used to estimate the value and volume of the trade in the area.

4 Robert Tittler, "Society and Social Relations in British Provincial Towns," in *A Companion to Tudor Britain*, ed. Robert Tittler and Norman Jones (Oxford: Wiley-Blackwell, 2009), 363–80, at 364.

5 Frank Meeres, *The Welcome Stranger* (Norwich, UK: Poppyland, 2018), 5–9.

6 Joan Thirsk, "The Fantastical Folly of Fashion: The English Stocking Knitting Industry, 1500–1700," in *Textile History and Economic History*, ed. Negley B. Harte and Kenneth G. Ponting (Manchester: Manchester University Press, 1973), 50–73; Pauline Croft, "The Rise of the English Stocking Export Trade," *Textile History* 18 (1987): 3–16; Lesley O'Connell Edwards, "The Stocking Knitting Industry of Later Sixteenth-Century Norwich," *Textile History* 52 (2021): 146–64.

7 A. R. Michell, "The Port and Town of Great Yarmouth and Its Economic and Social Relationships with Its Neighbours on Both Sides of the Seas 1550–1714" (Ph.D. diss., Cambridge University, 1978).

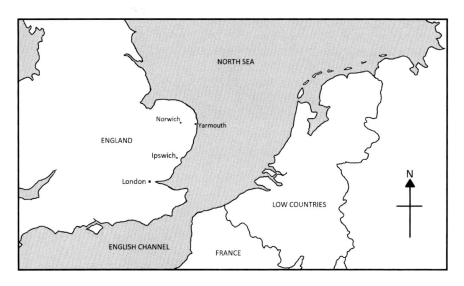

Fig. 6.1: Map of Norwich, showing its location in England and position relative to the Low Countries. Map: Copyright © Lesley O'Connell Edwards.

JERSEY STOCKINGS

Jersey stockings were wool stockings, hand knitted from what contemporaries termed fine yarn. There were three major types of yarn used for wool stockings in the sixteenth century—woollen, worsted, and jersey. Woollen was made from carded fibres, worsted was made from combed fibres, and jersey was finer than worsted and also made from combed fibres.[8]

A document dated December 1596, probably written by Thomas Caesar (1561–1610), brother of Sir Julius Caesar who held a number of government and legal offices between 1581 and 1636, states that jersey yarn was first spun in Jersey or Guernsey upon the "small wheele" and there could be several qualities.[9] By 1600 jersey was spun and knitted across England. Oil (or grease or a similar lubricant) was used to produce combed fibre for spinning: jersey yarn was spun from combed fibre which had the oil washed out of it, unlike worsted yarn which was spun from combed fibre which still had the lubricant in it. Caesar's 1596 document states that jersey yarn was used for the finest cloth, and sometimes as weft for silk warp.[10] The fine nature of the yarn was also reflected in its use in knitting fine stockings. The

8 J. de Lacy Mann, "Documents and Sources V: A Document Regarding Jersey Spinning in the P.R.O.," *Textile History* 4 (1973): 140.

9 *Notes on the diversities of wools, 1596*, London, The National Archives (henceforth TNA), SP 15/33, fols. 155–56, described in Mann, "Documents and Sources V."

10 Mann, "Documents and Sources V," 140–41.

Ipswich census of the poor drawn up in 1597 included a spinner of "jersie" as well as a spinner of hose yarn, which latter would have created yarn for stockings that were not made from jersey yarn.[11] (Knitted stockings could also be referred to as hose in this period.)

There are very few surviving stockings in museum collections, and none can be clearly identified as jersey. There has been little work on wool preparation for yarn construction of these stockings so it is not known if these were spun from combed or carded wool, and thus woolen or worsted. Most of the sixteenth-century wool stockings in the Museum of London have a gauge of around 30 wales (stitches) per 10 centimetres but there are a few that are 45 wales per 10 centimetres (approximately 7.5 and 11.5 wales per inch, respectively).[12] Fragments of two stockings found in Norwich dating from the end of the sixteenth century have a gauge of 40 to 50 wales per 10 centimetres (approximately 10 to 13 wales per inch).[13] Sandra Comis found a similar duality to the Museum of London stockings in fifty-four knitted fragments of wool stockings from whalers' graves dated to 1614 to 1650 in Smeerenburg in Spitsbergen: but she also found eight which had a much higher gauge of between 55 and 65 wales per 10 centimetres (approximately 14 to 16.5 wales per inch), which would be a finer finished fabric.[14] It is possible that some jersey stockings might have been as fine as silk ones.[15] A silk stocking foot in the Museum of London has a gauge of approximately 70 wales per 10 centimetres (18 wales per inch).[16] A study of silk stockings from the late sixteenth and early seventeenth centuries which were found with high-status burials in the Czech Republic produced a range of gauges from 50 to 100 wales per 10

11 John Webb, *Poor Relief in Elizabethan Ipswich*, Suffolk Record Society 9 (Ipswich, UK: Suffolk Record Society, 1966), 129, 123.

12 Lesley O'Connell Edwards, "Knitted Wool Stockings in the Museum of London: A Study of 16th Century Construction," *Archaeological Textiles Review* 60 (2018): 43. The terminology used to describe gauge for knitted fabrics is that recommended by Jane Malcolm-Davies, Ruth Gilbert, and Susanne Lervad, "Unravelling the Confusions: Defining Concepts to Record Archaeological and Historical Evidence for Knitting," *Archaeological Textiles Review* 60 (2018): 10–24.

13 Elisabeth Crowfoot, "Textiles," in *Norwich Households: The Medieval and Post-Medieval Finds from Norwich Survey Excavations 1971–1978*, ed. Sue Margeson, East Anglian Archaeology Report 58 (1993): 48–50, 54, 58.

14 Sandra Y. Comis, "Zeventiende- en achttiende-eeuwse Kleding van Walvisvaarders Opgegraven op Spitsbergen" (Ph.D. diss., Groningen University, 2017), 68, 356, 365–72. Smeerenburg was a seventeenth-century fishing outpost on the island of Spitsbergen, north of Norway.

15 Michael Zell and Heather Falvey, eds., *Walter Morrell's "Manufacture for the Newe Draperie" (1616)*, Hertfordshire Record Society 34 (Hertford, UK: Hertfordshire Record Society, 2018/9), 52.

16 Silk stocking foot, Museum of London, no. A13833, available online at https://collections.museumoflondon.org.uk (accessed May 22, 2023). Gauge is given as 18 wales per inch.

centimetres (approximately 13 to 25 wales per inch), but the majority were 70 wales or more per 10 centimetres (at least 18 wales per inch).[17]

Jersey stockings were seen as suitable for royalty. They are recorded as early as 1556/7, when four pairs of "hoosen of garsey [i.e. jersey] making" were included in the New Year's gift roll of Philip and Mary.[18] Queen Elizabeth received a box "full of Guernsey hoose and sleves knytt" from Francis, Chamberlain of Woodstock, as a New Year's gift in 1561/2.[19] The royal wardrobe accounts for later in the reign include payments for plain and ornamented jersey hose, and for their care.[20] Mary, Queen of Scots, wore jersey stockings under her worsted ones at her execution in 1587.[21]

The variation in yarn quality mentioned in Caesar's 1596 document above suggests that different qualities of jersey stockings might be made. This variation may be reflected in the prices paid by the Earl of Leicester and Queen Elizabeth: the former paid 9s [shillings] for two pairs of jersey hose in 1558, whilst the queen paid 26s 8d [old pence] for two pairs in 1588.[22] Although it is not possible to know if these were the same size, the difference is too large to be explained by inflation.[23] Size is probably the explanation for the different prices paid for four pairs of stockings by William Cavendish in 1598: two pairs for his heir, who was around eight years old, were 3s each; but the other two cost only 2s 6d each and were for his younger son who might have been as old as three years then.[24] Quality might be the explanation for the two different valuations put on the jersey stockings by those who drew up the inventory of Norwich hosier Henry Sheardley in 1617: out of 335 pairs recorded, there were seventy-six coloured jersey pairs valued at 3s 8d per pair, and twenty-three coloured jersey pairs valued at 2s 8d each.[25] Again, an alternative explanation for the two values

17 Sylvie Odstrčilová, "Early Modern Stockings in Museums in the Czech Republic," *Archaeological Textiles Review* 60 (2018): 51–52.
18 John Nichols, *The Progresses and Public Processions of Queen Elizabeth*, vol. 1 (London: J. Nichols, 1823), xxxiv n. 2.
19 Nichols, *Progresses*, 118.
20 Janet Arnold, *Queen Elizabeth's Wardrobe Unlock'd* (Leeds, UK: Maney, 1988), 209–10.
21 Richard Rutt, *A History of Hand Knitting* (London: Batsford, 1987), 66, notes that one of the original descriptions, by Robert Wingfield (ca. 1558–59), can be found in London, British Library, Harley MS 290, 205v: "her nether stockings worsted couloured watchet clocked wth siluer and edged on the topp wth siluer, and next her legge a paire of jerzie hose white."
22 Simon Adams, *Household Accounts and Disbursement Books of Robert Dudley, Earl of Leicester 1558–1561, 1584–1586* (London: Cambridge University Press, 1995), 91; Arnold, *Queen Elizabeth's Wardrobe Unlock'd*, 210. There were 20 shillings in a pound, and 12 pence in a shilling.
23 Joseph P. Ward considers that inflation ran at no more than 8% in the decades 1560 to 1590—and good harvests could depress prices; Ward, "Metropolitan London," in Tittler and Jones, *A Companion to Tudor Britain*, 347–62, at 354.
24 Philip Riden, ed., *The Household Accounts of William Cavendish, Lord Cavendish of Hardwick*, Derbyshire Record Society 40–42 (Chesterfield, UK: Derbyshire Record Society, 2016), 40:xxii, 41:80.
25 *Inventory of Henry Sheardley of Norwich, Hosier*, 1617, Norwich, UK, Norfolk Record Office, DN/INV 28/131.

is that they might have been different sizes: the appraisers clearly had a reason, but did not feel the need to note it on the inventory. These two types of stockings were by far the most expensive in this inventory: the next highest in value were 2s 2d.

Jersey stockings were one of the fine stocking types which the Puritan divine Philip Stubbes inveighed against in his complaint about the extravagancies of dress in the 1580s, along with silk and worsted stockings; he claimed all people tried to obtain as a fine a pair as possible.[26] Although Stubbes seems to imply jersey stockings were individual luxury items, other evidence suggests these might not be so exclusive. In 1602 Christien Adams was apprenticed to learn to knit jersey stockings for her master's wife in Berkhamsted, whilst in 1596 Leicester Corporation lent Thomas Clark's wife money on condition she kept many poor children in work spinning and knitting jersey.[27] Although there are records of other items knitted from jersey, such as waistcoats or sleeves, it is likely that it was jersey stockings that were knitted by the poor Leicester children: knitting stockings was seen as a suitable occupation for the poor in the Elizabethan period, suggesting that these could be made on a mass production basis.[28]

STOCKING PRODUCTION IN NORWICH AND YARMOUTH CA. 1600

Norwich was noted for its textile industries, which included knitting fine stockings. Both native-born Englishmen and the non-native "Strangers," or aliens, were involved in this industry.[29] The latter were recent economic migrants, virtually all from the Low Countries. Most of the textiles produced, including stockings, came under the category of New Draperies, which tended to be finer than traditional broadcloth.[30] Norwich city council collected the aulnage duty for the New Draperies being produced in the city for five years from 1580 to 1585: the duty was payable on any finished wool goods, including knitted stockings. In the last year the city's aulnage accounts recorded this duty being paid on 35,700 pairs of stockings, which clearly shows that stockings were being produced in quantity for sale on the open market. After that it lost the right to

26 Philip Stubbes, *The Anatomie of Abuses*, 3rd ed. (London, 1585; repr., London: W. Pickering, 1836), 47.

27 Nick Brown, ed., *Berkhamsted Saint Peter's Churchwardens Accounts 1584 –1660*, Hertfordshire Record Society 38 (Hertford, UK: Hertfordshire Record Society, 2022), 86; Mary Bateson, ed., *Records of the Borough of Leicester*, vol. 3, *1509–1603* (Cambridge: Cambridge University Press, 1905), 327.

28 Kay Staniland, "Thomas Deane's Shop in the Royal Exchange," in *The Royal Exchange*, ed. Ann Saunders, London Topographical Society 152 (London: London Topographical Society, 1997), 65, 67; Riden, *Household Accounts*, 41:267; Lesley O'Connell Edwards, "Knitting Schools in Elizabethan England," *Knitting Traditions* (Spring 2013): 30–31.

29 O'Connell Edwards, "The Stocking Knitting Industry," 145, 160.

30 Richard Wilson, "The Textile Industry," in *Norwich Since 1550*, ed. Carol Rawcliffe and Richard Wilson (London: Hambledon, 2004), 220–23.

collect the duty, and thus ceased to receive any income from this collection.[31] However, there is no indication of the type of wool yarn used for these stockings.

Fine stockings were being produced in Yarmouth by 1608 under the aegis of the Strangers. A document in the papers of magistrate Nathaniel Bacon, dated October 12, 1608, about the wool bought by the Strangers in Norwich, mentions that around four hundred tod of the "finer sorte" of "combed wool" was "sent to Yarmouth and there imployed for fine stockings onely."[32] It seems likely these could well have been similar to the fine jersey stockings mentioned by Wilson. A tod is usually taken as twenty-eight pounds in weight, so four hundred tod would equate to 11,200 pounds. The quantity being supplied suggests that knitting fine stockings was a source of income for many in Yarmouth and the surrounding area. Contemporary writers claimed a pound of raw wool would create two pairs of stockings (with no reference to size or yarn type).[33] In the process of turning raw wool into finished yarn a lot of weight is lost: modern hand-spinners expect to lose around 50 percent of the weight of a raw fleece by the time it becomes yarn; modern reconstructions of museum artefacts at a similar gauge also suggest this could be a reasonable assumption.[34]

On the basis of two pairs per pound of wool, 22,400 pairs of stockings could be created from the four hundred tod, but if the wool was already prepared then more pairs would be created. The description of the wool sent to Yarmouth is ambiguous: if the term "combed wool" means that the wool had undergone all the necessary preparation prior to spinning, then not much further weight would have been lost when it was spun. In fifteenth-century Colchester, the town ordnances stated that a "combing stone" put out to female wool combers should weigh five pounds, and a "spinning stone" put out to female spinners should weigh four-and-a-half pounds, suggesting that wool for combing was already part prepared, and there was only a weight loss of roughly 10 percent in the combing process.[35] (The record does not state how many pounds the raw wool initially weighed before it reached the combing weight.) In addition, if the yarn produced in Yarmouth was fine, then even more pairs might be made from a pound of wool. As part of his "Newe Draperie" project in the 1610s, Walter Morrell claimed that he had managed to make five pairs of stockings from a pound of wool, and that the fineness of these stockings could be compared to silk ones; however, it is not clear if he meant wool yarn or raw wool, but in either case the stockings made would still be fine, as a pair made from half a pound of wool would weigh 4 ounces, allowing

---

31 O'Connell Edwards, "The Stocking Knitting Industry," 156–59.

32 Alan Metters et al., eds., *The Papers of Nathaniel Bacon of Stiffkey*, vol. 6, *1608–1613*, Norfolk Record Society 81 (Norwich, UK: Norfolk Record Society, 2017), 79.

33 [Robert Payne], *A Brief Description of the True and Perfitt Making of Woad … A Note Concerning Our English Wolle Made into Jersey Yarne*, April 25, 1586, London, British Library, MS Lansdowne 121, fols. 165–72, at fol. 172. Payne's name is not on the document but his authorship can be presumed due to the inclusion of his address.

34 See, for instance, Jane Malcolm-Davies and Ninya Mikhaila, *The Typical Tudor* (Lightwater, UK: Fat Goose Press, 2022), 65.

35 W. Gurney Benham, *The Red Paper Book of Colchester* (Colchester, UK: *Essex County Standard* Office, 1902), 59.

for a 50% loss in the yarn-making process.[36] Therefore, whilst the exact number of pairs of stockings made in Yarmouth from this wool cannot be determined, what the amount of wool being supplied to Yarmouth for fine stockings does demonstrate is that such stockings were being made in quantity in Norfolk by 1608, and it is quite possible this was the case in 1600 as well, when Wilson was writing about fine jersey stockings in *The State of England*.

OVERSEAS TRADE IN JERSEY STOCKINGS

Evidence of stockings being exported can be traced in the Tudor overseas port books, including those for Yarmouth. Some of these books record all the items in a cargo being exported abroad by a merchant: many include the destination, and a few the duty paid, but other books do not include this level of detail. These books were created annually in local ports and sent to the central government in London.[37] However, not many port books have survived from the later sixteenth century and early seventeenth century—and those that have are often in too poor a state of preservation to be used. In addition, historians generally consider that the true extent of trade is under-recorded, so they may not be a complete listing.[38]

Jersey stockings were being exported as early as September 1576 when Roger Jenkins is recorded as exporting eighty pairs of "knitt jersey hose" from London to an unknown destination.[39] In 1597 Jacques de Hem sent fifty pairs of white jersey stockings from Yarmouth to Camphere in the Low Countries. These were valued by customs for export purposes at a total of £10, which equates to 4s a pair.[40]

Yarmouth was an international port at the end of the sixteenth century, and cargos went as far as the Baltic in the north and the Italian states in the Mediterranean: much of what was exported was cloth, but herring was frequently traded, too. Some of the export port books which have survived for the period 1600 to 1602 give full details of cargos, including jersey stockings, plus their destination and the person exporting the items, which enables an analysis of the cargos, an understanding of some of the traders' activities, and sometimes, using other evidence, their status in local society. One book for Michaelmas 1600 to Michaelmas 1601 lists 2,940 pairs of stockings in thirty separate cargos: all these are described as "corse jersey hose."[41] Two port books

---

36 Zell and Falvey, *Walter Morrell's "Manufacture,"* 52.
37 Gary Paul Baker, "Domestic Maritime Trade in Late Tudor England c. 1565–85: A Case Study of King's Lynn and Plymouth," in *The Routledge Companion to Marine and Maritime Worlds 1400–1800*, ed. Claire Jowitt, Craig Lambert, and Steve Mentz (London: Routledge, 2020), 96–101.
38 Baker, "Domestic Maritime Trade," 99–100.
39 *London. Official Collector of Tonnage and Poundage. Overseas, Exports Easter–Michaelmas 1576*, TNA E 190/6/4, Sept. 12, 1576, item 5.
40 *Yarmouth. Official: Customer Overseas 1597*, TNA E 190/479/9, 4v, item 2.
41 *Yarmouth. Official: Searcher Overseas Michaelmas 1600–Michaelmas 1601*, TNA E 190/481/2.

giving details of cargos have survived for the following year. One covers the period Easter to Michaelmas (April to September) 1602 and lists eighteen cargos, totalling 1,523 pairs: all these stockings are also "corse jersey."[42] The other covers the period October 1601 to September 1602, and lists the same cargos as that of the previous book for the summer period; in addition, although only a few cargos have their individual items listed for the winter period in this book, a further 351 pairs of "corse jersey" stockings are recorded in four cargos.[43] These totals obviously do not include smuggled pairs, which could account for nearly another thousand pairs, using Michell's estimate that around 20 percent more than the recorded total of stockings were smuggled from Yarmouth around 1600.[44] There are no stockings of any other type, such as woollen or worsted, recorded in these port books. Stockings were usually one item in a mixed cargo, but occasionally they were the only item: on eight occasions in 1600/1 and four occasions in 1601/2.[45] Six of these cargos were more than a hundred pairs,[46] but the lowest number was twenty-eight pairs in 1601/2.[47]

The majority of the 4,814 pairs of stockings recorded in these three books are described as white: there were thirty-seven pairs described as dyed or coloured in 1600/1, and 242 in 1601/2. There is no reason why the white stockings could not have been dyed at their destination: dyeing of finished stockings did occur, as shown in English household account books, such as those of Nathaniel Bacon, a prominent Norfolk justice of the peace, which list payments to two Norfolk tailors for dyeing twelve pairs in total. The minimum cost for dyeing a pair was 6d, and the maximum 1s 3d.[48]

The term "corse" in this period meant ordinary, common quality, or usual: the use of the term in the modern sense of coarse to mean less refined, or of large particles, was rare, and it is not certain when that became more common.[49] Wilson described the stockings the children were knitting as "fine," which also implies that "corse" means usual. It is also likely they were plain knitting: this was a simple process and would be easy to learn, and an efficient way of making stockings; reverse loop patterning would make the knitting process slower. Reverse loop patterning on silk stockings is known from the mid-sixteenth century, the best-known example being the stockings of Eleonora of Toledo.[50] Elisabeth Crowfoot considers it is possible that such patterning

42 *Yarmouth. Official: Customer Overseas Easter–Michaelmas 1602*, TNA E 190/482/14.

43 *Yarmouth. Official: Controller Overseas October–September 1601–1602*, TNA E 190/482/9.

44 Michell, "Port and Town," 30–31.

45 E 190/481/2, 2r, item 1; 6r, item 3; 6v, last item; 7v, item 7; 8r, item 6; 11r, item 4; 13r, item 1; 14r, item 6. E 190/482/9, 13r, item 5; 14v, item 2; 15r, item 3; 15v, item 7.

46 E 190/481/2, 2r, item 1; 6v, last item; 7v, item 7; 8r, item 6. E 190/482/9, 14v item 2; 15r, item 3.

47 E 190/482/9, 15v, item 7.

48 Elizabeth Stern, "Peckover and Gallyard, Two Sixteenth-Century Norfolk Tailors," *Costume* 3 (1981): 17, 19, 20, 22, 23.

49 OED, s.v. *coarse*, adj.

50 Rutt's examination of a relevant photograph reproduced in *A History of Hand Knitting* (72) suggests that at least some of the patterning was created by using reverse loop patterning, although Jane Malcolm-Davies considers that a full analysis of their construction and patterning is overdue; Malcolm-Davies, "Sticks, Stones, Fingers and Bones:

might have been used on wool stockings, too, in this period, and thus some jersey stockings might not have been described as "corse" or plain.[51] The fragments of one of the stockings found in Norwich did include reverse loop patterning, but these are dated to between 1620 and 1650.[52]

Whilst destinations are given in the Yarmouth export port books for 1600/1 and 1601/2, it is not always possible to link a ship to its destination. Although Wilson only listed France specifically as a destination for the Norwich jersey stockings, just 307 pairs out of 4,814 pairs (5.3 percent) are definitely recorded as being exported from Yarmouth to France. In reality, the vast majority of confirmed destinations for the stockings exported from Yarmouth were in the Low Countries: 4,116 pairs (85 percent). Of these pairs, over half (2,479 pairs, or 60 percent), went to Rotterdam, in twenty-eight cargos.[53]

The 1601/2 books give the values of the pairs of stockings. The value per pair on which duty was paid was 32d (2s 8d) for all the cargos of white stockings, and the value per pair for all cargos of the coloured stockings was 40d (3s 4d), presumably reflecting the additional value that dyeing added to the latter. On four occasions duty was not paid on some of the stockings in a cargo, although it was paid on all the other pairs in those cargos.[54] In each case, the duty was not paid on only a few pairs: twenty white ones on one occasion, thirteen coloured ones on another, and five white pairs on the other two. There is no obvious link with the number not attracting duty and the size of a cargo, and on other occasions duty was paid on all pairs of stockings in a cargo containing a similar number.

Only one other export of jersey stockings has been traced: the 1598/9 London port book of exports by native Englishmen records seven dozen pairs of short jersey stockings, which were probably stockings that came to the knee.[55] The term "jersey stockings" does not occur in other late-sixteenth- and early-seventeenth-century port books for London, King's Lynn, Boston, and Ulster which were examined for this research.[56] The terms "woollen" and "worsted" are used in these books, as in other official government documents, although the books of rates of the duty to be paid for exporting stockings in Elizabeth's reign do not include yarn descriptors. Jersey stockings are no longer recorded in Yarmouth port books after the early seventeenth

---

Nurturing Knitting and the Other Neglected Non-wovens," *Archaeological Textiles Review* 60 (2018): 5–6.

51 Crowfoot, "Textiles," 49.
52 Crowfoot, "Textiles," 48, 49, 58.
53 E 190/481/2, E 190/482/9, E 190/482/14.
54 E 190/482/9 14v, 15r (2), 18r.
55 *London. Official: Controller of Tonnage and Poundage Overseas Exports by Denizens Michaelmas 1598–Michaelmas 1599*, TNA E 190/10/11, 1r, item 5.
56 *London. Official: Surveyor Overseas: Exports by Denizens, Xmas 1608–Xmas 1609*, TNA E 190/14/7; G. A. Metters, *The King's Lynn Port Books 1610–1614* (Norwich, UK: Norfolk Record Society, 2009); R. W. K. Hinton, *The Port Books of Boston 1601–1640* (Hereford, UK: Lincolnshire Record Society, 1956); R. J. Horner and B. Scott, *The Ulster Port Books 1612–1615* (Belfast: Ulster Historical Foundation, 2012).

century. The 1611/2 book for exports uses the terms "woollen" and "worsted" as yarn descriptors: of the 11,604 pairs recorded, 11,190 were worsted and 414 were woollen.[57] The revised book of customs rates promulgated in 1604 under James I used the terms "worsted" and "woollen" as yarn descriptors to differentiate the types of stockings on which export duty was due: jersey does not appear as a category, and the Yarmouth port officials thus seem to have simply used the official terms, rather than any local variation.[58]

YARMOUTH EXPORT TRADERS AND JERSEY STOCKINGS FROM NORWICH

As the Yarmouth port books for 1600/1 and 1601/2 listed the traders who were exporting the stockings, it is possible to gain a sense of the people who were involved in the trade. This in turn enables a search of other records for the various traders mentioned, which can reveal information about their location, economic status, and social backgrounds. It was considered likely that these traders were local, and so records of Norwich and Yarmouth were examined for names that matched those of the traders. The Yarmouth port books distinguish between indigenous (native English) and alien (Stranger) traders. At this point in time, the trade from Yarmouth was dominated by the alien traders: there were few native English traders. Of the fifteen traders in the 1600/1 book, only four were native Englishmen; in the 1601/2 books, three were native Englishmen and twelve were aliens. (Ten years later, this had changed: thirty of the thirty-four traders were Englishmen in the 1611/2 export port book.)[59]

Table 6.1 shows the traders in the port books with traced links to Norwich or Yarmouth. Whilst there is often variation in the spelling of names in the port books and the sources used, the matches are sufficiently close to be credible. With one possible exception, the traders were Norwich based.

Two indigenous traders were located. A William Hearne appears in both the Yarmouth and Norwich records of freemen and city officials: either might be the exporter, as the Norwich one was a mercer and the Yarmouth one the son of a merchant. It is likely that only one was sending cargos in a specific year, as the officials would otherwise have needed to differentiate between them, given these were official documents.[60] The other native trader, Thomas Spendelowe, was an important person in Norwich, holding many offices at the beginning of the seventeenth century, including that of alderman

---

57 *Yarmouth Official: Searcher Overseas 25 Dec 1611–25 Dec 1612*, TNA E 190/484/2.
58 *The Rates of Merchandizes as they are Set Down in the Book of Rates for the Custome …* (London: G. Eld, 1604), 74.
59 E 190/484/2.
60 Timothy Hawes, ed., *Index to Norwich City Officers 1453–1835*, Norfolk Record Society 52 (Norwich, UK: Norfolk Record Society, 1986), 83; John Lestrange, ed., *Calendar of the Freemen of Norwich from 1317 to 1603* (London: Elliot Stock, 1888), 101; *A Calendar of the Freemen of Great Yarmouth 1429–1860* (Norwich, UK: Norfolk and Norwich Archaeological Society, 1910), 51.

Table 6.1: Exports of jersey stockings by traders with links to Norwich or Yarmouth

Name	National origin	Number of pairs exported	
		1600/1 port book	1601/2 port books
William Hearne	English	540 (in 3 cargos)	180 (in 2 cargos)
Thomas Spendelowe	English	385 (in 4 cargos)	624 (in 5 cargos)
Jacques de Hem	foreign	262 (in 3 cargos)	36
Oliver Dackett	foreign	716 (in 4 cargos)	—
Pasque Huberte	foreign	—	183
Jorge de May	foreign	72	—
Georgio Maye	foreign	—	210
John Goglier	foreign	17	—
Romens Rokingham	foreign	83	—
Joyce de Keysar	foreign	552 (in 5 cargos)	—
Total number of pairs exported by these men		2,627	1,233
Percentage of total pairs exported		89%	65%

and also of sheriff.[61] He was clearly a major trader, exporting and importing through Yarmouth: his name occurred with cargos that do not include stockings, and he was still recorded trading in the 1611/2 Yarmouth port book, although not in stockings.[62] Spendelowe was also a signatory to a letter from the mayor and council to the Privy Council in June 1623 asking them not to grant the borough of King's Lynn's request to set up a stocking knitting enterprise there, as it would mean less work for Norwich's poor who were struggling: it could be argued that this reflects his interest in trading in stockings, but might simply be an indication of his status in the city.[63]

Several Stranger, or alien, traders were found. In some cases there are several references to them in Norwich sources; in others there are only one or two. Jacques de Hem was probably the leading Stranger merchant in Norwich, from the 1580s to his death in 1624—and he was a very wealthy man.[64] Like Spendelowe, he was a major trader, exporting and importing through Yarmouth: many cargos he exported did not include stockings, and he was still recorded trading in the 1611/2 Yarmouth port book, although not in stockings.[65] He was also regularly listed paying tax as a Stranger on incoming goods, including sacks of wool and trusses of yarn.[66] On March 6, 1601,

61 Hawes, *Norwich City Officers*, 143. There is a range of spellings for Spendelowe's name.
62 E 190/484/2.
63 *Mayor and C. of Norwich [to King's Privy Council], 27 June 1623*, TNA SP 14/147, fol. 95.
64 Meeres, *The Welcome Stranger*, 65–66.
65 E 190/484/2.
66 D. L. Rickwood, *The Norwich Accounts for the Customs on Strangers' Goods and Merchandise 1582–1610*, Norfolk Record Society 39 (Norwich, UK: Norfolk Record Society, 1970), 81–111.

he became a freeman of Norwich as a merchant, purchasing this for £30: this entitled him to special trading rights and privileges on the same terms as native-born citizens who were freemen.[67]

Oliver Dackett, described as a hosier, was another wealthy Stranger merchant, although he only exported stockings in 1600/1. He clearly traded in stockings on other occasions: at Christmas 1605 he was recorded as paying the internal aulnage duty—required on all stockings offered for sale on the open market in England—on more than forty dozen pairs, and elsewhere he was described as a hosier.[68] Pasque Huberte was another merchant: he occurred regularly in the accounts for Strangers' goods from 1585/6 to 1600/1.[69] Frank Meeres identifies two Pasque Hubertes in Norwich around 1600, and links both to the Stranger Herbert family, one of whom was a wealthy cloth merchant.[70]

A George de Maye was listed in the 1600/1 accounts for Strangers' goods, paying duty on barrels of whey butter:[71] he may well be both the Jorge de May of the 1600/1 book who exported seventy-two pairs of stockings and the Georgio May[e] of 1601/2 who exported 210 pairs, as Jorge is the Spanish or Portuguese version of George, and part of the Low Countries was ruled by Spain in this period. Whey butter was used in combing wool, so George was very likely to have links to yarn production.[72] John Goglier and Romens Rokingham were both listed in the lay subsidy rolls (which assessed the wealth of individuals for tax purposes) for Norwich for the thirty-ninth and forty-first years of Elizabeth's reign (1596/7 and 1598/9), and were amongst the wealthier aliens, assessed on goods worth 20s and 40s, respectively.[73] Although Joyce de Keysar exported a total of 552 pairs of stockings, in five different cargos in 1600/1, no person of that name has been traced in Norwich records, but there were others with that surname who might well have been relatives.[74]

Given that these men all lived in Norwich (or perhaps Yarmouth in the case of Hearne) they would have been well placed to acquire quantities of jersey stockings knitted there. Seventy-seven percent of the total number of pairs exported in the two years between Michaelmas (September 29) 1600 and September 1602 have been linked to these men.

However, other evidence from the port books suggests that stockings were not purchased only by rich merchants: there was a wide range of buyers for jersey stockings.

67 Percy Millican, *The Register of the Freemen of Norwich 1548–1713* (Norwich, UK: Jarrold, 1934), 104.
68 *Cooke v Dutton, Response of William Paslew to Interrogatory 16, 19 September 1606,* TNA STAC 8/90/19; Millican, *Register,* 220.
69 Rickwood, *Norwich Accounts,* 91–100, 104, 108.
70 Meeres, *The Welcome Stranger,* 144.
71 Rickwood, *Norwich Accounts,* 105.
72 Thelma Morris, *"Made in Norwich": 700 Years of Textile Heritage* (Norwich, UK: Nick Williams, 2008), 13.
73 W. J. C. Moens, *The Walloons and Their Church at Norwich: 1565–1832 in Two Parts* (Lymington, UK: The Huguenot Society of London, 1887–88), 2:177, 178, 183.
74 Meeres, *The Welcome Stranger,* 71, 166.

The sizes of cargos were also analysed and showed that potentially anyone might export stockings. Severin Langlebecte sent five cargos which included stockings recorded in these port books: fifty-nine pairs in two cargos in 1600/1 and eighty-four pairs in three cargos in 1601/2. Whilst some traders exported cargos of stockings on more than one occasion, others did so only once, suggesting trading in stockings could be opportunistic. Table 6.2 shows the dominance of cargos with small numbers of stockings. Of the fifty-two cargos of stockings traced, 61.5 percent consisted of fewer than a hundred pairs, and a third of the total cargos were fewer than fifty pairs. Many traders originally from the Low Countries maintained their links with family members still there, and this could assist them in selling the goods they were exporting.[75]

Table 6.2: Sizes of cargos containing jersey stockings, 1600–2

Pairs of jersey stockings in a cargo	Less than 50	50–99	100–49	150–99	200–49	250–99
Number of cargos this size	18	14	9	3	5	3

The London port book of exports by native Englishmen shows the same dichotomy of many traders sending small quantities of pairs of stockings in a cargo, whilst a few traders were responsible for a large proportion of the stockings exported. Ten of the sixty-one cargos contained fewer than fifty pairs, and a further eleven contained between fifty and ninety-nine pairs. For example, Thomas Bostocke exported twenty pairs in March and fifty pairs in June, whilst Thomas Allport exported thirty-six pairs in April.[76] Conversely, the five largest cargos totalled 5,030 pairs, 36 percent of the total pairs of stockings.

Some cargos included only a very few pairs of jersey stockings. In 1600/1 one of Langlebecte's cargos included only six pairs, another trader exported only eight pairs in his cargo, and a third just twelve pairs; in 1601/2, three cargos included fewer than seventeen pairs each. Conversely, a small number of merchants accounted for the bulk of the pairs traded. In 1600/1 five merchants were responsible for 83 percent of the exports. The Strangers Oliver Dackett and Joyce de Keysar together sent nearly half the exports (24 percent and 19 percent respectively), whilst Jacques de Hem exported 9 percent; two native Englishmen, William Hearne and Thomas Spendelowe, were responsible for nearly a third of the exports (18 percent and 13 percent, respectively). In the 1601/2 books, Thomas Spendelowe was responsible

---

75 Meeres, *The Welcome Stranger*, 148–51.
76 E 190/10/11: Bostocke, 21r, item 2; 31v, item 4; Allport, 24v, item 5.

for a third of all the stockings listed, and William Hearne and three alien merchants were responsible for a further 44 percent.

INTERNAL TRADE WITHIN ENGLAND

There is much less evidence of internal trade within England than export trade, and what has survived has done so by chance. Contracts were made for the supply of stockings, but reference to them survives by accident: that of John Underwood and Peter Noxton because it is mentioned by the former in an extant letter, whilst that of Richard Stonham of King's Lynn and Nathaniel Michells of London because their arrangement broke down and resulted in several court cases.[77] Neither contract, though, suggests the number of pairs involved. The type of stocking was unspecified in the first case, and in the second worsted was specifically mentioned in addition to unspecified "other" stockings. The 1617 inventory of hosier Henry Sheardley of Norwich listed 335 pairs of stockings, of which ninety-nine pairs (around 30 percent) were jersey stockings: he was clearly trading in stockings.[78]

The 1598/9 London port book of exports by native Englishmen included a thousand pairs of Norwich short worsted stockings being exported on a single occasion.[79] This quantity of Norwich stockings exported by a London trader shows that there was clearly a trade in stockings between London and Norwich, but there is little evidence to show how this occurred. Norwich traders did not deal through the official London channels. The port books recording coastal trade from Yarmouth show very few cargos of stockings being sent to London by sea. Given these were not bulk goods like coal, it is much more likely that these were sent by road. Carriers regularly travelled from Norwich to the capital. Evidence from disputes about the payment of aulnage at the beginning of the seventeenth century clearly shows that stockings were transported to London from Norwich by cart.[80] Stockings appear with the various cloths woven in Norwich in other documentation about aulnage, which suggests that they were being produced in sufficient quantity for widespread sale.[81]

---

77 *John Underwood to his brother, 13 August 1580*, TNA SP 46/32, fol. 89, available at State Papers Online, 1509–1714 [database], https://www.gale.com/intl/primary-sources/state-papers-online (accessed Aug. 6, 2018); *Nathaniel Michells (plaintiff) Richard Stonham (defendant) Court of Requests 1597*, TNA REQ 2/239/52.

78 *Inventory of Henry Sheardley.*

79 E 190/10/11, 4v, item 5.

80 STAC 8/90/19.

81 For example, see *Exchequer: King's Remembrancer: Barons' Depositions: Lenox v Baker 1606*, TNA E 133/80/19.

CHILD KNITTERS AND EARNINGS: THE BACKGROUND TO *THE STATE OF ENGLAND*

Wilson's comments on the age of child knitters and earnings are worthy of serious consideration. Since he alone is the source of the numerical information on earnings of the Norwich child jersey knitters, the background to *An Account of the State of England in Anno Domini 1600* needs to be understood. The work covers English social and economic structures in 1600, providing details of the incomes of the crown and upper classes as well as the governance and defences of England and Ireland. It seems likely that it was written in early 1601. Wilson (1560s?–1629) was a government official, part of the Cecil faction at Queen Elizabeth's court, so he wrote *The State of England* from the perspective of one well versed in political and government matters.[82] There is no specific indication in the work for whom it was written. F. J. Fisher suggested it might have been written for an Italian friend or patron, whilst Sean Kelsey considered it was his pitch for gainful employment in the government but did not speculate for whom it was intended.[83]

The State of England survives in two manuscript versions.[84] It was eventually published in 1936, when it was edited by economic historian F. J. Fisher for a Camden Society *Miscellany* volume.[85] The words concerning the child jersey knitters of Norwich and their earnings are the same in both the original manuscripts, and the transcript is a precise copy.[86] Fisher commented in his introduction that it was difficult to say how accurate Wilson's monetary estimates were as there are no other contemporary sources, but that other information Wilson provided which is known from other sources, such as the wealth of merchants and lawyers or incomes of bishops, suggested the document was worthy of serious consideration.[87] In the later 1590s Wilson was heavily used as a foreign intelligencer by the Cecils and by Thomas Sackville, Lord Treasurer Buckhurst.

82 A. F. Pollard and Sean Kelsey, "Wilson, Sir Thomas (d. 1629), Record Keeper and Author," Jan. 3, 2008, in *Oxford Dictionary of National Biography*, online ed. (Oxford: Oxford University Press, 2004–), https://www.oxforddnb.com (accessed Feb. 27, 2023).

83 Fisher, *The State of England*, vii; Pollard and Kelsey, "Wilson, Sir Thomas." In the original *Oxford Dictionary of National Biography* entry (1904), Pollard suggested it was written for Sir Robert Cecil, but the revised version (2008) does not suggest this, and neither did Fisher in 1936.

84 Thomas Wilson, *An Account of the State of England in Anno Domini 1600*, TNA SP 12/280. Both manuscripts are bound into this volume. The manuscripts have been digitised and are available at State Papers Online, 1509–1714 (see note 77, above; accessed May 11, 2023).

85 Fisher, *The State of England*, vii.

86 Wilson, *Account of the State of England*, "The state of citizens," at 25 in the holograph version and 22 in the other version.

87 Fisher, *The State of England*, vii.

His repeated appointments suggested they found him a reliable informant, and it is likely he carried this trait into his reports and writing.[88]

CHILD KNITTERS IN ENGLAND AROUND 1600

Wilson's statement indicated very clearly that there were child knitters between the ages of six and ten years making jersey stockings in Norwich in 1600, and evidence from a range of other sources shows that young children were knitting stockings in this period.[89] Knitting was seen as a suitable occupation for poor children, and several knitting schools were set up in towns and cities in the 1590s to teach them this skill, including one in Norwich.[90]

There are three contemporary sources that provide age data on groups of child knitters: the Norwich census of the poor made in 1570, one in Ipswich made in 1597, and a civic project to provide the poor with training and work in Salisbury in 1625.[91] All of these were drawn up by local officials to answer a particular concern of the local civic authority: these were not generalised accounts, as the officials gave specific details of the individuals involved. Figure 6.2 shows the range of ages from these sources, revealing that fifty out of 124 children (40 percent) are in the age range of six to ten years.

The 1570 Norwich census of the poor listed seventy-five child knitters who were under twenty-one, twenty-nine of whom were between ages six and ten. In total, there were 995 people under twenty-one in the census: 926 children under sixteen and a further sixty-nine between ages sixteen and twenty.[92] The initiative to set the poor to work in Salisbury in 1625 included fourteen children under age sixteen being apprenticed to be knitters, of whom eleven were between ages six and ten.[93] Thirty child knitters are listed in the incomplete 1597 Ipswich census of the poor, of whom eight were between ages six and ten; another five children were learning to knit, of whom four fell into this age bracket.[94]

88 Pollard and Kelsey, "Wilson, Sir Thomas."
89 Fisher, *The State of England*, 20. For child knitters, see, for instance, J. F. Pound, *The Norwich Census of the Poor 1570*, Norfolk Record Society 40 (Norwich, UK: Norfolk Record Society, 1971).
90 O'Connell Edwards, "Knitting Schools," 30–33; Frank Meeres, *The Story of Norwich* (Andover, UK: Phillimore, 2011), 101.
91 Pound, *Norwich Census of the Poor*; Webb, *Poor Relief in Elizabethan Ipswich*, 119–40; Paul Slack, *Poverty in Early Stuart Salisbury*, Wiltshire Record Society 31 (Devizes, UK: Wiltshire Record Society, 1975), 65–75.
92 Pound, *Norwich Census of the Poor*, 95–96; O'Connell Edwards, "The Stocking Knitting Industry," 151–52.
93 Slack, *Poverty in Early Stuart Salisbury*, 65–75.
94 Webb, *Poor Relief in Elizabethan Ipswich*, 119–40.

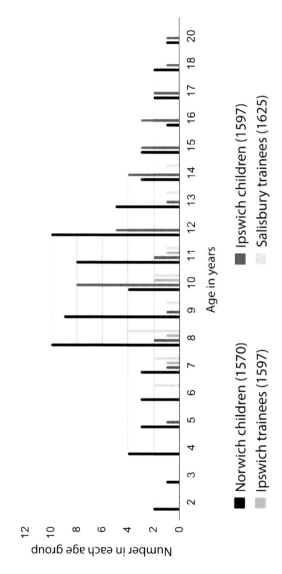

Fig. 6.2: Age ranges of child knitters. Sources: J. F. Pound, *The Norwich Census of the Poor 1570* (Norwich, UK: Norfolk Record Society, 1971); John Webb, *Poor Relief in Elizabethan Ipswich* (Ipswich, UK: Suffolk Record Society, 1966), 119–40; Paul Slack, *Poverty in Early Stuart Salisbury* (Devizes, UK: Wiltshire Record Society, 1975), 65–75. Graph: Copyright © Lesley O'Connell Edwards.

WAGES FOR CHILDREN; WAGES FOR KNITTERS

Thomas Wilson commented that any child age seven and over could earn four shillings a week knitting jersey stockings. Four shillings is a ridiculously high weekly wage for the period, especially for what is not very skilled labour, and is thus likely to be incorrect for the child jersey stocking knitters: it is much higher than recorded adult wages. Craig Muldrew estimated that a married woman working as a spinner could earn 1s 1½d in 1580 and 1s 4d in 1620 weekly.[95] Casual wages paid on a daily basis for non-regular work for women were around 3d per day in 1600, as was the casual wage for children.[96]

Evidence from Norwich in the early 1570s shows that poor children could earn 6d a week. In 1571 the city council imposed Orders for the Poor which included measures to prevent begging and provide work for those who were idle, both adults and children. Following the details of these orders is a comment noting that they had been put into practice and listing the benefits the city had reaped from this process, including that those children who were previously idle or begging were now kept in work and could earn 6d a week.[97]

Weekly wages were included for some knitters in the Ipswich census of the poor made in 1597. The wages of the eighteen children whose only source of income was knitting ranged from 1d to 11d weekly: twelve earned between 4d and 8d. Only one adult woman earned more than a shilling a week, and then only 2s.[98]

Knitting silk stockings cost more, but the little evidence available only refers to money paid for knitting a single pair. The fine gauge of silk stockings, plus the expertise needed to handle the silk yarn, suggest these would have been made by skilled workers and would take considerably more than a week to make. Writing in the 1580s, Stubbes claimed that just the knitting of silk stockings, or stockings made from the finest yarn, cost between a noble and a ryall, or possibly even more; this equates to between 6s 8d and 15s at least.[99] In 1594 the Bacon accounts recorded a payment of 15s for the knitting of a pair of tawny silk stockings for Nathaniel Bacon.[100] The Texel silk stocking reconstruction project estimated that re-creating a single stocking took around two

---

95 Craig Muldrew, "'Th'ancient Distaff' and 'Whirling Spindle': Measuring the Contribution of Spinning to Household Earnings and the National Economy in England, 1550–1770," *Economic History Review* 65 (2012): 519.

96 Jane Humphries and Jacob Weisdorf, "The Wages of Women in England, 1260–1850," *Journal of Economic History* 75, no. 2 (2015): 432; Sara Horrell and Jane Humphries, "Children's Work and Wages in Britain, 1280–1860," *Explorations in Economic History* 73 (2019), app. A: "Values of Children's Pay and Remuneration by Decade."

97 John C. Tingey, comp. and ed., *The Records of the City of Norwich*, vol. 2, *Containing Documents Relating to the Social and Economic Progress of the City* (Norwich, UK: Jarrold, 1910), 355.

98 Webb, *Poor Relief in Elizabethan Ipswich*, 119–40.

99 Stubbes, *The Anatomie of Abuses*, 47; Colin R. Chapman, *How Heavy, How Much and How Long?* (Dursley, UK: Lochin Publishing, 1995), 64.

100 Stern, "Peckover and Gallyard," 21.

hundred hours of knitting.[101] However, Wilson was very clear that the children earned a weekly amount, rather than a payment per pair; and that the stockings were made from jersey yarn, not silk.

OTHER POSSIBLE EXPLANATIONS FOR WILSON'S FOUR SHILLINGS

Tudor writers did not produce their figures in a vacuum, and there are other possible explanations for Wilson's figure of four shillings which need to be considered. It could be that when Wilson used the term "earn" he was thinking either of the total value of a pair of stockings, or what a child knitter earned for the city, not for him/herself.

It may be that Wilson confused the value or price of a pair of stockings with weekly earnings. The average customs value of the fifty pairs exported by Jacques de Hem from Yarmouth in 1597 was 4s per pair.[102] It is possible that Wilson saw this record and had it in his memory. The values placed on the white and coloured jersey stockings in the 1600/1 and 1601/2 Yarmouth port books are lower, at 2s 8d for a white pair and 3s 4d for a coloured pair, but not too dissimilar.[103] William Cavendish's accounts show that three pairs cost 4s 8d per pair in 1599.[104] The Norwich inventory of Henry Sheardley, hosier, made in 1617, shows two types of jersey stockings, valued at 2s 8d and 3s 8d per pair, respectively: the inventory values are likely to be wholesale prices.[105] The latter figure of 3s 8d is near Wilson's four shillings so it is possible that the four shillings includes the cost of the yarn, dressing, and other overheads, not just the cost of knitting the stockings.

However, it may be that Wilson's four shillings is a reference to a more theoretical economic concept of what the whole of the jersey stocking production process earned for the nation in general. Another sixteenth-century document clearly used the term "earn" in reference to the whole creation of a pair of jersey stockings, from raw fibre to finished product. Robert Payne's documentation concerning the establishment of a woad-growing project at Woollaton in 1586 states that 8s could be earned out of a pound of wool by women and children, by turning it into jersey yarn and then knitting two pairs of stockings from this yarn: half a pound of wool would thus earn 4s. The intention was to show that the New Draperies, which included stockings, kept more people in work than the older broadcloths and earned the country more money.[106] It may be that Wilson saw this document—or that both men were working from another source, now lost. This concept was clearly in circulation for a while: writing in 1616,

101 A pattern based on these stockings (from Shipwreck BZN17 Texel) has been made and is available through Ravelry as "17th Century Silk Stockings," https://www.ravelry.com/patterns/library/17th-century-silkstockings (accessed June 5, 2023). The pattern credits Chrystel Brandenburgh and Marialli Buitondijh.
102 E 190/479/9, 4v, item 2.
103 E 190/482/14; E 190/482/9.
104 Riden, *Household Accounts*, 41:197.
105 *Inventory of Henry Sheardley*.
106 Payne, *Brief Description*, fol. 172.

Walter Morrell mentioned the same calculation that a pound of wool would create two pairs of worsted stockings, again to prove that the New Draperies employed more people and earned the country more money. The value he placed on each pair was a little more, at 4s 6d per pair: possibly a reflection of the general rise in prices.[107]

The benefits listed in the Orders for the Poor of Norwich City in the 1570s were also based on the idea that providing work for those who had been idle or begged resulted in an annual financial benefit to the "common wealth" of the city. Although the author only mentioned that the poor children who begged or were idle now earned 6d a week, he produced an annual total of £1,235 to the benefit of the city, which is based on the calculation that 950 poor children were earning 6d a week (this number includes those who were listed with an occupation in the 1570 census of the poor).[108]

CHILD JERSEY STOCKING KNITTERS IN NORWICH: NUMBERS AND OUTPUTS

Contemporary writers considered that a knitter would make two pairs of stockings a week, although they did not take into account the size of the stockings or the fineness of yarn.[109] It is possible to produce an estimate of the number of child jersey stocking knitters based on Wilson's figures. A full-time knitter is likely to have knitted for fifty weeks a year, allowing for Christmas and other celebrations (although the author of the benefits of the Norwich Orders for the Poor based his calculations on a fifty-two-week year).[110] At 4s a week, in fifty weeks each child would earn £10. Wilson commented that jersey stocking knitting would be the chief part of the £12,000 the children gained, but did not define exactly what he meant by "chief part." If it is reasonable to assume that the "chief part" of the £12,000 earned towards the children's keep from knitting jersey stockings was £10,000, then that estimate means that a thousand children in Norwich between six or seven and ten years old were knitting jersey stockings. However, it should be borne in mind that some knitters might only knit for part of the year, such as when no agricultural work was available; or might have an additional occupation such as spinning, as was the case with eighteen of the seventy-five knitters under the age of twenty-one in the Norwich census of the poor.[111]

Given that the total population of Norwich at this time was around 15,000, this estimate suggests that approximately 6.7 percent of the population were children knitting jersey stockings.[112] Around 37.5 percent of the population in this period would be under sixteen, which equates to around 5,650 for Norwich: and given high infant mortality probably fewer than 1,500 would be in the six-to-ten-year age bracket.[113]

107 Zell and Falvey, *Walter Morrell's "Manufacture,"* 21.
108 Tingey, *Records of the City of Norwich*, 355.
109 Thirsk, "Fantastical Folly of Fashion," 64.
110 Thirsk, "Fantastical Folly of Fashion," 64.
111 O'Connell Edwards, "The Stocking Knitting Industry," 151–52.
112 Tittler, "Society and Social Relations," 364.
113 Nigel Goose and Andrew Hinde, "Estimating Local Population Sizes at Fixed Points In Time: Part II: Specific Sources," *Local Population Studies* 78 (2007): 79.

This would suggest a dearth of children in this age range available for all the other economic activities they might carry out, with consequences for the rest of the population. There are no contemporary comments that this was the case. In addition, this figure does not include all the other knitters of different ages who were making other types of stockings: the 1570 Norwich census of the poor and that of Ipswich in 1597 shows that all ages of the poor knitted, and this is likely to have been the case with other knitters who were not classed as poor.[114] This would suggest an even higher percentage of the city's population were stocking knitters, but again this is not confirmed by contemporary evidence.

However, there is an alternative explanation: it is quite possible that not all the child knitters (and the other knitters) lived in the city. Norfolk was a densely populated part of the country, with many who worked at least part time in the textile trades. A 1596 Norwich inventory confirmed that one trader was putting yarn out to knitters in the countryside to knit stockings, and it is very likely others did, too.[115] It is possible that Wilson made the error of assuming that because the stockings came from Norwich, all the knitters must have done, too.

If it is assumed each of the child knitters was making two pairs a week, like other knitters, then, continuing with the assumption of one thousand knitters, between them they were making 100,000 pairs annually. Whilst this seems a large number, it has been estimated that everyone wore out at least two pairs annually which means that given a minimum population of England of four-and-a-half million, at least nine million pairs of stockings were needed, so perhaps such a large number is not surprising.[116]

However, if jersey stockings were made from much finer yarn, the gauge at which the stockings were knitted would be finer. Fewer pairs would therefore be created by an individual knitter per year, as each stocking would contain more wales, and there is a limited number of these that can be created in a set time. Since there is no evidence, either archival or archaeological, concerning the gauge of jersey stockings, it is thus not possible to provide an accurate estimate of how many pairs the child jersey stocking knitters might have created.

CONCLUSION

The evidence for child knitters shows that children between the ages of six and ten were knitting stockings, both in Norwich and elsewhere in England. It confirms that children of these ages were expected to work and that knitting was seen as a suitable occupation for them. This paper has offered suggestions as to what could underlie Wil-

114 O'Connell Edwards, "The Stocking Knitting Industry," 148–49, 151–52; Webb, *Poor Relief in Elizabethan Ipswich*, 119–40.
115 *Inventory of Susanna Backowe*, 1598, Norwich, UK, Norfolk Record Office, DN/INV 15/233, fol. 1.
116 Thirsk, "Fantastical Folly of Fashion," 63–64.

son's statements about the wages earned by Norwich child knitters and also shown how his numerical data might be used to extrapolate statistics about the number of knitters.

Evidence for internal trade is circumstantial, but stockings knitted in Norwich were being sold elsewhere. Evidence from the port books of 1600/1 and 1601/2 for Yarmouth clearly shows that jersey stockings were traded overseas. Over three-quarters of the 4,814 pairs exported were handled by traders with proven links to Norwich or Yarmouth, with the vast majority going to the Low Countries. Combining the evidence from the port books with other local records from Norwich and Yarmouth has resulted in a greater understanding of trading networks between Norwich, Yarmouth, and the Low Countries.

In conclusion, this research has shown that hand-knitted jersey stockings were being produced in quantity in Norwich in a pre-mechanised age, and that channels existed to ensure that these were traded and sold, including abroad. It confirms the comments of contemporary writers that large numbers of stockings were being produced and thus could contribute to the overall economy of England.

Recent Books of Interest

Archaeological Footwear II: Sandals, Pattens and Mules, from the Roman, Mediaeval and Modern Periods, by Marquita Volken (Zwolle, Netherlands: SPA Uitgevers, 2022). ISBN 978-9089320704 (hardback), 978-9089320711 (paperback). 295 pages, 379 illustrations (31 in color).

Following Marquita Volken's first volume on shoes by eight years,[1] her new book immediately clarifies how she has adapted her earlier innovative approach in categorizing shoe uppers to cover three new types of footwear. Because the basic letter-shape codes she used previously do not apply to sandals, pattens, and mules, she encodes them according to the item type and the sole material, e.g., PC means patten with cork sole, MUL translates to mule with a leather sole.

She then explains the technical characteristics of each type and where and when they found favor by their European wearers. The chapters cover Roman sandals, Roman bath slippers and clogs, medieval-to-modern pattens, and mules (including chopines). Most of these include an introduction, sometimes coverage of relevant tools, written and iconographic sources, methodology and terminology, and detailed descriptions of various named types surviving in archaeological contexts. Throughout, diagrams and photos clarify many points, provide examples of finds, and demonstrate decorative details added by artisans of the past.

As in the earlier volume, Volken provides numerous well-drawn style and chronology diagrams that compare various kinds of footwear, visually conveying when each style comes into fashion and then fades away in favor of another one. Ninety primary cutting patterns provide isometric views of each style, top-down views of soles and upper components, and bibliographic references. Most conveniently, each entry on a diagram references its corresponding pattern, and vice versa, thus making it easy to find the details of a specific style either by function and shape or by time period.

In chapter 6, "Reconstructions," Volken provides helpful photographs to detail her steps in creating thirteen different projects over fifty pages, covering the range of footwear discussed earlier in the book. Further, a number of cutaway diagrams illustrate the construction of many examples, greatly facilitating understanding of how components fit together and the stitches used to secure them to each other. Clearly

---

1   Marquita Volken, *Archaeological Footwear: Development of Shoe Patterns and Styles from Prehistory till the 1600's* (Zwolle, Netherlands: SPA Uitgevers, 2014), reviewed by Gale R. Owen-Crocker, *Medieval Clothing and Textiles* 12 (2016): 195.

the author believes that reconstructions can inform us about the past a great deal, through both crafting and wearing these types of footwear.

This new book shines brilliantly. Anyone interested in making historically accurate footwear for performances or re-enactments will find this volume invaluable as both a guide to surviving artifacts and an instructional manual for turning raw materials into wearable products. Archaeologists will also find it helpful in identifying pieces of leather that turn up in excavations, providing a reference for both how they might fit as part of a larger item and, if they carry decoration, possibly an idea of when they were created. — *Ken Stuart, Cornell University*

***Byzantine Silk on the Silk Roads: Journeys Between East and West, Past and Present*,** edited by Sarah E. Braddock Clarke and Ryoko Yamanaka Kondo (London: Bloomsbury Visual Arts, 2022). ISBN 978-1350103740. 376 pages, 350 illustrations (323 in color).

Clarke and Kondo's well-edited book includes deep-dive articles covering the construction, history, and dissemination of silk textiles along the Silk Roads, from ancient China to twenty-first-century adaptations. While this may seem overly ambitious, the connecting threads between articles (loom technology and silk) make clear the continuous use and adaptation of structures such as brocade, lampas, and samite, woven on multi-shaft looms and drawlooms. Scholars looking to understand the antecedents of medieval Spanish, Portuguese, and Italian figured silks will find this book invaluable.

Each chapter covers a specific topic, from the Chinese origins of complex weaves and the looms that produced them to later innovations in the Mediterranean and Europe. For example, in chapter 2, "Ancient Chinese Silk Textiles: Focusing on Warp-Faced Silks," Sae Ogasawara explores the early warp-faced silks beginning in the Warring States period (475–221 BCE) through the Han dynasty (206 BCE–220 CE), crucially linking the multi-warp textiles with the gradual development of "drawloom devices" that allowed for complicated thread manipulation, creating the figured cloths that would become so popular during the European Middle Ages. In chapter 6, "Four Categories of Ancient and Medieval Classical Figured Textiles," Kazuko Yokohari compares the development of warp- and weft-faced twills, taqueté, and samite façonné, structures that figure heavily in textiles produced in Anatolia, the Iberian Peninsula, and Italian city-states. Chapters 9 and 11, both by Kondo, focus on textiles of Byzantine court dress and the patterns and dyes throughout the Byzantine Empire, respectively.

Chapter 10, "Collections of Museums, Cathedrals and Churches," consists of color photographs and detailed descriptions of specific, complex-woven textiles from collections such as the Victoria and Albert Museum in London, the Abegg-Stiftung in Switzerland, the Metropolitan Museum of Art in New York, and the Hirayama Ikuo Silk Road Museum in Japan (among others). This is an incredibly useful resource for anyone studying complex weave structures, as there are detail photos (taken by Kondo) that show interlacements. Photos of the backs of these items would have enhanced this chapter, but many of the museum websites include that information.

At the end of the book is a detailed comparative chart of textiles, cultures, and chronology that lets the reader place the textiles from Chapter 10 within the context of contemporaneous political, legislative, and trade events. This is followed by a glossary, extensive bibliography, and index.

Clarke and Kondo have produced a unique compilation that provides crucial information for understanding the dissemination of textile technology and complex weave structures from their invention in China to the East and West. — *Carla Tilghman, Lawrence, Kansas*

Clothes, Culture and Crafts: Dress and Fashion Among Artisans and Small Shop-keepers in the Danish town of Elsinore 1550–1650, by Anne-Kristine Sindvald Larsen (Espoo, Finland: Aalto University, 2023). ISBN 978-9526412726. 253 pages, 62 illustrations (58 in color).

Anne-Kristine Sindvald Larsen's study, written as a doctoral thesis, focuses on the dress of men and women of artisanal status in the early modern period in the Danish port town of Elsinore (Helsingør), located alongside the Sound, the strait that separates Zealand and Scania (now Denmark and Sweden). Based on a study of 294 inventories from Elsinore dating from 1573 to 1650, as well as visual images, material evidence, and printed sources, the dissertation provides unique insight into what these townspeople wore.

Sindvald Larsen brings attention to the culture of dress among Danish shop-keepers and tradespeople in this period, ranging from high-end artisans to small-end traders such as goldsmiths, bakers, butchers, barbers, smiths, shoemakers, drapers, clothmakers, and painters. She investigates the clothing these men and their wives wore in their everyday lives, on festive occasions, and for church.

The study explores what values and meanings might have been associated with fashion in daily life and public occasions, such as weddings and churchgoing. It shows how clothes mattered socially, professionally, and economically, and how they could be important for one's ambitions, rank, reputation, and identity. It also makes clear that even though Elsinore was a small town on a European scale, fashion was an integral part of the society, and that townspeople integrated fashionable details and objects into their wardrobes. This was true of both those who could afford the latest fashions and those who would copy them with less means.

The best chapters are undoubtedly those where Sindvald Larsen bases her conclusions on the material she has studied directly. She lists all the garments and textile accessories found in the archival sources from Elsinore, which shows what was available at the time as well as what terms were used. She also demonstrates that artisans and their wives in Elsinore owned clothes made by tailors, challenging former claims that only the wealthy could afford tailor-made garments. Elsewhere, however, she has relied heavily on non-Danish works that perhaps do not reflect the society she aims to describe. The same applies to images; for example, a chapter on church dress includes an image of bourgeois women of Elsinore, but also two images of villagers in remote parts of the kingdom. Even though all are dressed for church, one may ask whether the latter reflect the dress worn by townswomen in Elsinore.

In general, some discussion on how images were selected for the study, and how they relate to dress described in the archival sources, would have been very welcome. A large number of images of townspeople from around the Sound survive, including at least a dozen from Elsinore, from church panels to epitaphs, but this study shows only a single image of Elsinore townspeople. Perhaps more would have been useful.

Aside from these minor issues, the study offers a wealth of information on the dress of a group of people only rarely mentioned in scholarly work, as most literature on Scandinavian dress has focused on royalty and nobility. *Clothes, Culture and Crafts* is a welcome addition to the study of European dress in the early modern period and will be of particular interest to those studying the dress of townspeople and people of lower and middle classes. — *Camilla Luise Dahl, Historical Archive of Bornholm, Rønne, Denmark*

The Mitre: Its Origins and Early Development, by Nancy Spies (Leiden, Netherlands: Brill, 2024). ISBN 978-9004691049. 381 pages, 294 illustrations (about half in color).

The episcopal miter has long deserved deeper study, and this work makes a significant contribution to understanding it. It focuses on the origin of this ecclesiastical hat by clarifying its terminology, refining older theories of its physical evolution (ca. 1050 to ca. 1200), and proposing that it was a new creation, quite out of the blue, from central-southern Italy in the mid-eleventh century, which caught on because of cultural developments connected to the reform movement. The author is wise to situate the history of the artifact within broader cultural currents, approached through a variety of subdisciplines and types of evidence. The book primarily uses art history and material culture, but it also engages written evidence from a range of source genres, from liturgical to diplomatic to satirical, and thus will interest medievalists of many stripes.

Foundational to the study, and one of its greatest gifts, is the impressive collection of 534 medieval images of the miter, many of which are reproduced in 294 figures. Yet Spies is well aware of the pitfalls of artistic evidence and carefully accounts for them. Praiseworthy too is her use of "experimental archaeology," attempts to materially reproduce medieval miter styles, a process which can confirm or rule out theorized lines of development. She thereby posits two distinct styles of miter, lobed and peaked, neither of which was a stage in the evolution of the other, and one of which (the peaked) won out for the sensible reasons that she suggests. Her intriguing hypothesis that miter styles were inspired by two chess pieces may not convince everyone, but her reasoning deserves serious consideration.

Some cautions must be mentioned. The book's organization causes frequent repetitions and references to things to be discussed later. Sometimes the original Latin is provided, but sometimes not, and occasionally a translation is flawed. It is unclear why modern nations are used as geographical categories, and why "saints" is a separate category from ecclesiastical ranks. There are some factual errors (though not crippling to the argument) and some misunderstandings of the reform movement.

Certain assumptions about manuscript availability and some choices of sources were puzzling, and the liturgical commentaries could have been plumbed more thoroughly. Three matters would benefit from special attention. Though perhaps "impossible to know," can any hypothesis be advanced for the apparently total lack of archaeological and written evidence for the lobed and sideways peaked miter styles? Could the very early papal grants of the "Roman miter" indicate a privilege to dress as the pope dressed? And the abbatial miter (which did not end in 1200) requires fuller investigation and explanation.

The author nevertheless provides a great service by gathering together so much relevant evidence on a topic that has much to offer our understanding of ecclesiastical power and how it is culturally shaped and expressed. — *Steven A. Schoenig, S.J., Saint Louis University*

***Textilie z archeologických výzkumů na Pražském hradě: Památky po českých panovnících, jejich rodinných příslušnících, světcích a církevních hodnostářích** [Textiles from Archaeological Research at Prague Castle: Relics of the Czech Rulers, Their Family Members, Saints and Church Dignitaries]*, by Milena Bravermanová, Helena Březinová, and Jana Bureš Víchová; translated by David J. Gaul (Prague: Academia, 2023). ISBN 978-8020034045. 971 pages, approximately 800 illustrations (most in color).

This is the long-awaited and monumental catalog of textile finds from excavations within the Prague Castle complex, including religious buildings, grave sites, and other structures. The book documents a long-term project beginning in the 1980s to reexamine, analyze, and better conserve the site's textile remains. The work by Czech archaeologists and textile specialists was accomplished in cooperation with international experts, in particular the Abegg-Stiftung in Switzerland. This two-volume, bilingual (Czech and English) publication reports the results of those decades of work in extensive and careful detail.

Eight introductory chapters provide background for the items in the catalog, covering previous descriptions, publications, and conservation work; the history of each grave or tomb, detailing evidence for identification and any disturbances of the contents; the non-grave sites that yielded textile remains; and an overview of silk production and trade. Original text from non-Czech sources is given in footnotes with only a few exceptions. A chapter on fashion offers a high-level context for interpreting the construction and use of the garment finds.

The catalog itself is the heart of the publication, providing exceedingly detailed data on 170 finds, many of which involve multiple separate textiles. For each, it gives the physical context of the find, where it is held, evidence for dating, conservation work, dimensions, technical analysis (fiber, weave, color, pattern, and any evidence for tailoring), a summary of previous reports, relationships to similar fabrics, and a synthesis of the best current understanding of the textile's origins, provenance, and usage. Photographs and figures might illustrate the find's original state, the original arrangement of fragments, weaving diagrams, drawings of decorative motifs, the most likely reconstruction and any evidence of sewing, and in a few cases, modern replicas of the garment. A final table summarizes the key data.

Beyond the catalog is a concluding summary, references (organized by historic documentary sources, cited literature, and conservation reports), an index of historic personages, and a glossary (in Czech) of textile terminology.

The catalog is an amazing and exhaustive resource, especially when combined with the historic analysis of the individual graves and the collated references from previous publications. Readers interested in more details on garment construction may need to follow up in the cited conservation reports, which may not be easily accessible. But in general the level of detail is far above what is generally included in a catalog.

Although the volumes are bilingual, it's important to note that the organization of the text and images prioritizes the Czech reader—a feature that it is hard to fault. In some places, figures are interleaved with the Czech text, so reading in English involves much back-and-forth. The catalog itself has parallel columns in Czech and English and doesn't suffer the same awkwardness. The English translation is not complete: most of the initial chapters have a much condensed English translation, and (as noted above) there is no English glossary. There are occasional oddities in the translation of clothing terms, such as the use of "cloak" universally for overgarments, including caftan-style garments. The technical language of the textile descriptions in the English translation is standardized on French terminology used by the Centre International d'Etude des Textiles Anciens (CIETA).

One noteworthy feature of this project is an understanding of how international the textiles and clothing of the elite residing (or buried) in Prague Castle were. The textiles originated from across Europe, the Middle East, Central Asia, and possibly as far as China. Garment styles (where identifiable) reflect relatively international ecclesiastical fashions, and secular fashions have echoes from central Europe to Italy to the Ottoman-influenced Balkans. At the same time, there are some garment styles specific to the region, and concrete survivals of certain garments otherwise known only from art. We are enriched by this window into those connections. — *Heather Rose Jones, Concord, California*

Tracing Textile Production from the Viking Age to the Middle Ages: Tools, Textiles, Texts and Contexts, by Ingvild Øye (Oxford: Oxbow, 2022). ISBN 978-1789257779. 264 pages, 146 black-and-white illustrations.

Ingvild Øye presents a focused study of textile production in the Vestland region of Norway and the North Atlantic Norse settlements during the Viking and Middle Ages, analyzing information from extant textiles, tools, architecture, texts, and experimental archaeology to create a holistic view of the subject. Special attention is paid to the find context of textiles and tools, providing insights into the organization of labor at individual sites and in greater socioeconomic networks.

An initial short but thorough review of the resources, tools, and knowledge required for textile production prefaces the analysis of the tool and textile finds from predominantly female grave contexts in the study area. Øye demonstrates a correlation between the status of the graves and the number of tools as well as the number of work processes represented by those tools. She proposes that the the making of textiles required coordination of multiple physical and intangible resources by high-status women who acted as a node for the vast and interrelated networks that were necessary for textile production. Their furnished graves then disproportionately included textile tools as a symbol of their social power, obscuring "a large and archaeologically, largely invisible work force doing the manual work" (p. 112).

In the remaining chapters, Øye reviews working contexts where textile finds are rarer and tool finds include a greater proportion of lightweight whorls (small disks used for hand spinning) than in grave contexts. Urbanization and the development of technologies like the horizontal loom increased textile output and specialization, but neither rural production nor use of the vertical loom entirely disappeared during this period, most clearly seen in the increasing importance of decentralized manufacture of the woollen twill cloth known as *vaðmál* as a commodity good. Øye reports that an unusually high proportion of whorls found in waterlogged environments are organic, many of them very light, implying that the production of fine textiles could have been even more prominent than reflected by the surviving textiles and tool assemblages from dryer sites, which are unlikely to preserve organic materials. Her assessment of the Icelandic textiles and tools reveals that all qualities of textile, including fine and complex weaves, were produced from the very early Viking Age and actually decline at high-status sites as *vaðmál* as a commodity product increases later in the Viking Age.

This dense volume will provide insights for those interested in the archaeology of working contexts and tools or the socioeconomic networks of the period. The text includes a plethora of data, including alternative interpretations of finds when context or classification is unclear, which can cloud the writing, but the many tables, figures, and appendices provide invaluable clarity and organization. Indexes of contents, images, and tables as well a detailed grave-by-grave summary table with discrete columns for each type of artifact would have been helpful. *Tracing Textile Production* is a useful contribution to our understanding of textiles, female power, and socioeconomic structures in Western Norway during the Viking and Middle Ages. — *Jean Kveberg, Madison, Wisconsin*

Author Index, Volumes 1–18

Printed and bound by CPI Group (UK) Ltd, Croydon, CR0 4YY

10/06/2025

14686713-0001

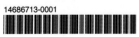